AF776325

Donors, technical assistance and public administration in Kosovo

MANCHESTER
1824

Manchester University Press

HUMANITARIANISM
Key debates and new approaches

This series offers a new interdisciplinary reflection on one of the most important and yet understudied areas in history, politics and cultural practices: humanitarian aid and its responses to crises and conflicts. The series seeks to define afresh the boundaries and methodologies applied to the study of humanitarian relief and so-called 'humanitarian events'. The series includes monographs and carefully selected thematic edited collections which will cross disciplinary boundaries and bring fresh perspectives to the historical, political and cultural understanding of the rationale and impact of humanitarian relief work.

Islamic charities and Islamic humanism in troubled times
Jonathan Benthall

Calculating compassion: Humanity and relief in war, Britain 1870–1914
Rebecca Gill

Humanitarian intervention in the long nineteenth century
Alexis Heraclides and Ada Dialla

The military–humanitarian complex in Afghanistan
Eric James and Tim Jacoby

Donors, technical assistance and public administration in Kosovo

Mary Venner

Manchester University Press

Copyright © Mary Venner 2016

The right of Mary Venner to be identified as the author of this work has been asserted by her in accordance with the Copyright, Designs and Patents Act 1988.

Published by Manchester University Press
Altrincham Street, Manchester M1 7JA
www.manchesteruniversitypress.co.uk

British Library Cataloguing-in-Publication Data
A catalogue record for this book is available from the British Library

Library of Congress Cataloging-in-Publication Data applied for

ISBN 978 1 7849 9272 9 hardback

First published 2016

The publisher has no responsibility for the persistence or accuracy of URLs for any external or third-party internet websites referred to in this book, and does not guarantee that any content on such websites is, or will remain, accurate or appropriate.

Typeset by Out of House Publishing
Printed in Great Britain
by CPI Group (UK) Ltd, Croydon, CR0 4YY

Contents

Acknowledgements

I am extremely grateful to everyone who contributed to this research, in particular the technical advisers and donor representatives who provided valuable insights, colourful comments, and access to otherwise unavailable documents, and the people in the Kosovo government who were prepared to talk to yet another foreigner with another list of questions. I would also like to thank colleagues at the University of New South Wales, in particular Gavin Kitching, Marc Williams and Elizabeth Thurbon, my friends who encouraged me to start this project, my husband David Morgan, and of course my parents for their investment in my education.

Abbreviations

AAK	Alliance for the Future of Kosovo
BPK	Banking and Payments Authority of Kosovo
CAFAO	Customs and Fiscal Assistance Office
CAM-K	Customs Assistance Mission – Kosovo
CARDS	Community Assistance for Reconstruction, Development and Stabilisation
CBAK	Central Banking Authority of Kosovo
CFA	Central Fiscal Authority
CIDA	Canadian International Development Agency
CMPS	Centre for Management and Policy Studies
CPE	Central Procurement Entity
DANIDA	Development cooperation, Ministry of Foreign Affairs, Denmark
DCSA	Department of Civil Service Administration
DFID	Department for International Development (UK)
DM	Deutsche Mark
DPS	JIAS Department of Public Services
EAR	European Agency for Reconstruction
EC	European Commission
ECLO	European Commission Liaison Office in Kosovo
EULEX	EU Law and Justice Mission in Kosovo
FAI	Finance Administrative Instruction
FRIDOM	Functional Review and Institutional Design of Ministries
FRY	Federal Republic of Yugoslavia
GDP	gross domestic product
GERAP	Group of Experts for Reform of Public Administration
IAC	Interim Administrative Council
ICG	International Crisis Group
ICO	International Civilian Office

ICTY	International Criminal Tribunal for the former Yugoslavia
IMF	International Monetary Fund
IOB	Independent Oversight Board
IPA	Instrument of Pre-accession Assistance
JCC	Joint Civilian Commission
JIAS	Joint Interim Administrative Structure
KCAP	UNDP report on Kosovo government capacity
KCB	Kosovo Consolidated Budget
KCSL	Kosovo Civil Service Law
KFOR	Kosovo Force
KLA	Kosovo Liberation Army
KTC	Kosovo Transition Council
LDK	Democratic League of Kosovo
MFE	Ministry of Finance and Economy
MPA	Ministry of Public Administration
MPS	PISG Ministry of Public Services
NATO	North Atlantic Treaty Organisation
NGO	non-governmental organisation
OECD	Organisation for Economic Co-operation and Development
OSCE	Organization for Security and Co-operation in Europe
PDK	Democratic Party of Kosovo
PEFA	Public Expenditure and Financial Accountability
PEMTAG	Public Expenditure Management Technical Assistance Grant
PFM	public finance management
PIFC	Public Internal Financial Control
PISG	Provisional Institutions for Self Government
PPA	Public Procurement Agency
PPP	Personnel Policies and Procedures Project
PPRB	Public Procurement Regulatory Body
PSMP	Public Sector Modernisation Project
SAP	stabilisation and association process
SDK	FRY Social Accounting Service
SIDA	Swedish International Development Agency
SIGMA	Support for Improvement in Governance and Management, OECD
SPAC	Senior Public Appointments Committee
SRSG	Special Representative of the Secretary General
TAFKO	Kosovo Task Force
UNCITRAL	UN Commission on International Trade Law
UNDESA	UN Department of Economic and Social Affairs

UNDP	United Nations Development Program
UNMIK	United Nations Mission in Kosovo
UNSC	United Nations Security Council
USAID	United States Agency for International Development
VAT	Value Added Tax
WBG	World Bank Group

Introduction

In June 1999, the United Nations, together with a large number of other international bodies, bilateral aid donors and non-governmental organisations (NGOs), embarked on a major programme of post-conflict reconstruction in the small, former Yugoslav province of Kosovo. To end the conflict between the ethnic Albanian population and the Yugoslav Government, an international security presence, Kosovo Force (KFOR), arrived to prevent renewed hostilities, and a UN-led international civilian mission, the United Nations Mission in Kosovo (UNMIK), came to support reconstruction, establish self government, maintain law and order and perform public administration functions. Within weeks, thousands of foreign UN staff and donor-funded consultants and advisers started arriving in the territory to begin what was, at the time, the largest ever post-conflict reconstruction operation.

In February 2000 I was one of them. I came knowing almost nothing about Kosovo and relatively little about peacekeeping or development assistance. I was recruited not by the UN but by one of the many participating aid donors as one of the technical experts engaged to set up new government institutions. Kosovo was my first experience of the implementation of development assistance and I found it significantly different from the well-ordered government administration with which I was familiar. As one of my Kosovar acquaintances succinctly expressed it some time later, 'The development world is a bit of chaos as far as I'm concerned. I don't think they operate in a very rational manner. They have good intentions, but the way they work – I'm still getting to grips with it.'[1]

The role I played in the reconstruction effort was relatively minor but during my three years there I worked for several donors in different parts of the interim administration, including some of those examined in this study, and was able to observe the performance of the major international actors. My impression was that what should have been a united effort to restore normalcy and to improve the lives of the people of Kosovo was mired in bureaucracy and riven with conflict between the different organisations and the individuals who worked for them. While some parts of the exercise forged ahead, pushed by people who seemed to know what they were doing, others lagged behind, or seemed to travel in circles.

I went on to work in other post-conflict countries and on other types of development assistance projects. In 2010 I returned to Kosovo planning to assess for myself the long-term outcomes of the intense international activity of the first post-conflict years. The scrawny young men and women who had started work in the new government departments in the first months after the conflict were by then older and plumper. They sat behind executive desks, inside newly renovated buildings that had previously been derelict and unusable, and discussed some of the more advanced issues in governance and finance with confidence. Foreign technical advisers still had a presence, but far fewer than the hundreds that had been there in 2000. It seemed to me that, in some areas at least, a lot had improved over the previous decade. In the political sphere, the outcomes of the post-conflict mission also seemed relatively positive, certainly when compared to some other state-building interventions. Over more than sixteen years since the start of the exercise, peace has been maintained and Kosovo is now a reasonably stable democracy with regular elections. Following its unilateral declaration of independence in 2008, it became a new nation, recognised by most major powers. On this basis it would appear that the post-conflict exercise in Kosovo has been a success.

This is not the impression given, however, in much of the academic literature on UNMIK and evaluations of governance and public administration in present-day Kosovo. Many accounts of the results of the international intervention create a general impression of failure and disappointment. Annual progress reviews produced by the European Commission, for example, list numerous ways in which the administration fails to meet expectations.[2] Yet few of the current public administration institutions in Kosovo existed before the arrival of foreign experts, certainly not in their current form. During the period of international supervision after 1999, UNMIK's interim civil administration, and the other international bodies that supported it, passed new legislation, established new administrative procedures and set up new organisations to provide public services. It was only some time later that these responsibilities were transferred to the control of the Kosovo government and they remained under some form of international supervision until late 2012. The successes and failures of today's government must owe something to the efforts of the international community. The purpose of this book is therefore to examine what donors and international organisations did to construct government administrative institutions in Kosovo and how this has contributed to the current performance of Kosovo's public administration.

Most of the international organisations and national governments that joined the UN as partners in the post-conflict Mission saw the exercise as something much more than peacekeeping and physical reconstruction. Their efforts extended well beyond humanitarian relief, physical reconstruction and temporary administration, as set out in the United Nations Security Council resolution that authorised the Mission. Their programme comprised the full 'liberal peace' agenda of rapid democratisation and market liberalisation and the creation of new public institutions with new policies in order to achieve and sustain the conditions considered necessary for lasting peace.[3] Many organisations arrived with an ambitious agenda of social, institutional, political and cultural transformation, from Yugoslav socialism to democracy and a market economy, which they had been formulating even while the conflict was still under way. They assumed that almost everything would have to change, and it would need to change immediately. Their proposed activities addressed multiple areas of economic and social reform all at once in the rush to take advantage of the opportunity to create the right kind of institutions, administrative practices and laws, and to influence the policies and behaviour of a future government.

Not all international participants, however, shared these social transformation and economic development goals, at least to begin with. In particular, the UN, which had overall leadership of the international exercise and responsibility for a large share of the administrative institutions that donors intended to reform, had much more limited aims in this respect. Many in the UN initially saw the peacekeeping task simply as a holding exercise, to prevent conflict pending a political resolution[4] and it was only some years later that the UN also began to adopt the language of development and to discuss the task in Kosovo clearly in terms of building governance institutions and state capacity.

Most non-UN actors approached Kosovo in the same way they approach all the other countries where they work, as somewhere in need of 'development'. The activities they implemented under the umbrella of post-conflict reconstruction were not all that different from the activities pursued by these international actors in any developing country. They were often implemented by the same organisations, drawing on the same sources of funding. They addressed much the same issues of 'institution building' and 'capacity development', and had the same ambitious objectives as development assistance programmes in other places. Ideas and theories from the development assistance literature provided the conceptual basis for donor programmes and influenced the attitudes and assumptions of the international personnel involved in the process. The methods they used, in particular the engagement of technical advisers to deliver 'projects', were essentially the same methods that have been used for decades to implement development assistance. Once the urgency of the immediate post-conflict period passed, the international intervention took on even more of the characteristics, methods, ideas and language of conventional aid programmes.

Understanding post-conflict Kosovo therefore requires an understanding of development assistance ideas and methods. But here also a large amount of the literature is exceedingly pessimistic, both about aid in general and about how it is implemented. The practices of assistance to developing countries are fraught with problems and failures to the extent that some argue it should not be done at all.[5] Most of the literature on development assistance, however, is based on the firm assumption that these problems can be fixed and that large amounts of money and expertise from the better-off nations ought to be able to solve the problems of poor countries.

This book is therefore also a study of the application of the practices of development assistance in a post-conflict setting. It focuses in particular on how different international organisations and bilateral donors approached the creation of Kosovo's public administration institutions in the immediate post-conflict period and how the combined actions of these organisations, working in the same space at the same time, led to the current reality in Kosovo. Development actors in Kosovo used the methods of development assistance, in particular technical assistance projects and foreign expert advisers, to construct new institutions, processes and systems in public finance and public administration. The shortcomings of these methods, which have been identified in the literature on development assistance many times in the past, also affected the performance of donors in Kosovo. In spite of this, in many areas international actors achieved considerable success against the goals they set themselves. The UN itself also had a large role to play in the creation of Kosovo's public administration structures but it did not wholeheartedly share the goals of the development actors or apply the same methods. The contrast between the activities of development organisations on the one hand and the actions of the UN on the other goes a long way to explaining the variations in the performance of Kosovo's administrative institutions today.

Kosovo as a case study of development assistance

Kosovo can be seen almost as a laboratory of development assistance practices. The post-conflict environment had several features that make it easier to examine questions about effectiveness and outcomes. In most other developing country contexts the effects of aid interventions are difficult to measure because the scale of activities is usually relatively small, the impacts are diffused and measurement is confused by the impacts of previous and subsequent projects. In Kosovo, many of these variables are controlled. There is a relatively clear 'before' benchmark and a precise start point for most international activity. Some of the largest and most influential development actors and international organisations were involved in the exercise, and a very large amount of assistance was invested in a relatively small place over a relatively short period of time. Moreover, all institution-building activities faced more or less the same contextual, political, historical and cultural challenges.

There is a tendency in much of the writing on Kosovo to treat the international presence as a single entity to which responsibility for all successes and failures should be attributed. Many writers refer to 'UNMIK', or more vaguely to the 'international community', as if they were clearly defined and had uniform motivations and interests. In fact, the collection of actors who made up the international presence in Kosovo, under the UN umbrella and outside it, had diverse objectives, motivations, strategies and methods, and sometimes disagreed strongly on the policies that should be pursued. Kosovo thus provides an opportunity to directly compare the activities and achievements of the major participants in the reconstruction exercise and the effects of the interactions between them.

The benchmark

The arrival of the first UN staff to set up the interim administration in mid-June 1999 marked the beginning of international development assistance in the territory.[6] Although Kosovo had received some World Bank funds in the past, through the former socialist Yugoslav Republic, and donors had provided humanitarian aid during the conflict, all institution building and public administration development activities started from this date. The UN, the European Union (EU), the World Bank, the International Monetary Fund (IMF), the United States Agency for International Development (USAID) and a host of other organisations and national governments became involved in efforts to restore and develop Kosovo's economy and society. These actors invested a considerable amount of resources in the task. Between 1999 and 2010 the UN spent around $2.7 billion (approximately €2.3 billion) on the civil administration, the European Commission contributed another €2.5 billion and significant amounts were provided by other donors.[7] There is thus a large amount of development activity in Kosovo that can be studied.

From a geographical perspective, Kosovo was a convenient place to mount a major international exercise. It is a small territory located close to European capitals, just a two-hour flight from Vienna and a few hours' drive from Greece. But despite its proximity to other parts of Europe it had most of the characteristics of other recipients of development assistance, including severe poverty, dilapidated infrastructure and a cultural and political environment that was considered to be an obstacle to economic advancement. Kosovo's economy had always been less developed than the rest of Yugoslavia. The economic distortions of the Yugoslav system of 'self-managed socialism', the effects of discriminatory measures against Kosovo Albanians after 1989, Yugoslav government mismanagement of the economy during the 1990s, UN economic sanctions and the violence of 1999, all made things much worse.[8] At the end of the conflict, almost half the population had fled from their homes, 120,000 houses had been destroyed, electricity, water and telephone services had stopped working and land mines made farm land unusable. Poverty and economic distress were obvious to the foreigners who arrived at that time and were clearly seen to justify a large programme of development activity.

Historical accounts of the Kosovo region describe a traditional Albanian culture based on strong patrilineal clans or extended family networks and customary legal codes and values which, if they were still influential in modern-day Kosovo, would be in clear conflict with many of the ideas promoted by international actors engaged in development assistance. Traditional laws were based on principles of personal honour, which created a tradition of blood feuds and honour killings.[9] Gender equity, modern legal codes, equality before the law and the state's monopoly on the use of power and punishment would be difficult to reconcile with this patriarchal, clan-based traditional culture, and many reports produced by donors imply that these traditions are still relevant.[10] News reports of the persistence of blood feuds and honour killings support these perceptions, as do stories of organised crime, political assassinations and illegal behaviour by some political leaders and businesses.[11]

The legacies of the socialist government were also identified as an impediment to plans for institutional development. As a province within socialist Yugoslavia, Kosovo's society and economy had been influenced by a style of administration based on extreme centralisation and hierarchical control, the absence of independent civil society organisations, and economic policies that included controlled food prices, below-cost utilities, expansive staffing of state-owned enterprises and generous pensions for employees.[12] These practices, which were regarded positively by many in the local population, were quite contrary to the market-based, open economy model proposed by the World Bank, the IMF and other lead actors in the reconstruction effort. At the same time, however, many international actors saw the post-conflict environment as an opportunity to overcome these obstacles and to implement reforms and institutional changes that would be politically or administratively more difficult in other contexts. They regarded Kosovo as a green-field site for the construction of new, modern, best-practice public-sector organisations.[13]

Public finance and the civil service

The international involvement in Kosovo encompassed all aspects of government, from the provision of municipal services to the administration of justice. This account focuses on two aspects in particular: the establishment of institutions and processes for the management of public finances; and the creation of the framework for managing the civil administration. Sound management in these two areas is regarded as essential for achieving economic development and poverty reduction objectives and are therefore frequent targets for donor-funded institution-building programmes. Public finance management (PFM), in particular, receives attention from organisations such as the IMF and the World Bank as a consequence of their concern for economic stability and growth, and from many other donors because of its importance for the sound management of their donated funds. An effective civil service is also considered the basis for good public administration performance and an important component of good governance. The concepts and processes introduced to Kosovo by international experts in these two fields were, however, significantly different from what had existed previously in this part of the world. The task of the international organisations was therefore not simply reform and incremental development of existing institutions, but the construction of completely new organisations, structures, processes and behaviours modelled on their ideas about 'best practice'.

Within UNMIK's 'pillar' structure, public finance was nominally the responsibility of the EU, with the United States, through USAID, also playing a significant role. Civil service development, on the other hand, was one of the many public-sector functions managed by the UN itself. This account documents what these international actors did to implement their ideas about the type of public finance and civil service institutions that would be best for Kosovo, and tracks developments in these two sectors over the period since 1999. It describes the gradual evolution and ongoing functioning of Kosovo's new institutions and the ultimate results, assessed in terms of the performance of the Kosovo government in these fields today.

The theory and practice of development

Official development assistance replaced colonial administration as the primary form of Western involvement in the affairs of less well-off nations after the Second World War. Over the decades since then academics and aid organisations have produced a vast amount of analysis and documentation debating questions about the best way to achieve development, and indeed how development itself should be defined.[14] Their theoretical discussions, however, often seem far removed from the practical issues and challenges of implementing development projects. Current dominant ideas from this body of literature underpinned the policies adopted by development actors in Kosovo, but their efforts to implement these policies were often undermined by defects in the methods of development assistance.

Theories of development

Since the 1970s, the 'neo-liberal' economic ideas that have influenced government policies in Western economies have also had an impact on development theory and have directed aid policy towards market-led development, a reduced role for the state and structural adjustment programmes to transfer economic power from the public to the private sector.[15] These policies have tended to portray government as an obstacle to development rather than its sponsor. Support for the extremes of neo-liberal policy prescriptions has retreated somewhat in recent decades in part as a response to the economic successes of a number of mostly East Asian economies under firm political direction, which appeared to challenge the idea that governments should simply leave economic development to market forces.[16] There has thus been renewed interest in the role of state institutions in supporting economic change, and a recognition of the need to ensure sufficient state capacity to perform this role.[17]

Nevertheless, the policies currently promoted by the international financial institutions and major developed country donors continue to be based on a more or less neo-liberal agenda of market-led development through fiscal discipline, rapid privatisation of state-owned enterprises, low taxes, trade liberalisation and foreign investment. The role of government is generally limited to regulating economic activity and implementing fiscal policies that will be conducive to private-sector growth. These were the ideas at the centre of the programmes of economic and institutional development implemented by the lead actors in Kosovo. They were not, however, necessarily the policies the Albanian population, including former socialist officials and employees of state-owned enterprises, had in mind as they returned to their homes after the conflict.

The activities of development actors are not limited to introducing the right economic policies. They also assume the need for changes in the political, social and cultural environment. Various formulations of ideas about the role of human motives and values in generating economic success have appeared in development policy literature including the concepts of 'social capability',[18] 'culture'[19] and 'social capital'.[20] Early post-war ideas about 'modernisation', for example, assumed the need for changes in social and political structures, ideas, values and ways of thinking as preconditions for economic 'take off'.[21] This underlying assumption of modernisation, it can be argued, has not changed all that much in recent thinking on development.[22] Several related and somewhat overlapping concepts of this kind dominate current discussions. Obstacles to economic progress are variously identified in terms of poor 'institutions',[23] inadequate 'governance',[24] or a lack of 'capacity' on the part of developing country governments and people requiring the implementation of 'capacity-building' projects.[25] The essential idea behind each of these concepts is that a large part of the task of development assistance is to replace the existing social, political and cultural systems with institutions, values and practices that donors consider necessary to sustain economic growth and improve social welfare.

Development and post-conflict reconstruction

Programmes of post-conflict peace building are also generally based on similar assumptions that democratisation and marketisation will create prosperity, stability and the conditions for a lasting 'liberal peace'.[26] The boundary between 'normal' development and post-conflict reconstruction is further blurred by the fact that many of the least-developed countries receiving development assistance have also experienced conflict at some time in the not-so-distant past, or remain at risk of falling into conflict. Both post-conflict and developing countries are therefore assumed to need a democratic government and regular, free elections, an active parliament, an independent, incorruptible judiciary, an effective, merit-based government bureaucracy, transparent, policy-based budgets, a free press, sound labour market policies, enforceable property rights, efficient social welfare programmes, active civil society organisations, anti-corruption measures and a raft of new government agencies to support them. Along with these institutions comes a set of values that the society is expected to embrace including, for example, the idea that individual merit should take precedence over kinship, clan or political allegiance in public employment; that government should serve the needs of the population as a whole rather than just the ruling group; that women are as entitled to education, employment, civil rights and justice as men; or that people of different faiths or different ethnic or racial backgrounds also have a right to participate in society. For most of the people who work for development organisations these are strongly held principles, but in many developing or post-conflict countries they amount to an ambitious and complex transformation of the existing society and culture. They also tend to identify the non-compliant attitudes, values and behaviour of the people of the recipient country as the major problem to be addressed by development programmes, setting up a clear divide between development actors and the subjects of development.

These donor expectations of institutional development and cultural change have generated an increasingly complex, demanding and sometimes internally contradictory agenda for change in developing and post-conflict countries. The reform agenda 'constitutes an overwhelming smorgasbord of changes deemed necessary to assure government effectiveness'.[27] In Kosovo, for example, while the World Bank, the IMF and their collaborators focused on new economic policies and institutions, other international actors saw a need to completely reorganise the education system, restructure higher education, transform the delivery of health services, regulate the media, revise the road rules and promote the concepts of gender equity and ethnic harmony.[28] The post-conflict environment itself, however, presents challenges to development assistance. The context is significantly more complex and the range of issues to be addressed, their urgency, the volume of assistance, the number of international actors and the level of public attention are all much greater than in more stable developing countries. Conflict and competition between the major international actors may also be more significant as they struggle to claim a prominent role for their organisation, their government or their policy agenda.

In literature on post-conflict reconstruction there is a clear divide between those who see the post-conflict enterprise as a special activity to which the normal public administration practices and rules of economic management might not apply, and those who regard it as no different from the situation in any other developing country. There is thus disagreement over the balance to be struck between short-term, pragmatic solutions to immediate problems and the desire to entrench good practices for long-term sustainable results. This tension is particularly significant in matters of economic policy. International actors often have different views on the importance of imposing fiscal discipline, controlling inflation, introducing new taxes and privatising public enterprises, on the one hand,[29] relative to the need to deliver a 'peace dividend', place former combatants in public employment, or provide short-term stimulus to the economy, on the other.[30] The post-conflict environment also highlights tension between the desire of foreign actors to take advantage of the opportunity to achieve rapid change and their expressed commitment to consultation and local ownership. The possibility of meaningful ownership of the reconstruction and development programme by the local population is significantly undermined by the disruption and uncertainty of the immediate post-conflict environment and the fact that international actors, under pressure to achieve results quickly, are reluctant to lose valuable time in consultation and negotiation.[31]

Critiques and alternatives to development

Within the relatively closed world of development assistance there is broad agreement on the value of development aid and the agenda it should pursue. In the wider context of academic and popular literature, however, there is considerable debate about the processes of economic and social change supported by aid donors. Some authors are enthusiastic about the benefits of capitalism, or of Western 'civilisation', and the inevitability of its spread around the world.[32] Others challenge the generally Eurocentric focus of these works, but nevertheless agree that the development of global markets necessarily brings standardisation and predictability in laws and practices, and changes in concepts, values and ideologies.[33]

For many, on the other hand, the practice of development assistance, which purports to help people in less developed parts of the world, is in fact intrinsically malign and destructive.[34] The activities of development actors are seen as a form of Western or liberal imperialism that seeks to exploit or subjugate fragile and disadvantaged communities, undermine local cultures, deepen deprivation and create relations of dependence.[35] Peace building and post-conflict reconstruction are also identified as part of this larger hegemonic project that has the ideological purpose, despite the good intentions of the individuals involved, of spreading the values and norms of dominant powers and implementing economic policies that would not be acceptable to the population in other circumstances.[36] The 'Europeanisation' policies of the EU have also been portrayed as a process of neo-liberal restructuring that reflects the interests of transnational capital.[37] Generally these criticisms are based on explicit opposition to capitalism, industrialisation and globalised economic relations and consequently reject the practices of development that intend to spread these systems further.

Another body of writing asserts that there must be alternative, more culturally appropriate paths to development than those promoted by conventional development programmes.[38] Rist, for example, argues that 'there are numerous ways of living the good life, and it is up to each society to invent its own.'[39] The imposition by donors of Western institutions and values on traditional societies, it is suggested, is preventing these alternatives from emerging. Arguments about the need for alternative approaches to development have been around for a long time. Essentially the same debates about the hardships resulting from economic development, the loss of traditional values and community life, and the need for alternative approaches, have recurred since the beginning of the industrial revolution, whenever traditional societies face change.[40]

Neither of these radical challenges have much impact on the practices of development assistance. On the contrary, most major international development organisations take it as given that the primary objective of development is to bring more countries into economic relations with the developed world, for their benefit. Promoting forms of social and economic organisation that are compatible with the global economy is thus one of the explicit and unquestioned intentions of their aid programmes. International actors are often well aware of available alternative non-Western modes of governance and behaviour, but explicitly reject them because of the risks they may pose to their strongly held beliefs about the value of transparency, equity, human rights and gender equality. In these circumstances, therefore, it is not at all clear how alternative paths to a better life, based on indigenous cultures and non-Western modes of behaviour, and without the imposition of foreign values and ideology, can be achieved given the power and dominance these critiques attribute to the Western model and its supporters.

Moreover, the 'Westernisation' and modernisation policies of donors often have strong support from within the developing countries themselves. Those on the receiving side of donor interventions, or at least the educated elites in these countries, share the transformation objectives of international actors and cooperate with the proposed change agenda. This was expressed, for example, by Tadeusz Mazowiecki, Poland's first prime minister after the end of communism, when he told his parliament 'We in Poland do not want a Polish way, a third way, because we know what works in the world and we know what doesn't work and we want what works.'[41] The elites do not, of course, always represent the views of other sectors of the society, and their reasons for supporting the proposed changes may be misguided, or self-interested. In some countries, their enthusiasm for the new policies may wane when they realise the full implications of democracy, transparency, the free market and the rule of law for their own power and influence.

Although development organisations generally support the broad 'liberal peace' institution-building agenda, they are also aware of its limitations and risks. There are numerous examples of the over-enthusiastic or inappropriate application of neo-liberal policies, and these have provided ample ammunition for their critics.[42] International intervention in post-conflict countries can be difficult to implement and can have adverse impacts.[43] Rapid development of a market economy and democratic politics can be destabilising. Paris argues, however, that the solution to this is not less intervention but an even more intrusive and longer-lasting involvement of outsiders in the domestic affairs of countries emerging from conflict in order to establish stable institutions and achieve phased reform.[44] Neo-liberal development programmes may not always work as well as donors hope they will, but there is no clear evidence that any other policy would achieve better results in terms of peace, political stability and individual welfare. Certainly most development actors are convinced that their ideas of best practice in government administration are what developing countries need.

Good enough governance

A critique of the current development model that is more likely to have an impact on aid practitioners questions whether many of the 'modern' practices promoted by donors are in fact essential for development. There is evidence, for example, that developed nations themselves did not necessarily have ideal, rational, Weberian government structures in place at the time of their rapid economic development. Many of the practices that development projects work hard to eradicate, such as nepotism, sinecures, tax farming, unaccountable public officials and political appointments to government posts, were common features of public life in Europe and the United States until relatively recently,[45] and a number of countries, such as China, Vietnam and Malaysia, have achieved significant economic success with institutions that are a long way from the ideals promoted by donors.[46] This suggests that, if institution building is required at all, it could be more effectively focused.

Grindle, for example, argues the case for donors to pursue 'good enough governance', a minimally acceptable level of government performance that at least does not hinder economic and political development and that enables poverty reduction initiatives to be implemented.[47] A realistic reform agenda, she argues, should set priorities among reforms, giving precedence to those that are essential over those that are less so, and those that are relatively easy to implement in the short term over those that are more difficult and longer term. The problem for donors, however, is deciding which aspects of governance should receive their attention and which can be ignored. 'Good enough governance' sounds sensible, but its implementation in aid practice inevitably produces conflict over what exactly constitutes an essential priority reform, as various advisers and policy entrepreneurs lobby on behalf of their particular field of interest or expertise, and donors pursue their strongly held ideas about the necessity for social change.

Development in practice

Donors' ideas about development as transformation set ambitious aims for their assistance programmes. Aid donors produce country strategy papers, multi-annual planning documents and logframes setting out how they propose to support the transformation of institutions, values and behaviours, and then conduct regular assessments of progress towards their goals. The means they have available for achieving their objectives, however, are actually quite limited and the impacts of their activities are always uncertain. The methods commonly used by donors to deliver aid have often been the subject of criticism in the literature on development.

The implementation of institution building generally relies on the formulation of targeted technical assistance 'projects' delivered by foreign advisers. The use of a project model for the delivery of aid has been the basis of development assistance for many decades. It has its origins in the idea of development as a largely mechanical process focused on capital formation and therefore amenable to an engineering approach. This means that complex development programmes, carefully formulated on sound analysis of local political, economic and cultural conditions, and agreed with the national government, are subsequently broken down into a sequence of smaller, manageable projects which more easily fit within the budget cycles and procurement plans of donor organisations, and which can be separately explained, approved, funded, contracted, reported on and accounted for.

This model has been widely and frequently criticised. Projects, it has been argued, make it difficult to take account of the wider context, past history or previous efforts, are inflexible, have fixed objectives that are difficult to change, and tend to be dominated by officials or advisers from the donor country. They are often badly designed, of insufficient duration, inadequately funded, poorly supervised and not well coordinated.[48] The alternatives to projects are not particularly obvious, however, and may have their own drawbacks. A longer term, less focused programme approach, for example, may lose sight of the objectives and mask a lack of activity.[49]

Institution building and capacity development projects almost always involve technical experts from more developed countries who are engaged to provide advice and transfer knowledge, abilities and attitudes to local counterparts. Like 'projects', technical assistance, also called technical cooperation, has always been a feature of development assistance and has attracted much the same criticisms. The US government initiated its first major programme to provide advisers to work abroad in 1949[50] and the United States continues to invest heavily in providing technical advice and expertise. UN-affiliated organisations, the World Bank and other bilateral and multilateral donors also established technical cooperation and training programmes at about the same time.[51] This type of donor activity has consistently made up around 20 per cent of all official development aid.[52]

Most of this technical assistance is delivered by private-sector consulting firms or non-profit non-governmental organisations (NGOs) under commercial contracting arrangements. These bodies, in turn, usually subcontract the actual work to independent consultants, generally self-employed professionals who are paid on a daily or monthly fee basis and who form a floating pool of specialist consultants moving from project to project, from firm to firm and from country to country, depending on the employment opportunities that become available. One of the crucial issues in the implementation of institution-building projects, therefore, is finding the right people to do it. Technical assistance employment is something of a closed shop. Consultant roles invariably require previous experience on similar projects, but there is no apprenticeship system through which to gain this experience. The pool of people who are both interested in this kind of employment and have the qualifications to do it is thus relatively limited, and experts with the necessary professional skills and experience in law, accounting, economics or information technology can rarely be expected to also have the right language skills, knowledge of the local culture, understanding of local politics or even the awareness of development policy issues that might be considered essential for this work.[53] Graduates of development studies courses, on the other hand, have the theoretical knowledge but lack real-world experience. The firms who are contracted to deliver donor-funded technical assistance projects are constantly searching for people to fill adviser roles, and projects with short timeframes multiply these difficulties.

Recipient governments and critics of development sometimes query the relative costs and benefits of technical assistance, noting the high fee rates of advisers and that very little of the money paid to consultants remains in the local economy.[54] The cost of technical assistance is easily identified in aid budgets but the benefits advisers provide through training, advice and competent management are generally less visible than tangible outputs such as roads and schools. There is thus a tendency to assume that the benefits of technical assistance are low or non-existent. Critics also argue that the presence of foreign advisers may erode ownership and create dependence, undermine the capabilities of local staff and encourage adoption of policies that are too complex, misguided or unsustainable, while failing to transfer skills to local counterparts.

In spite of these doubts about the value and effectiveness of technical assistance, donors continue to make extensive use of foreign experts, in part because of the lack of viable alternative methods, but also because technical advisers can have subsidiary benefits rarely referred to in project specifications. They often function as financial controllers and monitors, information gatherers and commercial ambassadors on behalf of the donor country or organisation. Reports submitted by advisers provide donors with information on the workings of the government, the performance of senior government officials and the rate of progress in implementing policies recommended by donors. International consultants can also, usually, be relied on to account accurately for the use of donor funds, to curtail opportunities for mismanagement and misappropriation, and to pursue the donors' political, economic or commercial interests.[55]

Most of the development actors operating in post-conflict Kosovo applied their normal aid 'modalities', or methods, to the task of institutional development and economic transformation. They implemented aid projects in various forms and engaged foreign technical experts to set up new government organisations and to provide advice and training. Although most UN and some EU staff were not recruited specifically as technical advisers, and may not have seen themselves in that role, their responsibilities in Kosovo's administrative departments and ministries were essentially the same as those of the technical consultants working alongside them. The decisions they made had the same long-term implications for the future Kosovo administration and their work faced the same challenges experienced by technical advisers in all developing country contexts.

Aid effectiveness and national interest

Despite the numerous reported deficiencies and failures of development assistance, many in the field are certain it could be much more effective if it was implemented correctly. Over the years various reports and studies have exhorted donors to change their aid delivery practices to address past criticisms.[56] The 2005 'Paris Declaration on Aid Effectiveness', one of the more recent initiatives in this direction, for example, committed donor signatories to modify their practices with a view to making their programmes more effective.[57] They agreed, among other things, to coordinate their activities, to minimise overheads and transaction costs, and to harmonise their procedures for reporting, procurement and disbursements. Donors also agreed they should support the recipient countries' own development strategies and base their programmes on them. A considerable investment in promoting and monitoring the achievement of aid effectiveness reform has been made since then including several more high-level conferences and agreements.[58]

Most of these aid effectiveness ideals are by no means new, however. Many have long been seen as best practice in aid administration. References to country ownership and donor coordination, for example, appear in some of the earliest literature on development assistance.[59] Donors have, however, found it difficult to put them into practice in their work. The results of the final 2011 monitoring survey on the Paris Declaration were described by the OECD as 'sobering'. Only one out of the thirteen measurable targets established in the 2005 agreement had been met, and that by a narrow margin.[60]

One of the main reasons for the poor results from efforts to reform aid implementation is that they ignore the political nature of development assistance as an instrument of donor country foreign policy. In addition to its stated goals of economic development and social transformation, official development aid has many other objectives which may include serving national interests through improved security, trade, national prestige, expanded spheres of interest and the ability to project national values. It was long ago observed that 'International politics lies at the heart of foreign aid and, indeed are the very reason for its existence'.[61] Little has happened in the intervening time to change this assessment. Harmonisation between donors in these circumstances is not easily achieved, and alignment of donor programmes with recipient country development plans is only possible when the recipients' plans are already largely compatible with those of donors.

The development agenda in Kosovo

Donor planning for post-conflict development in Kosovo largely accepted the premise that, in a globalised economy, adopting institutions and practices that meet the needs and expectations of foreign interests is increasingly unavoidable for any country, and that this might involve significant change in the existing culture and values.

In previous decades, Yugoslavia had also been engaged in a programme of transformation of this rural backwater of the Federation. Fifty years of socialism had already generated a significant amount of 'modernisation' of institutions and values. It had, for example, brought almost universal literacy and longer life expectancy, urbanisation, and employment opportunities for women. This socialist transformation had itself followed previous efforts to influence local ways of life and belief during five hundred years of Ottoman rule. The aim of most international actors now was to replace the socialist institutions of Yugoslavia with Western-style democracy and markets, following the apparently successful model already applied elsewhere in Eastern and Central Europe. The post-conflict situation gave them significant scope to do this. In the immediate post-conflict period international personnel were much more than simply technical advisers to the government: in effect they were the government. Kosovo's political leaders were also, on the whole, willing to go along with these reform and development plans of international actors in exchange for the prospect of independence and, in due course, a place in Europe.

The UN was the odd one out in this respect. Its multinational membership, representing all variations in political ideology, means it has no particular position on questions of economic policy or social change. UNMIK was thus not committed to the neo-liberal model promoted by some of its international partners and had no blueprint of its own. The successive Special Representatives of the Secretary General (SRSGs), who were always from Europe, and the Deputy SRSG, who was always American, were generally supportive, but the position of UN Headquarters staff and many of the officials within UNMIK itself was less clear.

All of the complex issues and debates in post-conflict reconstruction were encountered when international actors intervened in Kosovo. They were confronted with urgent problems and conflicting opinions on how they should be resolved. Donor representatives, technical consultants, and UN and EU officials found themselves embroiled in debates about the policies that should be adopted, the speed at which they should be implemented and the difficulty of balancing short-term expedience and long-term outcomes. The pursuit of political stability was given primacy by some actors, while others considered effective government institutions an equally important long-term priority. The desire by some international actors to restart the economy and provide employment ran up against concerns about future fiscal sustainability and the need for merit-based public-sector recruitment. While most international actors expressed a public commitment to consultation to achieve local ownership, they also acknowledged that the urgency of the situation, and the absence of a recognised government, would make this difficult.

Kosovo's institution-building outcomes

Measuring the results of any specific development assistance activity is difficult and ultimately largely subjective. For donors the success of a project could mean simply that the proposed outputs, such as training courses or reports, have been delivered, but this provides little indication of the wider or longer-term impacts. On the other hand, attempts to link development assistance inputs to improvements in high-level indicators such as gross domestic product (GDP) growth or poverty rates produce disappointing results. This study focuses on the extent to which international actors have produced the outcomes they intended to achieve, setting aside for now debates about the legitimacy of these objectives. Multiple sources of evidence are drawn on to judge their relative successes and failures in institutional development, including the views of donors on their own activities, the results of external assessments and progress reports, the opinions of technical advisers and other observers, and most importantly, the views of Kosovo's citizens on the performance of their own government institutions.

While these sources suggest that international actors have failed, so far, to achieve their more ambitious aim of transforming Kosovo into a smoothly functioning, ethnically harmonious and prosperous market democracy, there have been institution-building successes on a more modest scale. From a territory which in mid-1999 had no recognised government or established public institutions, Kosovo is now a self-governing entity with an elected parliament, government ministries, a civil service, a budget, a public revenue-raising regime and a body of enacted legislation. Many of these government institutions have been provided with trained and capable staff. In this respect, some international organisations and donors have achieved much of what they set out to do. However, the results of the development of public administration functions in the emerging Kosovo government have been very uneven. Some organisations and some functions are considered to perform satisfactorily, while others are well below expectations.

In the field of PFM the outcomes have generally been positive. Donors' own assessments, official reviews and evaluations, comments by independent observers and interviews with international advisers and Kosovars, all indicate that most of Kosovo's public finance institutions, including the revenue agencies, the Ministry of Finance, the central bank and expenditure management systems, are performing satisfactorily. Indeed public finance is widely regarded as a success of the international intervention. The Kosovo Customs Service, in particular, stands out as a professional organisation compared to its counterparts in neighbouring countries, despite having characteristics that would normally be expected to predispose it to poor performance and corruption.[62] It needs to be emphasised that these assessments refer to relative success, measured within the context of Kosovo, or the Balkan region more broadly. Even the best performing of Kosovo's institutions have shortcomings that, if considered in isolation, might be identified as signs of failure.

The performance of many other government functions, however, is regarded much less positively. These institutions are repeatedly cited as major problems needing further development assistance and reform. Serious weaknesses are found, for example, in the conduct of public procurement activities, and the Kosovo civil service in general is struggling to achieve the standards of performance expected by international observers. The more successful outcomes in many areas of public finance and the less positive results in civil service development are associated to a significant extent with the actions of the different international organisations involved in each sector.

It is, of course, always easy in hindsight to criticise actions taken, or not taken, by others in the past without appreciating the realities of the situation at the time. Any assessment of the achievements or failures of international actors in Kosovo needs to take account of the politically complex and physically challenging conditions in the early phases of the intervention, during which many difficult-to-reverse decisions were made. In conducting this research I noted a tendency for people who had only recently become involved in Kosovo to express an ideal view of how things should have been done by those who came before, failing to understand the obstacles that had existed at the time. Some of what happened in the early years of the intervention may have been, for political and financial reasons, unavoidable. This analysis shows, however, that some initial failures have had long-term consequences for contemporary Kosovo, while the focused early interventions of some actors produced good long-term results in key areas. Contrary to the assumptions of many critics, these findings support the value of institutional development programmes, the use of technical assistance and indeed the role of development assistance projects, for achieving the outcomes that donors pursue, and suggests that interventions of this kind in the right circumstances and with sufficient resources can have a lasting positive impact.

Outline of the book

This book tells the story of the development of several important public sector institutions in Kosovo during the period of international supervision. It describes what happened when various aid organisations put their ambitious reconstruction plans into effect and considers the extent to which the actions of these international agencies and aid donors during the rebuilding effort are responsible for the current performance of the Kosovo government. The main focus is on the early post-conflict years, but it also provides information on more recent developments that may have affected current public administration performance. The analysis deals with these events at several levels. It discusses the big-picture issues of why the various international actors became involved and what they hoped to achieve, and the more detailed questions about methods and process that are of interest to those who are responsible for delivering development and reconstruction. It pays particular attention to the effectiveness or otherwise of technical assistance and foreign expertise as a means of achieving change. The account of PFM and civil service development therefore provides considerable detail on exactly what was done, how it was done and the obstacles that were encountered, information that is often lost in more general discussions of ideas about post-conflict reconstruction.

Although these descriptions tend to highlight examples of disagreement and discord between international actors, it should be acknowledged that there were also many areas of cooperation.

International organisations and donors have produced a considerable amount of documentation on their activities in Kosovo, assessments of the performance of the public administration and proposals for further reform and assistance. Most of this material has been published on the internet, although some of it is now difficult to find as websites have been closed down or archived. Many academic works have also been written on the early years of Kosovo's reconstruction, some by people who were directly involved in various capacities.[63] Few of these independent studies have dealt in any detail with the development of public finance institutions and civil service management. Much of the information in the book is drawn from these published sources, but I also sought out many of the people I had met when I was working in Kosovo to get their first hand, unedited versions of what really happened. Some of these people shared their personal documents and unpublished papers. During a visit to Pristina in 2010 I also met the advisers who were implementing the latest iteration of donor technical assistance projects and talked to representatives of the major donor organisations, most of whom were in fact Kosovars, as well as some of the remaining UN staff in the downsized UNMIK. I also had formal meetings with senior government officials, some of whom had once been my trainees, and interviewed a range of other Kosovo government staff.

The following account of public administration development in Kosovo is a synthesis of information from all these sources. In this introduction I have argued that the intervention in Kosovo was essentially, for most actors, a development assistance exercise and have described the ideas about post-conflict reconstruction and development that informed their actions, the methods they used and the complaints frequently made about these methods. Chapter 1 briefly sets the scene for the reconstruction exercise and explains the intense donor interest in determining the direction of Kosovo's post-conflict development, which soon turned what may have initially been conceived as a relatively straightforward operation into a large and complex exercise. This chapter also describes the situation in Kosovo in the immediate aftermath of the conflict and provides a brief chronology of the development of Kosovo's independent government over the years of international supervision.

Chapter 2 identifies the lead players in the story. These comprised some of the largest and most influential international organisations, development bodies and bilateral donors. It examines each of their objectives and motivations, the methods they used, the resources they made available for the task, the relationships between them and how these all affected what they were able to achieve. Chapters 3 and 4 describe what happened when these actors applied their ideas and methods to creating new PFM institutions and a new civil service as the foundation for a future government. I explain the significance of these two issues for development and the difficult policy debates they sometimes generate, and then describe the steps taken to resolve these issues in Kosovo and the results achieved.

The conclusion to this book assesses the factors that contributed to successes or failures of donor activities and the implications for future post-conflict missions and for current debates on development assistance more broadly. Successful donor intervention required agreement on the objective and consistency in applying it, sufficient resources over an extended period, a focus on promoting merit-based recruitment and performance-based management of public sector staff, and a degree of insulation from the vested interests of politicians. Other factors were also relevant, however, in particular the opportunity presented by the post-conflict environment and the ability of international advisers to exercise control over the new institutions for an extended period, conditions that are rare in the world of development assistance.

Although the opinions of many Kosovars are included, this account is written largely from the point of view of the outsiders who intervened in Kosovo and in particular the technical advisers and the donors who engaged them. It recounts their experiences and addresses questions of concern to them about the effectiveness of their activities. All the individuals I spoke to were promised anonymity to allow them to express their personal views frankly. Some strong opinions were repeated in interview after interview, including torrents of complaint about EU aid management, an unexpected lack of criticism of USAID implementation practices, and generally negative views readily expressed by international actors about their Kosovar counterparts.

In this work I generally adopt the terminology used in the official documents of major international organisations and thus use 'Kosovo' rather than 'Kosova' for the name of the country, and 'Kosovar' rather than 'Kosovan' to refer to the people of Kosovo. In most instances, 'Kosovar' can be assumed to refer to Albanian Kosovars – despite the UN's vigorous pursuit of the idea of a harmonious multi-ethnic Kosovo, ethnic Albanians were the dominant local actors in the events described. Given the political evolution from the Federal Republic of Yugoslavia to the Republic of Serbia over the period, a reference to Yugoslavia can in most cases be taken as a reference to Serbia and vice versa. The term 'international actor' refers both to the multilateral and bilateral organisations that made up the international presence and to the individuals that worked for them or on their behalf. By discussing the development and performance of the current government administration the book necessarily accepts the present reality of Kosovo's separation from Serbia.

The story of what took place once UN officials and donor-funded technical experts arrived in Kosovo to put the plans of the international community into action has moments of triumph and glory, and elements of tragedy and occasionally farce. The people of Kosovo sometimes seem to have been merely the audience rather than actors in this play. The entire process was certainly much more complex than is sometimes suggested in official accounts. However, the overall conclusion of this investigation is reassuring. Although there were many failures and inadequacies in what was done by international actors, even those considered to be effective, the institution-building outcomes in some parts of the public administration were reasonably positive and at this point appear to be sustainable. Comparing these successes with the less positive outcomes in other areas of international involvement produces a fairly clear picture of the factors that contributed to relative success and the circumstances that generated relative failure.

Notes

1 Kosovar manager of a UNDP programme, Pristina.
2 European Commission, *Kosovo 2012 Progress Report* (Brussels: European Commission, 2012); European Commission, *Kosovo 2013 Progress Report*, (Brussels: European Commission, 2013); European Commission, *Kosovo 2014 Progress Report* (Brussels: European Commission, 2014).
3 R. Paris, *At War's End: Building Peace after Civil Conflict* (Cambridge: Cambridge University Press, 2004).
4 I. King and W. Mason, *Peace at any Price: How the World Failed Kosovo* (London: Hurst & Company, 2006) 73.
5 T. W. Dichter, *Despite Good Intentions: Why Development Assistance to the Third World has Failed* (Boston, MA: University of Massachusetts Press, 2003); D. Moyo, *Dead Aid: Why Aid is not Working and how there is Another Way for Africa* (London: Allen Lane, 2009).
6 The history of Kosovo and the events that led up to the post-conflict mission are described in A. J. Bellamy, *Kosovo and International Society* (Basingstoke: Palgrave Macmillan, 2002); T. Garton Ash, *History of the Present: Essays, Sketches and Despatches from Europe in the 1990s* (London: Penguin, 2000); M. Glenny, *The Fall of Yugoslavia* (London: Penguin, 1996); T. Judah, *Kosovo: War and Revenge* (New York, London: Yale University Press, 2000); N. Malcolm, *Kosovo: A Short History* (New York: Harper Perennial, 1999). Political events during the first five years of UNMIK have been comprehensively documented in King and Mason, *Peace at any Price*.
7 Information from UN General Assembly Kosovo budget reports 1999–2010 (www.un.org); European Commission/World Bank, *Donor Polling for Kosovo (Under UNSCR 1244)* (Brussels: Joint Office for South East Europe, 2006); European Commission, *Instrument for Pre-Accession Assistance (IPA) Multi-Annual Indicative Planning Document (MIPD) 2008–2010, Kosovo* (Brussels: European Commission, 2008); and www.eulex-kosovo.eu/en/info/whatisEulex.php, accessed 5 June 2014.
8 W. Bartlett, *Europe's Troubled Region: Economic Development, Institutional Reform and Social Welfare in the Western Balkans* (London: Routledge, 2006); ESI, *De-industrialisation and its Consequences: A Kosovo Story* (Pristina; Berlin: European Stability Initiative, 2002); V. Gligorov, 'The economics of Kosovo: Does viability matter?' *The International Spectator* 35: 2 (2000) 87–101; IMF, *Kosovo: Macroeconomic Issues and Fiscal Sustainability* (Washington DC: International Monetary Fund, 2001); IMF, *Kosovo: Progress in Institution-Building and the Economic Policy Challenges Ahead* (Washington, DC: International Monetary Fund, 2001); A. Nove, *The Economics of Feasible Socialism* (London; New York: Routledge, 2003); World Bank, *Kosovo Poverty Assessment Vol 1: Main Report* (Washington, DC: World Bank, 2001).
9 Malcolm, *Kosovo: A Short History* 17–21.

10 DFID, *Kosovo: Strategy Paper 2001–2004* (London: UK Department for International Development, 2001) 4; European Agency for Reconstruction, *Institutional Capacity Building Support (Kosovo) Executive Summary*, Evaluation (EU/11/05/07) (Thessaloniki: European Agency for Reconstruction, 2008) 3.

11 AFP, 'Blood feud cripples lives in Kosovo', *Agence France-Presse* (12 July 2011); IWPR, 'Blood Feuds Revive in Unstable Kosovo', *Institute for War and Peace Reporting* (21 February 2005); C. Jennings, 'New honour code aims to cut killings', *Scotsman* (23 April 2005). Also see coverage in UNMIK News Archives and UNDP Early Warning Reports.

12 M. Arandarenko and P. Golicin, 'Serbia' in B. Deacon and P. Stubbs (eds), *Social Policy and International Interventions in South East Europe* (Cheltenham, UK; Northampton, MA: Edward Elgar, 2007) 167–86.

13 World Bank, *Kosovo: Building Peace through Sustained Growth. The Economic and Social Policy Agenda* (Brussels: Joint Office for South East Europe, 1999) 17.

14 For summaries of the main ideas about development in this literature see J. Rapley, *Understanding Development: Theory and Practice in the Third World* (Boulder, CO: Lynne Rienner, 2002); K. Willis, *Theories and Practices of Development* (London; New York: Routledge, 2005).

15 H.-J. Chang, 'The market, the state and institutions in economic development' in H.-J. Chang (ed.), *Rethinking Development Economics* (London: Anthem Press, 2003) 41–60; J. E. Stiglitz, *Globalization and its Discontents* (New York; London: W W Norton & Company, 2002); J. Toye, *Dilemmas of Development: Reflections on the Counter-Revolution in Development Economics* (Oxford: Blackwell, 1993).

16 C. Johnson, *Japan, who Governs?: The Rise of the Developmental State* (New York: Norton, 1995); A. Leftwich, *States of Development: On the Primacy of Politics in Development* (Cambridge, UK; Malden, MA: Polity; Blackwell, 2000); R. Wade, *Governing the Market: Economic Theory and the Role of Government in East Asian Industrialization* (Princeton, NJ: Princeton University Press, 1990).

17 World Bank, *The State in a Changing World*, World Development Report 1997 (published for the World Bank by Oxford University Press, 1997).

18 M. Abramovitz, 'The elements of social capability' in B. H. Koo and D. H. Perkins (eds), *Social Capability and Long Term Economic Growth* (New York: St Martins Press/Korean Development Institute, 1995) 19–47; J. Temple and P. A. Johnson, 'Social capability and economic growth', *The Quarterly Journal of Economics* 113: 3 (1998) 965–90.

19 L. E. Harrison, *Underdevelopment is a State of Mind: The Latin American Case* (Centre for International Affairs, Harvard University and University Press of America, 1985); L. E. Harrison and J. Kagan (eds), *Developing Cultures: Essays on Cultural Change* (New York; London: Routledge, 2006).

20 P. Collier, *Social Capital and Poverty*, Social Capital Initiative Working Paper No. 4 (Washington, DC: World Bank, 1998); C. Grootaert, *Social Capital: The Missing Link?*, Social Capital Initiative Working Paper No. 3 (Washington, DC: World Bank, 1998).

21 W. W. Rostow, *The Stages of Economic Growth: A Non-communist Manifesto* (Cambridge: Cambridge University Press, 1960) 8.

22 L. Pritchett, M. Woolcock and M. Andrews, *Capability Traps? The Mechanisms of Persistent Implementation Failure*, Working Paper 234 (Washington, DC: Center for Global Development, 2010).

23 D. North, *An Introduction to Institutions and Institutional Change* (Cambridge; New York: Cambridge University Press, 1990).

24 F. Fukuyama, *State-building: Governance and World Order in the Twenty-first Century* (London: Profile Books, 2004); World Bank, *Governance Matters: A Decade of Measuring the Quality of Governance* (Washington, DC: World Bank, 2006).

25 OECD, *The Challenge of Capacity Development: Working Towards Good Practice*, DAC Guildelines and Reference Series (Paris: Organisation for Economic Co-operation and Development, 2006); UNDP, *Capacity Development*, Technical Advisory Paper 2 (New York: United Nations Development Program, 1997); M. Venner, 'The concept of 'capacity' in development assistance: new paradigm or more of the same?', *Global Change, Peace & Security* 27: 1 (2015) 85–96.

26 Paris, *At War's End*.

27 D. W. Brinkerhoff, 'Rebuilding governance in failed states and post-conflict societies: Core concepts and cross-cutting themes', *Public Administration and Development* 25 (2005) 3–14, 7.

28 L. Abdela, 'Kosovo: missed opportunities, lessons for the future', *Development in Practice* 13: 2–3 (2003) 208–16; I. Bache and A. Taylor, 'The politics of policy resistance: Reconstructing higher education in Kosovo', *Journal of Public Policy* 23: 3 (2003) 279–300; D. Buwa and H. Vuori, 'Rebuilding a health care system: War, reconstruction and health care reforms in Kosovo', *European Journal of Public Health* 17: 2 (2007) 226–30; J. Campbell, V. Percival and A. Zwi, 'Ministerial challenges: Post-conflict, post election issues in Kosovo's health sector', *European Journal of Public Health* 13: 2 (2003) 177–81; C. Corrin, 'Developing policy on integration and re/construction in Kosova', *Development in Practice* 13: 2–3 (2003) 189–207; A. Di Lellio, 'Empire lite as a swamp', *Transitions* XLV: 1 (2005) 63–80; A. Hehir, 'Autonomous province building: Identification theory and the failure of UNMIK', *International Peacekeeping* 13: 2 (2006) 200–13; S. G. Simonsen, 'Nationbuilding as peacebuilding: Racing to define the Kosovar', *International Peacekeeping* 11: 2 (2004) 289–311; M. Sommers and P. Buckland, 'Negotiating Kosovo's Education Minefield', *Forced Migration Review* 22 (2005) 38–9; UNMIK, *Kosovo: Reconstruction 2000*, Public Reconstruction and Investment Programme (Pristina: Department of Reconstruction, EU Pillar IV, 2000).

29 T. Addison, A. R. Chowdhury and S. M. Murshed, 'Financing reconstruction' in G. Junne and W. Verkoren (eds), *Postconflict Development: Meeting New Challenges* (Boulder, CO; London: Lynne Rienner Publishers, 2005) 211–22; R. Caplan, *International Governance of War-Torn Territories: Rule and Reconstruction* (New York: Oxford University Press, 2005); IMF, *Rebuilding Fiscal Institutions in Post Conflict Countries* (Washington, DC: Fiscal Affairs Department, International Monetary Fund, 2004).

30 G. del Castillo, *Rebuilding War-Torn States: The Challenge of Post-Conflict Economic Reconstruction* (Oxford: Oxford University Press, 2008); J. L. Herrero, 'Building state institutions' in G. Junne and W. Verkoren (eds), *Postconflict Development: Meeting New Challenges* (Boulder, CO; London: Lynne Rienner Publishers, 2005) 43–58; B. Kamphuis, 'Economic policy for building peace' in G. Junne and W. Verkoren (eds), *Postconflict Development: Meeting New Challenges* (Boulder, CO; London: Lynne Rienner Publishers, 2005) 185–210; M. Turner and M. Pugh, 'Towards a new agenda for transforming war economies', *Conflict, Security and Development* 6: 3 (2006) 471–9; S. L. Woodward, 'Economic priorities for successful peace implementation' in S. J. Stedman, D. Rothchild and E. M. Cousens (eds), *Ending Civil Wars: The Implementation of Peace Agreements* (Boulder, CO; London: Lynne Rienner, 2002) 183–214.

31 Caplan, *International Governance of War-Torn Territories*; S. Chesterman, *You, The People: The United Nations, Transitional Administration and State Building* (Oxford: Oxford University Press, 2004); J. Narten, 'Dilemmas of promoting 'local ownership': The case of postwar Kosovo' in R. Paris and T. Sisk (eds), *The Dilemmas of Statebuilding: Confronting the Contradictions of Postwar Peace Operations* (London; New York: Routledge, 2008) 252–83.

32 J. Appleby, *The Relentless Revolution: A History of Capitalism* (New York; London: W W Norton & Company, 2010); N. Ferguson, *Civilization: The West and the Rest* (London: Allen

Lane, 2011); D. S. Landes, *The Wealth and Poverty of Nations: Why some are so Rich and some so Poor* (New York: W W Norton, 1998).

33 P. Parthasarathi, *Why Europe Grew Rich and Asia Did Not: Global Economic Divergence, 1600–1850* (Cambridge: Cambridge University Press, 2011); K. Pomeranz and S. Topik, *The World That Trade Created* (Armonk, New York; London: M. E. Sharpe, 1999).

34 B. Weinstein, 'Developing inequality', *American Historical Review* 113: February (2008) 1–18.

35 R. Abrahamsen, 'The power of partnerships in global governance', *Third World Quarterly* 25: 8 (2004) 1453–67; J. Essex, 'The Neoliberalization of Development: Trade Capacity Building and Security at the US Agency for International Development', *Antipode* 40: 2 (2008) 229–51; S. Hameiri, 'Capacity and its Fallacies: International State Building as State Transformation', *Millennium – Journal of International Studies* 38: 1 (2009) 55–81; S. Ilcan and L. Phillips, 'Global Developmentalities: Keynote Address' (Technocracy@Development Conference, The University of Wageningen, The Netherlands. 26–28 June 2006); L. Phillips and S. Ilcan, 'Capacity-building: The neoliberal governance of development', *Canadian Journal of Development Studies* 23: 3 (2004) 393–409.

36 W. Bello, 'The Rise of the Relief and Reconstruction Complex', *Journal of International Affairs* 59: 2 (2006) 281–96; D. Chandler, *Empire in Denial: The Politics of Statebuilding* (London; Ann Arbor, MI: Pluto Press, 2006); M. Duffield, 'Social reconstruction and the radicalization of development: Aid as a relation of global liberal governance', *Development and Change* 33: 5 (2002) 1049–71; N. Klein, 'Baghdad Year Zero: Pillaging Iraq in pursuit of a neocon utopia', *Harpers Magazine* (September 2004) 43–53; D. Moore, 'Levelling the playing fields and embedding illusions: 'Post-conflict' discourse and neo-liberal 'development' in war-torn Africa', *Review of African Political Economy* 27: 83 (2000) 11–28; Turner and Pugh, 'Towards a new agenda for transforming war economies'.

37 D. Bohle, 'Neoliberal hegemony, transnational capital and the terms of the EU's eastward expansion', *Capital & Class* 30: 1 (2006) 57–86.

38 T. Banuri, 'Development and the politics of knowledge: A critical interpretation of the social role of modernization theories in the development of the third world' in F. A. Marglin and S. A. Marglin (eds), *Dominating Knowledge: Development, Culture and Resistance* (Oxford: Clarendon Press, 1990) 29–72; S. A. Marglin, 'Towards a decolonisation of the mind' in *ibid.* 1–28; O. Mehmet, *Westernizing the Third World: The Eurocentricity of Economic Development Theories* (London; New York: Routledge, 1999).

39 G. Rist, *The History of Development: from Western Origins to Global Faith* (Atlantic Highlands, NJ: Zed Books, 1997) 241.

40 G. N. Kitching, *Development and Underdevelopment in Historical Perspective: Populism, Nationalism and Industrialization* (London; New York: Routledge, 1989).

41 Quoted in C. R. Hill, *Outpost: Life on the Frontlines of American Diplomacy: A Memoir* (New York: Simon and Schuster, 2014) 321.

42 R. Paris, 'Saving liberal peacebuilding', *Review of International Studies* 36 (2010) 337–65.

43 R. MacGinty and O. P. Richmond, 'Myth or reality: Opposing views on the liberal peace and post-war reconstruction', *Global Society* 21: 4 (2007) 491–7.

44 Paris, *At War's End.*

45 H.-J. Chang, 'Institutional development in historical perspective' in H.-J. Chang (ed.), *Rethinking Development Economics* (London: Anthem Press, 2003) 499–521.

46 P. Evans, 'Development as institutional change: The pitfalls of monocropping and the potentials of deliberation', *Studies in Comparative International Development* 38: 4 (2004) 30–52, 34; M. H. Khan, 'Corruption and governance in early capitalism: World Bank strategies and their

limitations' in J. Pincus and J. Winters (eds), *Reinventing the World Bank* (Ithaca, NY: Cornell University Press, 2002) 164–84 165; Leftwich, *States of Development* 130.

47 M. S. Grindle, 'Good enough governance: Poverty reduction and reform in developing countries', *Governance: An International Journal of Policy, Administration, and Institutions* 17: 4 (2004) 525–48.

48 E. J. Berg, *Rethinking Technical Cooperation: Reforms for Capacity Building in Africa* (New York: United Nations Development Program, 1993) 153; T. Carothers, *Aiding Democracy Abroad: The Learning Curve* (Washington, DC: Carnegie Endowment for International Peace, 1999) 270; D. Conyers and R. Mellors, 'Aid effectiveness in Sub Saharan Africa: The problem of donor capacity', *IDS Bulletin* 36: 3 (2005) 83–9; Dichter, *Despite Good Intentions* 130; D. D. Gow and E. R. Morss, 'The notorious nine: Critical problems in project implementation', *World Development* 16: 12 (1988) 1399–418; D. Porter, B. Allen and G. Thompson, *Development in Practice: Paved with Good Intentions* (London; New York: Routledge, 1991); D. Seers, 'Why visiting economists fail', *The Journal of Political Economy* 70: 4 (1962) 325–38.

49 G. H. Honadle and J. K. Rosengard, 'Putting "projectized" development in perspective' *Public Administration and Development* 3: 4 (1983) 299–306.

50 Task Force on Overseas Economic Operations, *Report on Overseas Economic Operations for the Commission on Organisation of the Executive Branch of Government* (Washington, DC: United States Government, 1955).

51 A. Maddison, *Foreign Skills and Technical Assistance in Economic Development* (Paris: Development Centre of the Organisation for Economic Co-operation and Development, 1965); C. Murphy, *The United Nations Development Programme: A Better Way?* (Cambridge: Cambridge University Press, 2006); World Bank, *The International Bank for Reconstruction and Development, 1946–1953* (Baltimore, MD: Johns Hopkins Press, 1954).

52 The proportion of 'technical cooperation' reported in official development assistance peaked at 24.8 per cent in 1973 and continued to represent around 20 per cent of development aid. In 2005 this was worth around $21.6 billion (OECD International Development Statistics Online, www.oecd.org/dac/stats/data, accessed May 2007).

53 Dichter, *Despite Good Intentions*; P. Griffiths, *The Economist's Tale: A Consultant Encounters Hunger and the World Bank* (London; New York: Zed Books, 2003); M. W. Huddleston, 'Innocents abroad: Reflections of a public administration consultant in Bosnia', *Public Administration Review* 59: 2 (1999) 147–60; Seers, 'Why visiting economists fail'.

54 Aid/Watch, *Action for Aid Justice: Australian Aid Priorities and Technical Assistance*, Fact Sheet (Erskineville, NSW: Aid Watch, no date); P. Morgan, 'Technical assistance: correcting the precedents', *UNDP Development Policy Journal* 2 (2002) 1–22; OECD, 'Technical Cooperation' in *2005 Development Cooperation Report* (Paris: Organisation for Economic Co-operation and Development, 2006) 111–29.

55 T. Land, *Joint Evaluation Study of the Provision of Technical Assistance Personnel: What Can we Learn from Promising Experiences? Synthesis Report*, ECDPM Discussion Paper No. 78 (Maastricht: European Centre for Development Policy Management, 2007) 15; Morgan, 'Technical assistance'.

56 Berg, *Rethinking Technical Cooperation*; N. Birdsall, *Seven Deadly Sins: Reflections on Donor Failings*, Working Paper No. 50 (Washington, DC: Center for Global Development, 2004); R. Cassen, *Does Aid Work? Report to an Intergovernmental Task Force* (Oxford; New York: Clarendon Press; Oxford University Press, 1986); OECD, *DAC Principles for Effective Aid: Development Assistance Manual* (Paris: Organisation for Economic Co-operation and Development,1992); OECD, *Harmonising Donor Practices for Effective Aid Delivery: Good*

Practice Papers, DAC Guidelines and Reference Series (Paris: Organisation for Economic Co-operation and Development, 2003); L. B. Pearson, *Partners in Development: Report of the Commission on International Development* (New York: Praeger, 1969).

57 OECD, *Paris Declaration on Aid Effectiveness*, High Level Forum, 28 February–2 March (Paris: Organisation for Economic Co-operation and Development, 2005).

58 3rd High Level Forum on Aid Effectiveness, *Accra Agenda for Action* (2008); 4th High Level Forum on Aid Effectiveness, *Busan Partnership for Effective Development Cooperation* (2011).

59 R. F. Mikesell, 'The emergence of the World Bank as a development institution' in K. Acheson, J. F. Chant and M. Prachowny (eds), *Bretton Woods Revisited: Evaluations of the IMF and the IBRD* (Toronto: University of Toronto Press, 1972) 70–84; Pearson, *Partners in Development*; Task Force on Overseas Economic Operations, *Report on Overseas Economic Operations*; US International Development Advisory Board, *Partners in Progress: A Report to the President* (Washington, DC: Govt. Printer, 1951); World Bank, *The International Bank for Reconstruction and Development, 1946–1953*.

60 OECD, *Aid Effectiveness 2005–2010: Progress in Implementing the Paris Declaration* (Paris: Organisation for Economic Co-operation and Development, 2011) 15.

61 J. D. Montgomery, *The Politics of Foreign Aid: American Experience in Southeast Asia* (New York: published for the Council on Foreign Relations by Praeger, 1962) 4.

62 E. Skendaj, *Creating Kosovo: International Oversight and the Making of Ethical Institutions* (Ithaca, NY: Cornell University Press, 2014).

63 A. Holohan, *Networks of Democracy: Lessons from Kosovo for Afghanistan, Iraq and beyond* (Stanford, CA: Stanford University Press, 2005); King and Mason, *Peace at any Price*; D. Magalachvili, 'Kosovo: A critique of a failed mission', *Mediterranean Quarterly* Summer (2005) 118–41; B. Pula, 'The UN in Kosova: Administering democratization?' in F. Bieber and Z. Daskalovski (eds), *Understanding the War in Kosovo* (London; Portland, OH: Frank Cass, 2003) 199–216.

1

The setting

Kosovo's post-conflict era began on 9 June 1999 when a military-technical agreement was signed between NATO and the Governments of the Federal Republic of Yugoslavia and the Republic of Serbia on terms for the withdrawal of the Yugoslav army and Serbian police from Kosovo. The next day, the UN Security Council adopted Resolution 1244 (UNSCR 1244) and the UN began rapid preparations for a large-scale peacekeeping mission. Many of those engaged in negotiating the resolution may not have fully grasped the magnitude and difficulty of the task they were handing to the UN. The Security Council debate made few references to the implementation arrangements for the peace agreement.[1]

Major aid donors and international aid bodies, however, had very clear ideas about what international action in post-conflict Kosovo should involve and had already developed quite detailed plans. Their proposed development and reform agenda was significantly more expansive than the UN's modest ideas about transitional administration and placed Kosovo firmly on a path to economic transformation. Events unfolding on the ground from the moment the peace agreement was signed, however, rapidly made the job of all parties much harder. Ongoing inter-ethnic hostility and the flight of most of the Serb population, a complex political situation with competing groups claiming to be the legitimate government, and a desire by many in the local population to return to the certainties of the past rather than to embrace rapid transformation presented significant challenges to the international intervention.

How Kosovo became an aid project

The UN scrambled to organise the Kosovo Mission in the days after the Security Council decision, but other organisations had been planning for the post-conflict period long before the conflict ended. On 2 April 1999, shortly after the start of NATO military action against Yugoslavia, the World Bank and the IMF held an emergency donor meeting to discuss the impact of the conflict on the region. This was followed a few weeks later by a high-level meeting of international financial institutions and donor countries to discuss their responses to the conflict.[2] The subject matter of these meetings went well beyond the immediate humanitarian crisis and included an exchange of views 'on a medium to long-term approach for economic reconstruction and recovery, growth and progress in reaching social stability in the region once peace is achieved'.[3]

In May, a joint World Bank/European Union office was set up in Brussels to coordinate aid in South East Europe, including Kosovo, with the goal of implementing a comprehensive regional framework for economic development.[4] In the same month, the European Commission announced a new 'stabilisation and association' process (SAP) for South East Europe. The SAP would provide financial assistance and cooperation to the countries of the former Yugoslavia and Albania in order to 'draw the region closer to the perspective of full integration into EU structures'.[5] In addition, in June 1999, G8 leaders endorsed the EU's proposal for a 'Stability Pact' which would provide a political framework for Balkan countries to integrate into 'the Euro Atlantic Structures'.[6] So, while the conflict was still under way and a large part of the population was scattered across the region in refugee camps, the major international powers and donor institutions were already drawing up plans for Kosovo's economic future and integration with the EU.

Defining the 'liberal peace'

As soon as the UN Security Council resolution was passed, a succession of donor meetings and press conferences, and numerous World Bank, IMF and European Commission reports further developed the agenda for the post-conflict period. A High Level Steering Group on Kosovo Reconstruction, comprising Ministers of major donor countries and senior officials of the lead international organisations, met on 13 July to discuss the strategic direction for economic reconstruction, stabilisation, reform and development in the region.[7] A donor conference to mobilise aid resources was held in late July in Brussels, attended by over 100 donor countries and international bodies.[8] The World Bank prepared a paper on 'Strategic Directions for Economic Recovery' for discussion at the conference, and outlined its own plans to provide policy advice and donor coordination.[9]

The World Bank and the European Commission produced further documents on economic reconstruction and development priorities for a second donor conference held in November 1999, also in Brussels. These reports defined the main policy tasks facing the interim civil administration, with a concentration on establishing economic institutions, strengthening the public administration, rapid transition to a market economy, reforms in education, health and social protection, and setting the stage for private-sector-led recovery.[10] The conference participants confirmed donor support for the programme set out in these papers.[11]

This reconstruction agenda in Kosovo was well within the parameters of the 'liberal peace' strategy. The World Bank argued that 'economic growth and prosperity in

Kosovo is clearly a pre-requisite to its stability'[12] and the theme of economic development as the path to peace is repeated often in the documents and speeches of donors. The World Bank's Johannes Linn argued that 'our efforts to help rebuild Kosovo must be comprehensive and not limited to the reconstruction of damaged economic assets',[13] and a paper presented to the conference by the EU official who would head up UNMIK's 'Pillar IV', Joly Dixon, boldly stated that 'UNMIK's mission is to turn Kosovo into a multi-ethnic democracy with a well-functioning economy firmly based on market principles and the rule of law'.[14] In his remarks to the conference he added 'the idea of just putting the thing back as it was before is not very attractive. We must have a higher aspiration than that'.[15]

Putting development into UNSCR 1244

The only legal authority for any international organisation or donor government to act in Kosovo without the agreement of the Federal Republic of Yugoslavia (FRY), however, was UNSCR 1244, so the statements of international and bilateral donors made it clear that their activities could in some way be linked to or justified by reference to that document. This required some expansive interpretation of the wording of the resolution. The stated function of the UN civilian presence in the Resolution was to provide:

> an interim administration for Kosovo under which the people of Kosovo can enjoy substantial autonomy within the Federal Republic of Yugoslavia, and which will provide transitional administration while establishing and overseeing the development of provisional democratic self governing institutions to ensure conditions for a peaceful and normal life for all inhabitants of Kosovo.[16]

The Resolution made only passing reference to economic prosperity and no reference at all to markets or the private sector. The documents produced by donors and international financial institutions, however, linked 'a peaceful and normal life' in Kosovo with economic reform and development and thus cited UNSCR 1244 as the authority to implement development programmes beyond immediate transitional administration.

These aspirations for Kosovo, it was clear, would require the application of significant amounts of donor funds. The World Bank and the EU envisaged a large, multi-year assistance programme of reconstruction and economic recovery to put Kosovo on the path of sustained economic and social development. At the second donor conference they proposed a comprehensive reconstruction and recovery framework over a period of four to five years at an estimated cost of US$2.3 billion.[17] Their reports acknowledged that such a large programme would be an ambitious and complex exercise and would involve a large number of actors and a substantial amount of technical assistance and training. The ideas and methods of development assistance were thus brought to bear on the post-conflict recovery exercise and the major international aid organisations and leading bilateral development agencies all saw a role for themselves.

While economic development dominated the discussions at donor conferences, the range of issues that were of concern to other donors and non-government bodies was much broader and rapidly expanding. A report on activities implemented during 1999 and 2000 describes donor initiatives in the environment, sport, media, culture, road safety and the preservation of historical monuments, among other things.[18] While some of these projects involved restoring or restarting institutions and facilities that had existed before the conflict, many had wider objectives of modernising, restructuring, reforming or establishing for the first time major components of daily life in Kosovo. There was thus a significant gap between the initial peacekeeping concept encapsulated in UNSCR 1244 and what donors wanted to see done.

There were other ways in which donors' ideas about the programme in Kosovo deviated from the words negotiated in the Security Council. As well as extending the scope of the task, the main donors, including the EU, the World Bank and USAID, showed little hesitation in their reports and press conferences in discussing Kosovo as a separate entity from Yugoslavia or Serbia, in spite of the wording of the Security Council resolution, which emphasised that Kosovo's autonomy would be 'within the Federal Republic of Yugoslavia'.[19] They generally took the view that what Kosovo needed was a complete break with the past. In this respect there is a significant difference in tone and approach between the carefully neutral stance of UN documents and the language in many donor statements. Although World Bank reports occasionally refer to the status of Kosovo as an entity within Serbia, and note the need for cooperation with Serbia and Yugoslavia on the degree to which 'substantial autonomy' will be exercised, they also note that UNMIK and KFOR are responsible for relations with Yugoslavia and leave these issues to them to resolve, while pressing on with calls for significant reform.[20]

The intransigence of the Milošević regime in Yugoslavia at the time and Serbia's poor image in international affairs following the conflicts in Bosnia and Kosovo made it easy for donors to take this position on Kosovo's assumed separation from Serbia. Had the Yugoslav authorities been prepared to cooperate more actively with the UN and encouraged Serbs in Kosovo to participate in the interim administration, things may have been different. However, in effect Kosovo was treated by many international aid bodies as an independent entity from the start. UNMIK, operating under the constraints of UNSCR 1244 and subject to scrutiny by the Security Council, was obliged to take a more conservative stance on this question. The extent of institutional change that should be pursued and the degree of autonomy that should be allowed to Kosovo's administration was an ongoing source of conflict between the UN, which had a more limited interpretation of the objective, and many other actors, who saw their task as the creation of an independent Kosovo administration.

The 'blank slate', the 'lost decade' and the 'window of opportunity'

The reports produced by the World Bank, the IMF, the European Commission and other organisations expressed a particular set of ideas about Kosovo's history, the conflict and its implications, and these ideas influenced the activities and attitudes of donors and technical advisers. The use of 'dominant narratives' by international actors to make sense of complex situations has been noted as a feature of foreign intervention in post-conflict and developing countries.[21] Although these donor accounts of the Kosovo context are factually based, they present a relatively selective view of the situation. A common theme is the idea of the territory as a 'blank slate', more or less devoid of political and economic institutions and ready to be reformed along lines favoured by donors. It was argued that Kosovo had no existing institutions, policies or administrative capacity, or what it did have was not what was needed. The World Bank's special representative to South East Europe, Rory O'Sullivan, at a press conference in July 1999 noted that 'The problem in Kosovo is that there is nothing there. There is no administration. There is no civil administration which comes from the local people, if you like ... Imagine the difficulty of setting up a totally new administration, a totally new country.'[22] Another World Bank report argued:

> The removal of Kosovo's autonomy and the consequent centralization of financial management functions in Belgrade ... have created an institutional vacuum for the public administration in Kosovo ... Essential functions of any public administration system ... either do not exist or exist in a rudimentary form that does not ensure adequate effectiveness and transparency in the use of resources.[23]

The importance of the 'blank slate' and 'institutional vacuum' concepts was that they created a 'window of opportunity' for donors to implement rapid and substantial social and economic reform, and to create new, ideal institutions from the ground up.

The cause of this blank slate was generally identified as the 'lost decade' resulting from the actions of Serbia and the consequent conflict, decline and neglect of the 1990s. The World Bank's paper on strategic directions for recovery in July 1999, for example, describes at length the loss of managerial and technical expertise, the looting of assets and pervasive neglect of maintenance over the decade as a result of the dismantling of Kosovo's autonomous structures in 1989 and the dismissal of Albanian staff.[24] The terms 'lost decade' and 'decade of neglect' appear in many subsequent documents produced by the World Bank and other donors. The actions of the Serb authorities under the Milošević regime of the 1990s certainly had an adverse impact on the Kosovo economy, as well as on the civil rights and well-being of the Albanian population, and few people in the immediate aftermath of the conflict were willing to absolve the Serb government of blame. However, at the same time these statements largely ignored Kosovo's long history of economic disadvantage and other factors that contributed to economic decline such as international sanctions and the general effects of socialism and economic mismanagement.[25] They also attributed blame for the economic situation almost entirely to Serbia and by association the ethnic Serbs in Kosovo. Statements such as these most likely did little to encourage future ethnic reconciliation within Kosovo.

The question of 'ownership'

At donor conferences and other meetings the lead donors reached agreement on the institutions and reforms that would be essential for successful reconstruction and development. At the same time, however, they also made reference to the importance of local participation in developing and implementing the reconstruction programme. The World Bank's *Strategic Directions* paper in July 1999, for example, argued that:

> Kosovo's people should be responsible for the economic and social recovery of their region. Expatriates should assist, rather than substitute themselves to local authorities in the identification of needs and priorities. Donors should empower and support Kosovo's emerging authorities for the successful implementation of the Priority Recovery Programme.[26]

The UN Secretary General's first report to the Security Council also stated that 'it is clearly an essential requirement for the success of UNMIK that the people of Kosovo be included fully and effectively in its work, particularly that of the interim administration, so that the transition to self-governing institutions is both smooth and timely.'[27]

Despite these expressed intentions to involve the local population in setting priorities and coordinating development programmes, the opportunities to achieve this in the absence of a recognised local government were limited. A World Bank/European Commission report acknowledged that 'in view of the tight timetable, involving Kosovars to the extent desirable in the preparation of the emergency projects may be difficult'.[28] USAID also noted that 'tradeoffs between rapid donor-led reform and more time-consuming consultative approaches loom large as donors attempt to accomplish as much as possible while funding levels and the international presence remain large'.[29]

Donor statements generally asserted that Kosovo's politicians were committed to the economic reform policies being proposed, and Kosovar representatives and officials occasionally made public statements of support.[30] A significant proportion of the wider Kosovar population, however, supported a return to the socialist era of state-controlled production. The 1970s and 1980s, when the province had been a self-governing autonomous region of Serbia, had seemed to many Kosovo Albanians to be the best of times. They had had their own Assembly, police force, university and national bank, and the administration had been primarily in the hands of Albanians.[31] It was the closest they had ever been to the goal of independence. The hardships of the Milošević era led many Kosovo Albanians to believe that life would be good again if everything returned to the way it was before 1989. In the immediate aftermath of the conflict, therefore, workers who had lost their jobs in former government departments and state-owned enterprises in 1989 returned to their posts and reinstated the system of socialist self-management that had applied a decade earlier. Albanian judges, appointed by the UN's judicial affairs office, refused to recognise the legal framework that applied in 1999, under Serbian rule, and instead applied laws that were current in 1989, forcing the UN to formally change its policy on applicable law.[32] There was a widespread view that government institutions, utilities and enterprises ought to be restored to what they were, with the guaranteed employment that implied.[33]

The World Bank reported to the second donor's conference in November 1999 that 'there is a long way to go before local opinion moves away from a simple wish to recreate economic life as it existed before the abrogation of Kosovo's autonomy towards modern economic and social policies, with high government standards'.[34] This was, however, seen primarily as a public education issue:

> the articulation of a clear vision and the path of transition that Kosovo must follow are tasks that the political leadership must now address ... A major task for UNMIK and the international institutions will be to help develop viable transition strategies and institutions, and build public support for them.[35]

Similarly, although USAID claimed that it had consulted closely with Kosovar community leaders on its programmes, including through a 'Democracy and Governance retreat' in November 1999 and through local 'Community Improvement Councils', the purpose of these meetings was not to seek the views of local representatives and develop policies and projects based on their preferences, but to ensure 'strong buy-in to, and support for the type of economic policy and institutional reforms being pursued'.[36]

Kosovo in June 1999

While UN officials in New York were developing their plans for the transitional administration mission, and the lead development organisations were conferring in Washington and Brussels, events in Kosovo moved rapidly. As the Yugoslav forces withdrew some Kosovars began implementing their own ideas about the post-conflict political, institutional and demographic environment, which did not conform to the plans of either group of international actors. The initial concept for UNMIK, presented to the Security Council by the Secretary General Kofi Annan two days after UNSCR 1244 was passed, clearly underestimated its complexity. The general assumption seemed to be that all parties – Serb and Albanian – would return to the status quo of three months earlier and the UN would simply take over from the Belgrade government in overseeing the administration while starting to re-engage Albanians in the public sector. The UN appeared to be still working on the basis of the model proposed at the Rambouillet negotiations in February 1999, which had envisaged an orderly transfer of responsibility from the Serbian government to local autonomous entities.[37] There were several reasons, however, why this approach would not now be possible. The chaos and lawlessness that followed the departure of Yugoslav and Serb forces and the flight of most of the Serb officials who had previously administered the territory made a peaceful and orderly transition unlikely. The security vacuum between the departure of the Yugoslav authorities and the arrival of KFOR troops and UN police also provided an opportunity for manoeuvring by various Albanian political factions to gain control of public resources, and for some Kosovars to implement their own interpretation of reconstruction.

Serb exodus

At the end of earlier Balkan conflicts of the 1990s, the return of refugees to their former multi-ethnic neighbourhoods had been slow. The Albanian Kosovars, however, who were mostly living in tents just across the border in Macedonia or Albania, returned to their homes in a matter of days, taking the international community by surprise. Just as promptly, most of the Serb population fled. The likelihood of a mass departure of Kosovo Serbs at the end of the conflict had been identified by a number of people well beforehand. The International Crisis Group, in May 1999, reported that Serbs 'are very likely to withdraw into Serbia proper as foreign forces move into Kosovo ... any Serbs who remain or return may need to be protected from armed Albanians – this must be a task for KFOR.'[38] The UN's Sergio Viera de Mello, who led a UN Interagency Needs Assessment Mission in late May 1999, also noted that the return of Kosovo Albanian refugees could cause the departure of Serb residents from Kosovo and that every effort must be made to assure their security.[39] Nevertheless, the NATO military forces which made up KFOR were either not aware of this problem or unable to do anything about it, and the six thousand civilian police planned for UNMIK to keep public order did not arrive until many months later. The ferocity of revenge attacks on Serbs that followed the departure of Yugoslav forces seemed to come as a surprise to both the UN and KFOR. As Timothy Garton Ash reported, 'young Kosovars manifest a thirst for revenge that sickens not just foreigners but also many among the older generation of Kosovars who still have memories of peaceful coexistence. Ethnic cleansing has been carried out under the very noses and tank barrels of more than 40,000 international troops.'[40]

The violence persuaded Kosovo Serbs who may have thought of staying to leave. By mid-August it was estimated that no more than 2,000 Serbs remained in Pristina, which previously had a Serb population of at least 20,000.[41] The sudden departure of the people who had until then been in charge of almost all public administration functions left a large gap in the workforce. The UN had been instructed to ensure a multi-ethnic society in Kosovo but several months after the arrival of UNMIK, Garton Ash concluded 'It is now entirely clear that our intervention had decisively resolved, in favour of the Albanians, a Serb Albanian struggle for control of this territory that goes back at least one hundred and twenty years. This was neither the stated nor the real intention of Western policymakers.'[42]

Albanian political factions

Setting up a new administration in Kosovo may also have been easier if there had been a stable and united government-in-waiting. However, this was not the case. The high probability of conflict between the various factions within the Albanian political community had also been widely predicted. During the early 1990s, Albanian Kosovars had largely been united behind their elected unofficial President, Ibrahim Rugova, and the Democratic League of Kosovo (LDK). Later, however, dissatisfaction with Rugova's policy of non-violence spurred the creation of the Kosovo Liberation Army (KLA) and other militia groups. The LDK leadership had also started to splinter. Diplomats who sponsored efforts to end the conflict found that the Kosovo Albanian side appeared to spend more time attacking one another than concentrating on forming a common negotiating team and uniting behind a shared position. The group that had assembled at Rambouillet in February 1999 included people who 'had hated each other for years and some of whom had recently been making death threats against the others.'[43]

Once NATO's actions had removed the Serb threat, the factions turned to fighting each other and the outbreak of civil war appeared a real possibility. During the first days and weeks, each group claimed authority over local administrative structures. Various branches of the KLA seized effective power over municipal administration and a 'provisional government', led by the KLA's Hashim Thaci, established offices in Pristina. The parallel government of Rugova's 'Republic of Kosovo' still existed and former LDK Prime Minister, Bujar Bukoshi, who had fallen out with President Rugova but retained control of large amounts of the administration's funds, returned from exile in Germany still claiming to lead the government. Kosovo thus soon had several putative governments, including multiple police forces. In the municipalities it controlled, the KLA collected taxes and customs payments and issued car registration plates. It was also reportedly involved in the expanding 'grey' economy, trading in oil, cigarettes and alcohol.[44] This situation was considered to pose a serious threat to UN authority in the early days of the Mission.[45]

The challenge of civil administration

All these developments – the flight of Serb government officials and workers, the political contests between Albanian factions and the rejection of existing Serb government institutions by the Albanian population – meant that the UN could not simply take control of an existing, functioning public administration. Neither did it feel able to recognise any of the alternative administrative structures, such as the LDK's parallel administration or the new KLA-backed 'provisional government', without prejudging the political future of the territory. Rather than simply overseeing a transfer of authority over existing institutions, therefore, the UN needed to create a completely new civil administration. The Secretary General's report in mid-July, after one month of work by the Mission, indicated the extent of the problems it was facing:

> The public service structures of Kosovo are largely inoperative due to a combination of neglect, war damage and the departure of trained staff. The municipalities are functioning inadequately or not at all. While water and electricity are usually available, the telephone lines are down, schools are not open and there is practically no public transport service.[46]

As Garton Ash noted, 'If you occasionally wonder why we need a state at all, you should visit a place like Kosovo that has none'.[47] He described Kosovo as a state of anarchy with unregistered cars and unpoliced drivers, organised crime and up to twenty-two murders a week. Even six months later, when I arrived in the winter of UNMIK's first year, the capital Pristina was a city of potholed streets, leaking sewers, intermittent power and piles of uncollected garbage. It was against this background that the various international actors set about their tasks of not only ensuring peace, rebuilding infrastructure and restoring normal living conditions, but also establishing modern institutions, creating a democratic political system, supporting local civil society organisations, building local capacity, promoting gender equality and ensuring long-term economic development.

Political developments since 1999

In spite of the many criticisms that have been made of it, UNMIK nevertheless had significant success in the sphere of political development. Since June 1999 Kosovo has passed through several distinct phases of political evolution, marking a progressive transfer of responsibility to local authorities. Understanding these political developments is relevant for assessing the extent to which donors and foreign advisers can claim responsibility, or should be held accountable, for the successes and failures of the post-conflict period, and to what extent local actors had opportunities to influence policies and outcomes. The main turning points in this development process were the creation of the Joint Interim Administrative Structure (JIAS) in January 2000, six months into the Mission; agreement on a 'Constitutional Framework' and the formation of Provisional Institutions for Self Government (PISG) in 2001; and the provisional government's unilateral declaration of independence in February 2008. Each of these transitions was fraught with conflict between the international mission and local politicians and sometimes between different international actors.

The first six months (July–December 1999)

Although UNMIK took a long time to establish itself, a significant amount was achieved in the first few weeks. The Secretary General's interim Special Representative, Sergio Viera de Mello, arrived on 13 June, three days after the passage of UNSCR 1244, and over the next month his small advance team of UN officials dealt with an extensive range of issues including establishing regional and municipal administrations, appointing local judges and prosecutors, liaising with Kosovar and Yugoslav politicians, assessing the state of public administration structures and utilities, and re-establishing local radio broadcasts, as well as liaising with the numerous international organisations, NGOs and journalists who also arrived in the province at that time. The International Criminal Tribunal for the former Yugoslavia (ICTY) began investigating war crimes, and the UN Mine Action Service started clearing mines.[48] Bernard Kouchner took up the job of SRSG in July. The major preoccupations of the Mission during this period included the humanitarian needs of returning refugees, preventing inter-ethnic retribution, and dealing with the emerging political violence between Albanian factions. The SRSG also had to find time for important visitors including US Secretary of State, Madeleine Albright, British Prime Minister, Tony Blair, and the Foreign Ministers of France and Germany, who all arrived during July and August.

The most significant political initiative during the first weeks was the establishment of a Kosovo Transition Council (KTC), a consultative body intended to allow participation of the people of Kosovo in the decisions and actions of UNMIK. It was not until August, however, that the two major contenders for political leadership, the LDK's Ibrahim Rugova and the KLA's Hashim Thaci, now leader of the Democratic Party of Kosovo (PDK), joined the Council. This was regarded as a major step forward by UN officials.[49] KFOR's demobilisation of the KLA and its reconstitution as the non-military Kosovo Protection Corps in September was also a significant milestone.

The Joint Interim Administrative Structure (January 2000 to March 2002)

In December 1999, UNMIK reached agreement with Kosovar representatives to set up a Joint Interim Administrative Structure (JIAS), which enlarged the KTC to represent a wider range of political and community interests and created an Interim Administrative Council (IAC) comprising four representatives from UNMIK and four Kosovars, all to be appointed by the SRSG.[50] A number of Administrative Departments were also created, to be jointly led by appointed Co-Heads, one Kosovar and one international. In exchange for positions in the new administrative structure, local political leaders were expected to give up their existing parallel governments, including the PDK 'provisional government' and the LDK 'Republic of Kosovo'. The JIAS brought some order and chain of command into what had appeared in initial UN plans to be a confused allocation of responsibilities. The KTC, IAC and Administrative Departments in effect created an unelected interim government with a parliament, a cabinet and an executive administration. However, Kosovars were outnumbered by internationals in all these bodies.

Provisional Institutions for Self Government (February 2002 to February 2008)

During 2000, SRSG Kouchner proposed a contract or 'pact' for provisional self government which would include an interim constitution and an elected government. This continued the idea of granting greater self government and autonomy in exchange for good behaviour on the part of Albanian Kosovars, which had been initiated with the JIAS agreement and has been a continuing theme in the international community's relations with Kosovo's leaders. Negotiations on a 'Constitutional Framework' and 'Provisional Institutions for Self Government' (PISG) were completed in May 2001 by Kouchner's successor, Hans Haekkerup, and Kosovo-wide elections for a parliamentary assembly were held in November 2001. Under the proportional representation electoral system put in place by UNMIK, no single party won enough seats to form a government and, after three months of negotiations, a coalition was formed comprising the three largest parties, the LDK, the PDK and the newly formed Alliance for the Future of Kosovo (AAK). Ibrahim Rugova, leader of the LDK, became President, and Bajram Rexhepi, from the PDK, was appointed Prime Minister. Ministerial responsibilities in the new administration were divided between the political parties, just as they had been in the JIAS.

Early performance of the PISG government was disappointing. Almost none of the members of the Assembly had any previous experience in government and, after ten years of resisting Serb authority, were more familiar with the politics of rebellion than the constructive work of government. The electoral system, which was based on a single electorate and closed party lists, had been devised to deter local political fiefdoms but meant that members of the Assembly were answerable to their party rather than to a local constituency, and with an all-party coalition government there was no real opposition. As a result, Kosovo's government 'had little authority, little experience in how to use it, little sense of overall direction and little political incentive to improve'.[51] UNMIK continued to have final authority over all legislation passed by the Assembly, and most of the areas of policy that Albanian politicians considered important, including security, policing, external affairs, justice and many aspects of economic policy, were reserved for UNMIK.

The crisis of March 2004

The idea of trading increased political authority for compliance with the expectations of international actors was continued with the 'Standards before Status' concept, introduced in 2002. The 'Standards' set out eight policy areas against which progress in Kosovo was to be measured as a precondition for talks on resolving Kosovo's 'final status'. In March 2004, however, a sudden outbreak of violence against Serb Kosovars, which spread to attacks on international forces, stimulated a formal review of UN strategy. In his report to the Security Council, Kai Eide, a Norwegian diplomat, questioned the 'Standards before Status' policy, suggesting that it had led to frustration and stagnation and recommended overall reform of UNMIK including setting a clear goal for the Mission, accelerating the transfer of competencies to the PISG, and increased international effort to improve local capacity for governance.[52] Relations between UNMIK and the Kosovo government improved considerably following the implementation of Eide's recommendations.

A second general election was held in October 2004 and this time the coalition government that resulted comprised only two of the three main political parties, the LDK and AAK, leaving Thaci's PDK to form an opposition. A third general election was held in late 2007. This time the coalition was formed by the LDK and the PDK with the AAK in opposition. PDK leader Hashim Thaci became Prime Minister. A joint LDK/PDK government must be seen as a significant improvement on the situation in 1999 when members of the two parties were reportedly reluctant to be in the same room with each other.

Supervised independence (February 2008 to September 2012)

Many Kosovo Albanians believed they had already declared independence in 1990 when they had established a parallel government and elected Ibrahim Rugova as President. Some international observers had always considered independence inevitable. UNSCR 1244, however, affirmed the sovereignty and territorial integrity of the Federal Republic of Yugoslavia, of which Serbia was the successor state. In October 2005, the UN Security Council agreed to sponsor talks between Serbia and Kosovo on the question of the final status of the territory. The negotiations were coordinated by Maarti Ahtisaari, a Finnish politician. After more than a year of discussion, however, Ahtisaari reported that agreement was impossible. The Albanians refused to accept anything less than full independence; Serbia would accept almost anything but independence. He proposed a 'supervised independence' arrangement, the 'Ahtisaari Plan', under which UNSCR 1244 would be replaced and the EU would take over from the UN in ensuring the rule of law, protection of minorities, human rights and the preservation of cultural and religious heritage in an independent Kosovo.[53] The Kosovo government was prepared to accept this compromise but

Serbia was not and had the support of Russia in the Security Council, thus ensuring that UNSCR 1244 remained in effect.

On 17 February 2008, in response to this impasse, the Government unilaterally declared independence but nevertheless committed itself to implementing the supervised independence arrangement. This step had been widely anticipated and a number of major powers immediately recognised the new country, most notably the US, Germany and France. UNMIK remained in place, but in November 2008 was significantly reduced in size and scope of operations. The reconfigured UNMIK had just 146 international staff and several hundred local personnel engaged primarily in monitoring political developments and minority community welfare.[54] Many of its functions were transferred to the new EU Law and Justice Mission (EULEX). An International Steering Group and an International Civilian Office (ICO) were established to oversee implementation of the Ahtisaari Plan. The International Steering Group formally ended the period of supervised independence in September 2012.[55]

From a political perspective, therefore, the UN-led intervention in Kosovo following the conflict has made significant progress. A democratic government has been established, elections are held regularly and relations between Serb and Albanian Kosovars have been stabilised, although by no means resolved. The number of countries that recognise Kosovo's sovereignty has gradually increased,[56] and Kosovo has been accepted as a member of the IMF and the World Bank. The UN no longer has close involvement in the governance of the territory. However, the international community's objectives in Kosovo have not yet been fully achieved and donor organisations continue to pursue economic, political and social transformation.

Notes

1 UNSC, *Security Council Minutes, 4011th Meeting, Thursday 10 June 1999* (New York: United Nations Security Council, 1999).

2 IMF/World Bank, *The Economic Consequences of the Kosovo Crisis: A Preliminary Assessment of External Financing Needs and the Role of the Fund and the World Bank in the International Response* (Washington, DC: International Monetary Fund, 16 April 1999); IMF/World Bank, International Community Responds to the Kosovo Crisis, Press Release, 27 April (Washington, DC: International Monetary Fund, 1999).

3 IMF/World Bank, *International Community Responds to the Kosovo Crisis*, Press Release, 27 April, para 3.

4 World Bank/European Commission, Press releases and documents on World Bank/European Commission activities in Kosovo web page (Brussels: Joint Office for South East Europe, 1999).

5 European Commission, Commission proposes a Stabilisation and Association process for countries of South-Eastern Europe, Press Release (Brussels: European Commission, 1999) 1.

6 Stability Pact for South East Europe, *About the Stability Pact* web page.

7 World Bank/European Commission, High Level Steering Group Inaugural Meeting, 13 July, Press Release (Brussels: Joint Office for South East Europe, 1999).

8 World Bank/European Commission, The First Donors Conference for Kosovo, Brussels 27 July, Press Release (Brussels: Joint Office for South East Europe, 1999).
9 World Bank, *Strategic Directions for the Economic Recovery of Kosovo: First Donors' Conference for Kosovo, Brussels, 26 July* (Washington, DC: World Bank, 1999); World Bank, *World Bank Group Response to Post Conflict Reconstruction in Kosovo: General Framework for an Emergency Assistance Strategy* (Washington, DC: World Bank, 1999).
10 World Bank, *Economic Statement by the World Bank*, Second Donors' Conference for Kosovo, Brussels, 17 November (Brussels: Joint Office for South East Europe, 1999); World Bank, *Kosovo: Building Peace through Sustained Growth*; World Bank, *World Bank Group Transitional Support Strategy for Kosovo* (Washington, DC: World Bank, 1999); World Bank/European Commission, *Towards Stability and Prosperity: A Program for Reconstruction and Recovery in Kosovo* (Brussels: Joint Office for South East Europe, 1999).
11 World Bank/European Commission, *Kosovo: Donors Pledge US$1 Billion in Support of the Reconstruction and Recovery Programme*, Press Release, Second Donors' Conference for Kosovo, Brussels, 17 November (Brussels: Joint Office for South East Europe, 1999).
12 World Bank, *World Bank Group Response to Post Conflict Reconstruction in Kosovo*, para 15.
13 J. Linn, *Statement by Vice President of the World Bank*, First Donors' Conference for Kosovo, 28 July (Brussels: Joint Office for South East Europe, 1999) para 7.
14 J. Dixon, *Pillar IV's Role within UNMIK*, Paper prepared for the first donor conference, 28 July (Brussels: Joint Office for South East Europe, 1999) para 1.
15 J. Dixon, *Speech at first donor's conference for Kosovo, Brussels, July 28*, Joint Office for South East Europe, 1999) para 5.
16 UNSCR 1244, para 10.
17 World Bank/European Commission, *Towards Stability and Prosperity* 3.
18 UNMIK, *Partnership in Kosovo: Reconstruction 1999–2000, An Overview by the Department of Reconstruction* (Pristina: United Nations Mission in Kosovo, 2001).
19 UNSCR 1244, para 10.
20 World Bank, *Kosovo: Building Peace through Sustained Growth* 3; World Bank, *Strategic Directions for the Economic Recovery of Kosovo* 4.
21 S. Autesserre, *Peaceland: Conflict Resolution and the Everyday Politics of International Intervention* (New York: Cambridge University Press, 2014).
22 World Bank, *Rebuilding Kosovo: A Complicated Challenge for the International Community*, Press Conference Transcript (Brussels), 12 July (Washington, DC: World Bank, 1999) para 17.
23 World Bank, *Kosovo: Building Peace through Sustained Growth* 20.
24 Ibid. 3–6.
25 Glenny, *The Fall of Yugoslavia* 66–7; Judah, *Kosovo: War and Revenge* 46.
26 World Bank, *Strategic Directions for the Economic Recovery of Kosovo* para 46.
27 UNSC, *Report of the Secretary-General pursuant to paragraph 10 of Security Council Resolution 1244 (1999) 12 June 1999* (New York: United Nations Security Council, 1999) para 16.
28 World Bank/European Commission, *Towards Stability and Prosperity* 33.
29 USAID, *Kosovo: Results Review and Resource Request* (Washington, DC: United States Agency for International Development, 2001) 4.
30 AFP, 'Official pleads for urgent aid for Kosovo', *Agence France-Presse* (21 September 1999); A. Begu, *Statement by Mr. Ajri Begu, Economic Policy Advisory Board, Kosovo, Second Donors' Conference, Brussels, November 17* (Brussels: Joint Office for South Eastern Europe, 1999); M. Hajrizi, *The Donor Community's Assistance: A Strong Foundation for a Prosperous Future for Kosova*, Speech by Mehmet Hajrizi, Co-Head of the Department of Reconstruction, UNMIK, Kosovo Donors' Meeting 25–26 February (Pristina: Joint Office for South East Europe, 2001).

31 Judah, *Kosovo: War and Revenge* 44.
32 UNMIK/REG/1999/24, 12 December 1999.
33 World Bank, *Kosovo: Building Peace through Sustained Growth* 4.
34 World Bank, *Economic Statement by the World Bank* para 3.
35 World Bank, *Kosovo: Building Peace through Sustained Growth* 2–3.
36 USAID, *Strategy for Kosovo 2001–2003* (Washington, DC: United States Agency for International Development, 2000) 10.
37 The text of the draft Rambouillet Accords is available at http://peacemaker.un.org/kosovo-rambouilletagreement99 and at www.alb-net.com/kcc/interim.htm, accessed 22 January 2016.
38 ICG, *Kosovo: Let's learn from Bosnia. Models and Methods of International Administration*, ICG Balkans Report N° 66 (Sarajevo: International Crisis Group, 1999) 14.
39 UNSC, *Report of the Inter-Agency Needs Assessment Mission Dispatched by the Secretary-General of the United Nations to the Federal Republic of Yugoslavia* (New York: United Nations Security Council, 1999).
40 Garton Ash, *History of the Present* 446.
41 UNMIK, *UNMIK News Archive 1999* (Pristina: United Nations Mission in Kosovo, 1999).
42 Garton Ash, *History of the Present* 445.
43 Judah, *Kosovo: War and Revenge* 200.
44 L. J. Cohen, 'Kosovo: "Nobody's country"', *Current History* 99: 635 (2000) 117–23, 120; ICG, *Who's Who in Kosovo*, ICG Balkans Report No. 76 (Pristina: International Crisis Group, 1999); Judah, *Kosovo: War and Revenge*.
45 M. Hirsh and J. Terzieff, 'Holbrooke's Ultimatum: Perform or Perish', *Newsweek* (30 August 1999) 27.
46 UNSC, *Report of the Secretary General on the United Nations Interim Administration Mission in Kosovo, 12 July 1999* (New York: United Nations Security Council, 1999) 4.
47 Garton Ash, *History of the Present* 435.
48 UNSC, *Report of the Secretary General on the United Nations Interim Administration Mission in Kosovo, 12 July 1999*.
49 J. Covey, 'Making a viable peace: Moderating political conflict' in J. Covey, M. J. Dziedzic and L. Hawley (eds), *The Quest for Viable Peace: International Intervention and Strategies for Conflict Transformation* (Washington, DC; Arlington, VA: United States Institute of Peace Press; Association of the United States Army, 2005) 99–122, 112.
50 UNMIK/REG/2000/1, 14 January 2000.
51 King and Mason, *Peace at any Price* 165.
52 UNSC, *A Comprehensive Review of the Situation in Kosovo (Eide Report)* (New York: United Nations Security Council, 2005).
53 UNSC, *Report of the Special Envoy of the Secretary General on Kosovo's Future Status (Ahtisaari Report)* (New York: United Nations Security Council, 2007).
54 UNSC, *Report of the Secretary-General on the United Nations Interim Administration Mission in Kosovo, 24 November 2008* (New York: United Nations Security Council, 2008).
55 ICO, *State Building and Exit. The International Civilian Office and Kosovo's Supervised Independence 2008–2012* (Pristina: Kosovo International Civilian Office, 2012).
56 One source claims 111 countries have now recognised Kosovo's independence (www.kosovothanksyou.com/, accessed 2 June 2015).

2

The actors

Official reports on the UN Mission in Kosovo generally refer to UNMIK as the only significant actor in the territory during its post-conflict reconstruction. In the field of public administration development, however, several large and influential international organisations and bilateral donors in addition to the UN played leading roles. Although the majority of these actors broadly agreed with each other on the overall goals of the international intervention, each also pursued their unique national or institutional interests and competed for status and influence. They had their own particular motives for becoming involved, as well as their own ways of working, funding limitations and organisational challenges. On the ground in Kosovo the work of these organisations and the relations between them were sometimes influenced by completely unrelated events in other places or at other times. In this respect the situation in post-conflict Kosovo was not that different from the complex relations between international donors and aid organisations in any developing country as they pursue their own ideas about what should be done and their own institutional interests. In Kosovo, however, the international presence was larger and much more intrusive, making divisions more obvious and ideological rifts more pronounced.

In this chapter I examine the roles played by the half-dozen organisations that had the largest influence on the future public administration in Kosovo, their objectives, the policies they promoted and how they worked together. The UN had overall authority over the Mission and was also responsible, through its civil administration component, for establishing the Kosovo Civil Service and its management procedures, rules and standards. Behind the scenes, however, there was considerable conflict between UNMIK and many of the other international actors. The EU was involved in public administration and public finance through several separate entities, the two most important being UNMIK's 'Pillar IV' and the European Agency for Reconstruction (EAR). Although these were both EU agencies they were quite distinct in their funding, organisation, staffing and procedures. Among the bilateral agencies, the US government was a significant donor, and USAID was particularly important in PFM development. Through its ability to deploy significant funding and large numbers of technical experts quickly it became the lead actor in this field. The UK's Department for International Development (DFID) was a much smaller donor in financial terms, but took a particular interest in the development of the civil service. The World Bank and the IMF provided limited financial assistance but between them played an important role in setting the agenda for institutional development. The combined activities of these international actors and the results they were able to achieve have had a significant impact on the conduct of public administration in Kosovo today.[1]

The United Nations

It had been by no means inevitable that the UN would take the lead role in the post-conflict period in Kosovo. In the complex negotiations between NATO and the Federal Republic of Yugoslavia in mid-1999, the idea that the UN should be responsible for administering Kosovo emerged more or less at the last minute. The peace agreement was the culmination of more than twelve months of diplomatic negotiations on the situation in Kosovo, beginning with discussions led by Richard Holbrooke in early 1989, and continuing through the 'Hill process' in late 1989 and the Rambouillet Conference in February 1999. Numerous peace proposals had been drafted and debated during this time, each involving some form of civilian implementation mission, but none involving the UN.[2] Several international missions had already been sent to Kosovo including the Kosovo Diplomatic Observer Mission in mid-1998 and the Kosovo Verification Mission, established under the auspices of the Organization for Security and Co-operation in Europe (OSCE), in October 1998.[3]

A detailed peace settlement proposal developed at the Rambouillet Conference in France in February 1999 had not envisaged a role for the UN, or for any international civil administration. It had assumed that all existing laws and institutions would remain in place and an OSCE-appointed Civil Implementation Mission, working with a Serb-Albanian Joint Commission, would oversee an orderly transition to an autonomous Kosovo government and administrative structure.[4] The Rambouillet concept was developed at a time when both the Serb government and the Albanian parallel administration were in place and relatively stable, and it would obviously only have been effective with the cooperation of the Yugoslav authorities and both the Serb and Albanian communities in Kosovo. By the time the final peace agreement was signed, however, the situation in Kosovo had changed considerably so this approach was no longer feasible. An ICG report published in May, during the negotiations on the peace agreement, recommended that there should be a single lead agency for the post-conflict international presence, but suggested that the OSCE should be given this role arguing that 'the UN has too often failed to provide decisive leadership in troubled times in the Balkans'.[5]

The UN had been largely excluded from formal discussions on the Kosovo question up to this point. The diplomatic alliance that had supported NATO military involvement had avoided raising the conflict in the UN Security Council because Russia and China would have certainly vetoed any resolution authorising action against Yugoslavia.[6] Deterioration in the relationship between the Clinton administration and the UN at that time has also been suggested as a factor that kept the UN out of the negotiation process.[7] However, as the hostilities escalated, the Yugoslav army indicated a willingness to agree to a settlement that involved a UN mission. Madeleine Albright believed that Milošević was too 'stubborn and emotional' to give in to NATO but would find it less humiliating to negotiate with the UN. UN involvement was also necessary to secure Russia's agreement to the post-conflict arrangement. It was thus the UN's advantages in terms of international legitimacy and perceived impartiality that gave it the edge over other contenders to become the lead institution in the post-conflict phase, rather than considerations of administrative competence. Another benefit of UN Security Council involvement was that neither the Belgrade government nor any of the Albanian Kosovar leaders had to agree the text of the agreement.[8] The reference to international civil and security presences 'endorsed and adopted by the United Nations' was formally incorporated into a draft document at a G8 meeting in early May 1999, and this text formed the basis of the agreement with Yugoslavia and the drafting of Security Council Resolution 1244 in June, which authorised a civil administration presence under UN auspices.

The UN Mission in Kosovo (UNMIK)

The Mission in Kosovo was a departure in peacekeeping activities for the UN. During the Cold War, most UN missions had been relatively limited in scope, largely involving ceasefire monitoring activities. The UN's reputation in peacekeeping operations had declined during the 1990s as a consequence of failures in Somalia and Bosnia-Herzegovina, where poorly resourced UN forces had been unable to impose peace.[9] The organisation was thus keen to demonstrate its ability to manage this large post-conflict exercise. The newly appointed US ambassador to the UN, Richard Holbrooke, declared that 'The U.N.'s future in international crises is going to be determined in very large part by what it achieves in Kosovo'.[10]

Like many other aspects of the international response to the Kosovo crisis, the provisions of UNSCR 1244 were influenced by the experience in Bosnia where it was considered that the implementation arrangements for the Dayton Agreement had suffered from 'diffusion of responsibilities between implementing agencies who have too often been rivals rather than partners'.[11] UNMIK was thus set up with four 'pillars', each led by a different international body, but all reporting to the UN-appointed SRSG. The pillar structure and the concentration of civilian powers under the UN, it was suggested, would make the Mission 'less vulnerable to rivalries among organisations and conflicts of institutional dignity'.[12] As with the decision to put the UN in charge, the allocation of responsibilities between the pillars was decided through high-level political negotiations in European capitals, rather than on the capabilities of each organisation. The pillars were thus designed more to address concerns about the institutional 'turf' of the multilateral organisations than to create a clear division of labour.[13]

The UN's responsibilities, as overall manager of the Mission, were extensive and included diplomatic relations with Yugoslavia and security and human rights issues as well as civil administration functions.[14] The Office of the SRSG, with 138 international staff, would deal with all the functions appropriate to the UN's senior diplomatic representative including political affairs, military and regional liaison, planning and coordination, legal advice, public information and an office of gender affairs. More than 2,000 international officials and local personnel, around 40 per cent of the UN staff, were dedicated to providing administrative and technical services to the Mission, including budget control, human resource management, procurement, language services, property control, registry and archives, contract management, medical services, engineering services, information technology, communications and transport. These administrative staff supported another 2,700 personnel who were assigned to provide more or less the same services for the administration of Kosovo. A succession of SRSGs have been responsible for leading the Mission since its inception, each with their own style of management and their own ideas about how the territory should be handled and there were significant changes in UNMIK policy and direction with each change of leadership. Until the appointment in 2011 of Farid Zarif, an Afghan national and career UN diplomat, all SRSGs had been from countries in Europe. Zarif was replaced in 2015 by Zahir Tanin, another Afghan.

UN performance

The UN Mission has managed to maintain peace and establish political stability in Kosovo despite serious operational shortcomings. Before the Kosovo Mission the UN had frequently been criticised for deficiencies in the management of its peacekeeping operations, the uneven quality of its police and civil administration personnel, and under-funding relative to the agreed mandate.[15] These organisational and logistical difficulties continued in Kosovo. While other international bodies such as OSCE had been active in Kosovo before the conflict and therefore already had significant in-country resources and on-the-ground experience, the UN had to mobilise its Mission with limited prior planning in a very short period of time. As a result there were considerable delays in staffing and logistics. Three months after the conflict, UNMIK did not have a presence in all of the municipalities, and a year into the Mission it had deployed less than three-quarters of its authorised professional staff.[16] Although the situation improved subsequently, the ICG noted that cumbersome UN personnel procedures meant that staffing was a constant problem.[17]

In addition to the initial mobilisation problems, the administrative traditions of the UN bureaucracy have been frequently identified as an obstacle to the Mission's effectiveness. The UN's internal management practices, despite efforts at reform, are founded on the administrative philosophies of the 1940s, when the organisation was established. The pressures that have been felt by public administrations in many countries to increase flexibility and responsiveness and to improve performance have largely passed the UN by. Magalachvili, who worked with UNMIK as a municipal administrator, accuses UNMIK of 'unimaginative, pedantic and self serving bureaucratic management' and is critical of the UN's 'Byzantine' personnel system.[18] Holohan, who also worked in UNMIK's municipal administration bureaucracy, notes a perception that people were hired through contacts or inside information rather than on merit, and that national representation in staffing often takes precedence over merit. She also suggests that 'Many of the operations of UN agencies are hostage to special interest international politics and are ransomed to whims of the member states that provide financial support.'[19] Wedgwood and Jacobson argue that

> The jealousies of member countries have led to a centralized model of administration and a reluctance to delegate financial decisions to UN mission chiefs, which does not favour the real time delivery of public goods in distant locales ... The overlay of redundant officials, the rate-limiting pace of the most laggard political process, the ability to play one agency against the other, and the absence of singular responsibility for the mission, all conspire to hobble the project of reconstruction.[20]

Many other accounts of the early phases of UNMIK are equally scathing in their criticisms of UN performance.[21] Similar views on UN staffing and competence were repeated in discussions with technical advisers and donor representatives, including a suggestion that some of the people seconded by national governments to work with the Mission may have been sent to Kosovo primarily because they posed a problem at home.

The UN Office of Civil Affairs (Pillar II)

The Mission in Kosovo and the similar exercise in East Timor several months later were the first to involve the UN in providing comprehensive civil administration functions rather than simply overseeing them. This was a major new direction for the UN. The relatively successful Mission in Cambodia in the early 1990s had made the UN nominally responsible for civil administration functions, but actual UN authority over the Cambodian government administration had been limited.[22] The small transitional mission in Eastern Slavonia from 1996 to 1998, which implemented an agreement to transfer territory from Yugoslavia to Croatia, had been quite successful. The main civil administration task of that mission had been to integrate existing

Yugoslav institutions with their existing Croatian equivalents.[23] Although there were numerous political challenges in this exercise it was considerably less complex than the situation the UN confronted in Kosovo where it was given the major share of responsibility for establishing a new public administration.

However, just as it had not been inevitable that the UN would lead the post-conflict intervention, the wording of UNSCR 1244 did not make it inevitable that the UN bureaucracy would itself dominate civil administration activities. There were other options. The OSCE already had a presence and had at one stage expected to play the lead role after the conflict. The EU could also have been given a broader scope of activities. However, in negotiations over the post-conflict arrangements, the UN took the task of managing interim civil administration functions. Albright suggests that 'the Alliance had turned to the UN for help in an area where that organization had proven expertise – civilian reconstruction'.[24] It is not clear what proven expertise she is referring to. The ICG took a different view and argued that 'the UN bureaucracy lacks political sophistication and is also too heavy, providing an extra layer of decision making and paperwork between the field operation and its sponsoring governments'.[25]

An Office for Civil Affairs, designated as Pillar II in the UNMIK structure, was established to manage this component of the Mission. It comprised 650 international UN officials and more than 2,000 locally engaged UN staff reporting to a Deputy SRSG. The Office was to be responsible for 'overseeing and where necessary conducting a number of civil affairs functions … as well as supporting the restoration and provision in the short run of basic public services.'[26] This brief description significantly understated the amount of work that would be required. Pillar II's responsibilities encompassed agriculture, environmental protection, industry, trade and commerce, police and judicial affairs, transport, education, social welfare and health, plus twenty-nine Municipal Administrations and five Regional Offices. An EU report shortly after the start of the Mission noted that 'The Civil Administration Pillar faces considerable challenges. It has to take on responsibility for practically all public services and departments of government at provincial, regional and municipal level. It is woefully under-resourced so to do.'[27]

During the first months a number of Joint Civilian Commissions (JCCs) were established to 'facilitate the process of a mediated and controlled transition to integrated public institutions and to address such contentious issues as administration and staffing of various public facilities'.[28] JCCs were established for health, education, municipalities, telecommunications and electricity. The description of the role of the JCCs is reminiscent of the Joint Commission envisaged in the Rambouillet proposal several months earlier and appears to assume that there would be a set of public institutions ready for 'mediated and controlled' transition. This was far from the actual situation by June 1999. Former public service structures were inoperative and political factions had captured many public facilities. Nevertheless, during the first six months of the Mission the UN civil administration successfully reopened hospitals, restored post-office services and rubbish collection, and started the new school year for thousands of primary and secondary students.

UN civil administration officials continued to play a significant role in public administration in Kosovo for a considerable period, even after the election of a provisional government and the appointment of Kosovar ministers. With the creation of the JIAS, at the start of 2000, UN staff in Pillar II became responsible for most of the new administrative departments, nominally sharing their authority with politically appointed Kosovar counterparts, although the extent of actual day-to-day interaction between the international Co-Heads and their Kosovar counterparts has been questioned and, according to observers, international officials generally remained in control of policy.[29] In 2002, the JIAS administrative departments became ministries of the PISG. International officials stayed on, however, and in some cases, due to the lengthy time taken to appoint permanent secretaries and other senior posts, effectively continued to run the ministries. Eventually, however, progressive reductions in the UNMIK budget led to restructuring and downsizing of the Civil Administration Pillar and accelerated the pace of the transfer of responsibilities to Kosovo government officials.[30] In 2006, UNMIK formally withdrew its staff from most ministries.[31] From then on responsibility for public administration policies and legislation clearly rested with the PISG government. After Kosovo's unilateral declaration of independence in February 2008, UNMIK closed its Civil Administration component and ceased having direct involvement in public administration.[32]

Pillar II performance

The absence of a local political regime considered acceptable to the international community meant that the UN civil administration was, in effect, the government in the territory. To those with experience in public administration, including SRSG Bernard Kouchner, with his background in the French government, the implications of this were clear. The UN headquarters bureaucracy in New York, however, appeared to many to be reluctant to accept this role, and most UN staff assigned to the Mission lacked the administrative experience to fulfil it. A former public finance adviser reported that, at one point during this period, Kouchner and his East Timor equivalent, Sergio Viera de Mello, wrote a joint letter to the UN Secretary General pointing out that in both places the UN 'had to be able to do the things a government does'. 'I was constantly confronted with the situation that this decision cannot be made because it is political, when clearly we were standing *in loco* the politicians so the political decision had to be made, and the structure was there to make that decision.'[33] Donor-funded technical advisers also complained about Pillar II's reluctance to take decisions. One commented that the UN 'had no sense of urgency in that respect. The UN was just running a peacekeeping mission and all you had to do was to keep the peace. And the peace was not going to be kept if the teachers weren't paid.'[34]

The UN has acknowledged that few of those recruited to its peacekeeping missions have had previous experience in public administration.[35] The civil administration in Kosovo was staffed by a mixture of career UN officials, short-term contract staff and UN volunteers, as well as personnel seconded from UN member governments, and many were on relatively short-term contracts. Some non-UN advisers had a low opinion of the competence and performance of the UN's civil administration personnel. UN staff, one said, 'were earning pretty good salaries and I don't think there were many performance indicators for them'.[36] Another suggested 'they have worked in areas where process was much more important than results, where there was never any focus on results, just inputs',[37] while one described senior UN staff as 'the ones who would throw their arms around but nothing would ever get done and they'd procrastinate about everything.'[38]

Relations between the UN and other international actors

There was a pronounced difference in approach and priorities between the UN component of the Mission and other international actors involved in the development of public administration. The wording of UNSCR 1244 – 'the "paper bridge" between Western and Russian/Chinese positions in the Security Council'[39] – was intentionally vague about the ultimate goal of the exercise, allowing the various organisations and individuals brought together in UNMIK to adopt different interpretations. While the EU, the US and many other actors saw the objective as long-term development and had a policy agenda that implied severing Kosovo's institutional links with Serbia and Yugoslavia, the UN attempted to adhere as far as possible to the Security Council commitment to maintain Yugoslav sovereignty, to cooperate with the Federal Republic of Yugoslavia (FRY), and to maintain the pre-conflict status quo wherever possible.[40] These differences generated an atmosphere of conflict between the two camps. Advisers working in Pillar IV tended to see the UN as an obstacle to achieving their goals, while a UN official dismissed Pillar IV as merely 'a bunch of experts. It wasn't a workforce like UNMIK.'[41]

During the early phases of the reconstruction exercise, attitudes to the UN may have been affected by the generally poor relationship between the US government and the UN at this time. Tension between the US and the UN started well before the Kosovo conflict, dating to the Clinton government's failed engagement in Somalia in 1993, and exacerbated by disagreement in the Security Council over weapons inspections in Iraq in 1998:

> recounting tales of UN incompetence is water-cooler sport in the State Department and the Pentagon. Washington's collective sneer has helped delegitimize the organization that Woodrow Wilson, FDR, and Harry Truman once dreamed would bind the world into a new structure of international relations.[42]

It was not only US-funded staff in Kosovo who were critical of the UN's approach, however. Pillar IV's 'end of mission' report, produced by the EU, also identified, rather more obliquely, their differences with the UN over the reconstruction of Kosovo:

> While the 'traditional' approach to Mission policy focused on the interim character of UNMIK's mandate and cautioned to engage into new areas alien to past UN peace-keeping activities ... the EU Pillar pointed out the necessity to create viable competitive economic institutions and the costs of non action in terms of development and stability foregone.[43]

The slow pace at which UN lawyers reviewed and enacted UNMIK regulations was a particular source of contention. Advisers felt that draft laws sent to UN headquarters for approval 'went into a black hole'.[44] USAID complained frequently about the UN's cumbersome processes for vetting and issuing regulations and decrees, and its slowness to implement agreed regulations after they were approved.[45] The World Bank and the IMF shared this concern about the pace of UNMIK's regulatory activity. The IMF reported that

> In a number of cases, notably insurance and privatization, important regulations take months of legal review, or budget decisions are not implemented by spending agencies due to differences in policy priorities or interpretation within UNMIK. These incidents have real economic costs for donors and Kosovars alike.[46]

UN legal staff, on the other hand, felt they were being pressured by donors and advisers, intent on achieving project objectives at all costs, to adopt complex new legal statutes that were not regarded by the UN as priorities for the Mission:

> The various organisations constituting UNMIK and the funding agencies brought numerous experts with an enormous number of proposals for legislation – which were the 'results' expected for the donation. These persons were experts in their fields, such as banking or finance, with a determination to propose the very best legislation as they saw it. An example is the lengthy and highly complex banking laws promulgated very early in the Mission. It was far from clear that such overly complex and detailed laws had any chance of being effectively administered.[47]

The European Union

The EU has been the largest donor to Kosovo's reconstruction and is today the major international influence on the policies of the Kosovo government. In many ways, however, its activities have been more concerned with the development of the EU than the development of Kosovo. Its policies towards Kosovo and other countries in the region are also the most explicit expression of the idea of development as economic, social and political transformation. The EU is engaged in a process of reform and transformation in the less-developed countries on its borders in order for them to adopt 'European standards'.[48] The EU was a significant participant in events during the conflict in 1999 and in the negotiation of the peace agreement and its response to the conflict has been identified as a turning point in EU foreign policy and its relations with the region.[49] In the post-conflict phase, the EU established a number of separate agencies in Kosovo with quite different functions, policy priorities and administrative methods. Between 1999 and 2008 the EU was in charge of Pillar IV of UNMIK, which was responsible for 'economic reconstruction'. It also provided more than €1.1 billion in reconstruction and development aid through EAR. After 2008, the European Commission Liaison Office (ECLO), since then rebranded as the European Union Office in Kosovo, replaced EAR as the management agency for EU technical assistance and development projects. Since independence in 2008, EULEX has taken responsibility for some of the work previously done by UNMIK, supporting and overseeing the police, the justice sector and the customs service, despite the fact that the UN still, technically, retains responsibility for these functions under UNSCR 1244. From 1999 to 2010 the EU provided around €2.5 billion for its activities in Kosovo.[50]

The Europeanisation objective of EU assistance

EU activities in Kosovo and in the Western Balkans more generally need to be understood against the background of the progressive development of the EU's 'internal market', as well as its prior involvement in the economic and political transition of other former socialist countries to EU membership. From its origins as a limited free trade agreement in the 1950s, the EU has evolved into a comprehensive economic and political union, if not quite yet a formal federation. The 1986 'Single Europe Act' intensified the process of removing all barriers to trade and commerce between EU member states and required the 'approximation' or harmonisation of all market-related legislation in member states. In 1992, the Maastricht Treaty established the basis for monetary union and also initiated a Common Foreign and Security Policy, which enabled the EU to act externally to promote democracy, the rule of law and human rights.[51]

The internal harmonisation process generated the *acquis communautaire*, an 80,000-page volume of EU directives which must be adopted into the legislation of each EU member. Accepting and enacting all elements of the *acquis*, translating EU legislation into national legislation, and demonstrating that it is implemented and enforced effectively through the appropriate administrative structures, is thus a precondition for EU membership.[52] In 1995, the Madrid Council introduced further conditions for post-communist transition countries including a 'bureaucracy criteria', which requires candidate countries to adjust their administrative structures to demonstrate that they have the capacity to apply the *acquis*.[53] This process of EU enlargement through adoption of the EU *acquis* was successfully applied to newly democratic states of Central and Eastern Europe after the fall of the Berlin Wall in 1989 resulting in their accession to the EU.[54] Since 1999 a similar approach has been extended to the countries of the Western Balkans, including Kosovo. 'Association Agreements' signed with each Balkan candidate country contain further specific conditions, such as, for example, requirements to comply with the ICTY and the requirement for Serbia to improve its relations with Kosovo.[55]

While some authors have praised this EU approach to state building, arguing that it has stimulated revolutionary changes in laws, policies and institutional structures in candidate and potential candidate states,[56] others have criticised the asymmetrical, hierarchical and coercive relationship between the EU and enlargement candidates, and the increasingly demanding reform agenda, and noted the danger that new rules and procedures introduced under EU pressure will not have strong political support and may subsequently be disregarded, contested or changed.[57] While the enlargement policy in the Balkans has so far seen Croatia achieve EU membership, doubts have been raised about the likely effectiveness of EU conditionality in the political environments in other parts of the former Yugoslavia, as well as the EU's actual level of commitment to membership for these countries.[58] In the case of Kosovo, these doubts about EU commitment are particularly strong in view of the fact that five of its member states have not yet recognised Kosovo's independence.

Europeanisation in Kosovo

In 1999, many of these EU enlargement policies had not yet been clearly formulated, and Kosovo was a long way from being able to comply with the requirements of the *acquis communautaire*, so initial institutional development under UN administration did not necessarily follow the EU's preferred models. Since then, however, the activities of international actors have been increasingly influenced by the prospect of Kosovo one day joining the EU, and in some sectors this has meant that international actors have had to go back and redo some of the 'sub optimal and non EU-compliant' legislation and institutional development actions of the early years.[59]

Geography aside, the justification for Kosovo's Europeanisation is not as obvious as in other places in the region. Kosovo and neighbouring Albania were part of the Ottoman Empire for almost five centuries and economic, cultural and religious ties with Turkey remain strong, so the idea of a 'return to Europe', common in many Central and Eastern European countries, has less relevance.[60] Nevertheless, the promise of EU membership, or a vaguer concept of European integration, has been seen by many donors as the strongest incentive for the institutional transformations they see necessary in Kosovo. DFID, for example, has argued that Europeanisation means Kosovo 'would have to abandon non-transparent social and political arrangements that have developed over many years and accept international norms of public administration and public life'.[61]

A 'SAP Tracking Mechanism' was established in November 2002 to monitor progress towards the goal of EU integration and since 2005 the European Commission has published annual Progress Reports monitoring Kosovo's efforts towards conforming with the requirements of the EU in the many areas of government administration considered important for accession. These range from the procedures of the Assembly and the conduct of elections, to policies on health, education, agriculture and trade, safety at work, food standards, nuclear safety, environmental protection and climate change. Advancement in all these areas appears to be equally necessary for Kosovo to achieve its 'European perspective'. Compliance with the requirements of the EU *acquis* has thus come to dominate public sector policy development in Kosovo. In 2006, the Kosovo government established an Office of European Integration Processes in the Prime Minister's Office and drafted a Kosovo Action Plan for the Implementation of the European Partnership. Much of the technical assistance funded by the EU has been explicitly linked to bringing Kosovo's administrative practices closer to European standards and ensuring that laws and policies are EU-compatible.

Whether the Europeanisation of public administration and EU compatible legislation and policies are the best or most direct way to improve the lives of the people of Kosovo is, however, debatable. Keukeleire *et al.* suggest that the EU's focus on accession criteria means that inadequate assistance has been provided in those areas that would address Kosovo's economic development.[62] EU documents rarely present an explicit argument that the comprehensive reforms required for EU integration will in themselves address economic development issues. The purpose of adopting a 'European perspective' and 'approximation to European standards' is to qualify Kosovo for closer trade relations with the EU, which would then be expected to bring economic benefits.[63] It is also expected to benefit existing EU members through actions to combat organised crime, improve border control, regulate migration and reduce environmental pollution.[64] The distribution of EU funds under the IPA has been weighted towards issues such as democratic institutions, law enforcement, human rights, minority rights, gender equality and public administration reform, rather than immediate economic development needs.[65]

The policies set out in the *acquis* are based on the historical legacies of Western Europe and are the result of negotiation over the years between existing EU member states. They are not necessarily the current 'state of the art' in public administration, and may not always be suitable for countries, such as Kosovo, with weak economic conditions, fragile governance and underdeveloped administrative capacities. International technical experts suggested, for example, that EU procurement law is excessively complex and difficult to implement efficiently, and that the EU Value Added Tax (VAT) model is not what would be recommended to a developing country in the absence of the requirement to align with EU policy. Moreover, attempting to adopt the full range of the EU's complex and demanding administrative policies may add significant costs to public administration.[66]

In spite of the amount of EU integration activity by the government, Kosovo is still a long way from achieving the institutional structures, capacity and standards expected by the EU and international advisers working with government agencies were quite pessimistic about the likelihood of Kosovo's current administrative deficiencies being addressed sufficiently to meet the requirements of membership in the foreseeable future.

The EU in UNMIK (Pillar IV)

The European Commission lobbied strongly during preparation for the UN Mission for control of the economic reconstruction portfolio and succeeded in being awarded responsibility for Pillar IV of UNMIK's four-pillar structure.[67] The remit of Pillar IV was the rebuilding of 'physical, economic and social infrastructure and systems'.[68] This statement did not, however, draw a sufficiently clear distinction between the functions of Pillar IV and Pillar II, the UN's civil administration component. In particular, the description of Pillar II's responsibilities included 'economic and budgetary affairs'[69] so it was initially unclear which of the two pillars would be responsible for public finance policy and institutions. Although this was resolved over the next few months in favour of Pillar IV, there were reportedly several efforts subsequently by Pillar II to establish a parallel Budget Office, and recurring disputes over the division of responsibility for budget functions between Pillar II and Pillar IV.

Joly Dixon, an EU official, was appointed to lead Pillar IV and at the donors' conference in July 1999 he was already able to announce plans for economic development and institution building in areas such as customs and taxation, budget policy and expenditure management.[70] However, although a handful of other EU personnel arrived very promptly to join the Pillar, the funding initially made available by the Commission proved inadequate and the EU was unable to identify all the technical staff needed for economic reconstruction activities within a reasonable timeframe. One of the reasons for the European Commission's problems in mobilising funds was the tightening of procedures following the discovery of financing irregularities in the European Commission shortly before.[71]

According to most sources it was due to this delay that the US government became heavily involved in Pillar IV activities.[72] A USAID-funded technical adviser provided an account of the events:

> It dragged for about two months, I think, from when Joly [Dixon] got there, from July ... to August and Joly in absolute, I think, frustration with the European Union's inability to mobilise turned to USAID who could see that if this wasn't done, particularly the Central Fiscal Authority and the Banking and Payments Authority, if they weren't staffed and operational then Kosovo would go down the tubes because there was just nothing happening. So he turned to USAID and asked if they could assist.[73]

Thus the majority of the international experts who implemented EU Pillar IV activities in UNMIK in the early months of the Mission were not, in fact, appointed or paid by the EU, but were contracted consultants engaged by an American firm on behalf of USAID. This produced a very complex staffing arrangement in the Pillar, with USAID-funded advisers often representing the EU within UNMIK. USAID technical advisers, for example, held the senior executive positions in the Central Fiscal Authority and the Tax Administration, under Pillar IV jurisdiction.

Nine months later the EU had still only filled 13 positions in the Pillar.[74] The number of EU-appointed staff steadily increased, however. In 2005 there were 130 international staff and a further 320 local employees and the Pillar had an annual budget of around €20 million.[75] Most of the EU Pillar staff were recruited directly to specific jobs on the basis of technical expertise rather than being seconded from the EU or member government bureaucracies. Pillar IV staff continued, however, to work alongside a large contingent of USAID-funded experts throughout its existence.

Development of the Kosovo Customs Service was also under the umbrella of Pillar IV but was delivered through a separate funding mechanism. The €3 million Kosovo Customs Assistance Mission (CAM-K) comprised seconded customs officials from EU countries who provided technical training and mentoring to locally recruited customs staff.[76] Several senior management positions in the Customs Service, including the post of Director-General, were filled by officials seconded from UK Customs and funded by DFID, but they also reported to Pillar IV. The work of CAM-K was later continued by the Customs and Fiscal Assistance Office (CAFAO), a Balkan-wide EU-funded programme.

Pillar IV's work accelerated rapidly after the arrival of USAID-funded staff in September 1999. By the end of the year it had created the Customs Service and the Tax Administration, established budget and treasury functions, set up the Kosovo Banking and Payments Authority (BPK), and started collecting customs revenue. At the beginning of 2000, under the JIAS arrangement, Pillar IV had oversight of the Central Fiscal Authority (CFA), the Customs Service and the JIAS Departments of Reconstruction, Trade and Industry, and Public Utilities. Two years later, with the election of the PISG government, many of these responsibilities were transferred to the new ministries, together with their associated international and Kosovar staff. Other Pillar IV staff continued to work on the 'reserved power' functions that were retained by UNMIK, in particular the management and privatisation of socially owned enterprises, the Customs Service and final authority over the Kosovo Consolidated Budget (KCB).

In February 2008, after the Kosovo Government's declaration of independence, the European Commission decided to disband its component of UNMIK. This decision had apparently not been anticipated by the UN, or indeed by the EU staff of the Pillar, and created a number of administrative and logistical problems.[77] The Customs Service, which was already largely 'Kosovarised', was handed to the government. Other functions, including management of the accumulated proceeds from the privatisation of socially owned enterprises, became a UN responsibility. Pillar IV's final report, subtitled 'Job Done!', identified ten major achievements during the nine years of its existence including establishing the foundations of a market economy, creating a self-sustaining Kosovo budget, establishing the Customs Service and the Central Banking Authority of Kosovo (CBAK), successful privatisation of state-owned enterprises and modernisation of public utilities.[78] However, while the EU had overall responsibility for these tasks, USAID could, and does, also claim a substantial share of the credit for many of these achievements.

EU development assistance: EAR and ECLO

In addition to its involvement in Pillar IV, the EU provided substantial amounts of direct funding for rebuilding and development projects through the European Agency for Reconstruction (EAR), a body established specifically for this purpose. EAR had a different mandate and a completely different way of working, although some of its activities in public administration and finance overlapped with Pillar IV responsibilities. The decision to establish a specialised agency to deliver EU aid for Kosovo, rather than using existing EU mechanisms, was a reaction to the EU's prior experience of implementing reconstruction activities in Bosnia, which had used different sets of procedures under various EU regulations.[79] The Agency was initially established to deal with reconstruction in Kosovo, but its mandate was subsequently expanded to include Serbia and Montenegro, after the fall of the Milošević regime in late 2000, and the Former Yugoslav Republic of Macedonia, after the inter-ethnic conflict of 2001.

While the bureaucratic formalities of establishing EAR were being concluded in Brussels, the European Commission set up a Task Force (TAFKO) to manage its initial funding, including the continuation of €10 million of humanitarian assistance projects that had been under way before the escalation of the conflict. Perhaps as a consequence of this previous involvement, TAFKO, unlike Pillar IV, was able to mobilise very quickly. The first members of the Task Force arrived on 5 July and by September 1999 it had 30 staff working in Pristina, had initiated around €50 million-worth of reconstruction activities and had begun making administrative preparations for the establishment of EAR.[80] EAR started operations at the end of December with 40 international staff and 42 'local agents' in Pristina and a budget of €626 million to spend on reconstruction.[81] The balance between international and local staff changed considerably over the next few years and in 2004 the Kosovo office had only 19 international staff, working with 46 local employees.

Early EAR funding was mainly directed towards repairing physical infrastructure and included projects in housing, electricity and de-mining. Funding for public administration functions at this stage consisted primarily of assistance in municipal administration through the secondment of officials from EU member governments.[82] The focus of EAR's work changed in subsequent years, however, with a larger share going to projects to support public administration development and institutional capacity. Although most of these activities were classified by EAR as 'Public Administration Reform', in the majority of cases they were in fact setting up functions, laws and institutions that had not previously existed in Kosovo, such as the Prime Minister's Office and the Office of the Auditor General, or further developing institutions that had been in existence for a few years, at most, and had been established by previous rounds of technical assistance.

EAR assistance for institution building concentrated on EU accession issues and compliance with the *acquis communautaire*. Most of the funds channelled through EAR were drawn initially from the Community Assistance for Reconstruction, Development and Stabilisation (CARDS) programme, which was explicitly linked to the requirements of EU 'approximation'. The Instrument of Pre-accession Assistance (IPA), which replaced CARDS after 2006, was even more clearly focused on the eventual integration of recipient countries into the European Union. EAR thus provided experts to help the government draft laws compatible with the *acquis* and encouraged the adoption of 'EU best practice' in other areas of public administration. Between 2002 and 2008, EAR allocated approximately €47 million to numerous projects in public administration and public finance including around €14.8 million to support 'European Integration' activities, and technical assistance contracts in the Ministry of Finance and Economy (€7.1 million), customs and taxation (€4.9 million), procurement (€4.2 million) and audit (€7.7 million). Although the total amount spent over the period was large, the funds allocated for each project were usually quite small, some as little as a few hundred thousand Euro, sufficient to fund one adviser for a few months' work. Most activities also had relatively short time frames, usually either eighteen months or two years.

EAR was always intended to be a temporary institution. Its original mandate was extended several times but it was eventually wound up at the end of 2008. Responsibility for managing EU assistance to Kosovo was transferred to the European Commission Liaison Office (ECLO) which continued to implement a similar programme of projects in public administration, budget preparation, internal audit, procurement and EU integration.

EAR performance

Internal assessments of the impact of EAR's work were largely positive. An evaluation in 2008, for example, found that EAR support had been important in establishing democratic governance structures and enabling a substantial upgrading of human resources.[83] Discussions with current and former international advisers and local observers, however, generated considerable criticism of the implementation procedures of both EAR and ECLO. The amount of criticism of EU projects from technical advisers may partly reflect the fact that the EU is now the most active donor and most advisers have been involved in EU-funded projects. Several people, however, specifically compared the EU adversely with other donors they had worked with, in Kosovo and elsewhere. Problems they identified included long lead times for planning new projects, short timeframes for implementing each activity, inadequate financial commitments, excessive administrative overheads, and inadequate skills among EU project management staff.

Planning processes for projects funded under CARDS and IPA involve lengthy preparation procedures beginning with a three-year Multi Annual Indicative Planning Document, preparation of a 'project fiche' for each activity, and further development of detailed terms of reference. Tendering the project to select an implementing firm may take a further six months so the total time required to establish each project can be up to eighteen months. Technical advisers complained that the time taken in project preparation often meant that the terms of reference were no longer relevant by the time the project started, and the average project duration of one to two years was considered insufficient to deliver the expected outputs:

> The bureaucracy of the thing is such that it probably takes up to six months to get to implementation which means that there's probably only a year to get it done before you are starting to wrap it up if you're a two year project … If you are trying to introduce new systems and structures and get them embedded you really need longer.[84]

Short projects also generated higher transaction costs, interruptions while tender processes were under way, and the negative effects of 'the tap being turned on and turned off': 'If you suddenly stop what you're doing there is an assumption that this rather cash strapped government can take it over, and even if there's a will to do that, I have examples where they don't and the thing just stops.'[85]

EAR and ECLO projects were also considered to be under-resourced relative to what was required, and funding levels appeared arbitrary, apparently based on a formula of 'one year equals one million Euros,' without a clear view of what that sum would actually buy.[86] Many advisers also complained bitterly about onerous reporting requirements:

> Under the EU system there is so much bloody bureaucratic paperwork, it bogs you down. You have to report according to all these different things. They have all these benchmarks, not really related to the project. Also I found that the benchmarks for the project were set eighteen months ahead and when I got there they weren't really relevant.[87]
>
> They look minutely at everything. We have to agree everything we do with them. I don't like it. All EU consultants complain. This process doesn't produce better results … There are lots of reports with very defined formats, not what you think you need to report on.[88]

EAR directly recruited international staff, on contract, to work on administering its development programmes and considered it was able to engage 'world class' professionals and specialists.[89] Although ECLO inherited many former EAR staff, it was suggested that the level of expertise in project management had declined since the transition and staff lacked the technical expertise or authority to manage projects effectively. This concern was expressed both by international advisers and Kosovars:

> There is a really ironic thing. They find the best [technical advisers] they can find in the world to do these jobs, maybe not the best but the best they can get, and then they don't trust them with their judgements. They don't trust our judgements ... The focus is on activities rather than outcomes.[90]
>
> It's not run by qualified people but by administrators, and administrators in a typical administrative thing will say 'have you produced a report?' and 'has the report been approved by the beneficiary?', but never add the question, has the report been read and understood by anybody.[91]

Some of these criticisms have been reflected in external evaluations of EAR and ECLO activities. In 2007 it was suggested that too much emphasis had been placed on project cycle management, rather than on strategic orientation and policy making, resulting in a fragmented approach and a focus on short-term project completion rather than long-term outcomes.[92] A 2009 evaluation identified similar deficiencies: among other things, projects were too ambitious and had too many components and activities, implementation periods were too short and project indicators were too focused on the delivery of specific outputs rather than outcomes such as capacity and sustainability.[93] An evaluation of IPA funding reported that the programme was 'heavy' in terms of managerial resources required, that planning and implementation procedures were relatively complex, deployment of funds had been slow and implementation had been insufficiently results oriented.[94] A 2014 review continued to criticise the intensive involvement by the EU Office in internal management of IPA projects which, it argued, is not efficient, is demotivating for contractors and beneficiaries, and is detrimental to ownership.[95] The message from these evaluations has been consistent and clear and the European Commission claims to have made changes to its IPA implementation practices in response, including moving to a more strategic approach and streamlining processes with fewer, larger projects.[96] A new IPA framework adopted for the 2014–2020 period makes further changes including the introduction of 'country strategy papers' and a sector-based approach focused on financing policy strategies rather than individual projects.[97]

The United States

Globally the United States has usually been the largest aid donor. In Kosovo, however, it came a distant second behind the EU in terms of financial contribution. The US nevertheless had a significant impact in several sectors and particularly in PFM development. The US government has also had a strong influence on developments in Kosovo in other ways, largely as a result of the positive attitudes of Albanian

Kosovars towards the US, but its activities have sometimes brought it into conflict with other international actors.

National interest and US assistance

The US has generally been relatively open about the national interest objectives of its foreign aid programmes. Until the 1990s, foreign aid was identified as a weapon in the fight against communism. The US was subsequently heavily involved in the political transition in former communist countries of East and Central Europe during the 1990s. The stated aim of US assistance in these places was to transform them from authoritarian, centrally planned societies into 'market-led democracies with vibrant economies, open political systems, and a strong civil society'.[98] A 2002 statement of US aid policy, in fact titled 'Foreign Aid in the National Interest',[99] identified development as one of the three pillars of US security policy and cited other national benefits of foreign assistance including opening markets for US goods, creating allies with similar values, and affirming US values and ideals. The US government is thus explicit about the ideological motives of its foreign aid and the essentially 'neo-liberal' economic and institutional development policies it promotes.

The size of the US aid programme tends to give it significant influence in most countries over the aid agendas of other donors. At the same time, however, the dominance of US foreign assistance and the history of its use to promote US national interest generates tension between the US and other actors and suspicions about US motives. In particular, relations between the UN and the EU have often been strained by their differing perspectives on foreign relations and the US belief that the countries of Europe are dependent on the military strength of the US.[100] These differences have also found expression in Kosovo.

Relations between the US and other actors in Kosovo are also conditioned by the fact that Albanian Kosovars generally have very positive attitudes towards the US, based on perceptions of stronger US support for the cause of Kosovo's independence compared to some other international powers. As one international adviser observed, 'They are extremely pro-US ... They thought they won the war. NATO had nothing to do with it. It was the US and Bill Clinton.'[101] Apparent overt support by the US for the KLA leadership immediately after the conflict contributed to this perception,[102] but a Kosovar consultant suggested that the stronger regard for the US compared to some European nations has a longer history:

> There is a cultural respect that the people of Kosovo have felt over the ages and this respect goes to the US and to the UK and then all the other Europeans and all the rest because of our past historical experience with these nations over the past hundred years. But also our experience since 1912, the whole Woodrow Wilson and London Accords and all this. Germans are much more respected because we have a big diaspora there, but when it comes to French, Italian, and all the rest, not really.[103]

There is clearly a close ongoing relationship between the US and the Kosovo government. The ICG has claimed that Prime Minister Thaci relied heavily on US Embassy guidance in the lead-up to independence in 2008, and that the independence declaration was in fact largely written by the US State Department.[104] A number of international advisers working in Kosovo, including Americans not directly associated with the US government, expressed the view that the Kosovo government is to some extent controlled by the US, that US diplomats intervene in government decisions and that the Prime Minister only acts with US approval.

USAID and PFM

The US became a major donor to the reconstruction effort despite the view in Congress that, because the US bore the largest military burden in the war, the EU and its member states should be the principal contributors to reconstruction. Congress therefore rejected President Clinton's initial request for large supplemental appropriations for Kosovo in the 1999 and 2000 budgets and stipulated that US funding would not exceed 15 per cent of total international spending.[105] This was, nevertheless, quite a large sum. Over the period to 2006 the US spent around $450 million (roughly €530 million).[106] Congress also placed restrictions on what US funds could be used for, which meant the programme was focused on technical assistance rather than infrastructure.

USAID established an office in Pristina in July 1999 and began providing funding in a range of sectors including agriculture, business development, community infrastructure and media development. Initially, however, assistance in public finance was not part of the USAID programme. This responsibility had been assigned by UNMIK to the EU's Pillar IV. Not everyone, however, fully accepts the story that USAID became involved in Pillar IV simply at the request of the EU. There had certainly been some prior planning for US engagement in economic reconstruction and several reports prepared by USAID during and immediately after the conflict dealt with these issues.[107] The speed at which USAID implemented its economic reconstruction activities in Kosovo certainly suggests that some thought had already been given to US participation in this field.

USAID was at the time engaged in implementing similar programmes in a large number of other countries around the world, and in particular in the former Soviet Union. A number of the people who came to work in Kosovo for the US government and USAID, as well as many of the technical advisers they engaged, transferred there from these countries. US personnel thus arrived with clear ideas about what should be done and what they wished to achieve and were well prepared to apply the same blueprint in Kosovo. Once agreement was reached with the EU Pillar on the US contribution, USAID procurement, based on an 'Indefinite Quantity Contract' procedure, which limited the bidding to six pre-selected firms, was completed in record-breaking time. The successful bidder did not need to conduct the formal recruitment procedures required by the EU but drew on its existing pool of consultants and subcontractors, many of whom had been working on USAID-funded technical assistance activities elsewhere and were able to deploy very rapidly. As one consultant recounted, 'To give you an idea of the lightning speed at which it worked … we were sitting in an apartment in Bangkok at whatever date it was in August and I had a fax pushed under my door which was the terms of reference issued by USAID for this assignment … Two weeks later, I got out of the car in Pristina.'[108] This rapid commitment of resources by USAID is unlikely to be possible in future, however, following subsequent controversies over contracting processes in Iraq.[109]

The first USAID contract to support public finance development was for a period of six months at a total cost of $6.4 million. Around $4 million of this was used for international consultants. Between September 1999 and March 2000 the consulting firm fielded around thirty specialists in various aspects of public finance and economic policy including customs, taxation, budget, treasury, procurement, banking, privatisation and commercial law. Only about half the consultants employed by USAID in Pillar IV were US citizens but, in contrast with the UN and the EU, there was a definite Anglo-Saxon and Anglophone dominance. Most experts were recruited from the UK, Canada and Australia as well as the US. During the first six months it was largely these advisers who were responsible for Pillar IV's achievements in public finance, in particular establishing the Central Fiscal Authority, the Tax Administration and the Banking and Payments Authority.[110]

At the end of the first six-month period, the EU Head of Pillar IV requested continuation of what had initially been seen as short-term support and a second, eighteen-month project, valued at $18 million, was contracted to the same firm. In spite of an increase in the number of EU staff working in Pillar IV in subsequent years and the later involvement of EAR and the World Bank in providing technical assistance, USAID continued to be a major donor in this field. Between 1999 and 2010, six successive multi-year economic governance projects were implemented, at a total cost of $104.5 million.[111] Not all these funds were used for developing government institutions, however. Because the overall objective was private sector development, the projects also included significant activities in commercial banking, commercial law, private sector accounting standards and privatisation of state-owned entities. The exact value of the assistance provided to develop public finance institutions is difficult to quantify.

After the election of the PISG government, USAID's priority became 'refining and calibrating' the new institutions, which were now considered to be under the control of elected ministers.[112] From then on, USAID strongly advocated the transfer of responsibilities to the Kosovo government. There was a significant reduction in overall USAID funding for Kosovo in the period from 2004, echoing a general withdrawal of support by all donors at that time, but USAID focused its reduced budget on areas where it considered it had established expertise and a proven record, namely public finance, financial system regulation, commercial law, trade policy and privatisation.[113]

USAID has continued to have a significant role in PFM development in Kosovo. It began several new multi-year projects in 2010 including a $10.2 million 'Growth and Fiscal Stability Initiative' and a tax administration project worth $5.7 million. These projects, however, progressively moved away from employing large numbers of resident international advisers in favour of intermittent visits by technical experts and more reliance on Kosovo or Albanian nationals in adviser roles.[114] USAID launched a new four-year programme for Kosovo in 2014 but, based on the good results claimed for previous assistance, planned to significantly reduce its involvement in the central public finance institutions.[115]

USAID performance

Literature on post-conflict development in Kosovo is, for the most part, remarkably lacking in criticism of the projects and implementation practices of USAID assistance. Interviews with both international technical advisers and Kosovars also produced relatively few negative comments about US-funded technical assistance. Former USAID consultants were, in fact, often very positive about their experiences. One consultant compared the approaches of the EU and USAID:

> From what I've seen here, I've seen USAID, in various projects, get results. And I see the EU sometimes dither around and waste resources. You just have to find people who have worked in both camps and ask them. I haven't found one person who doesn't say they greatly prefer the US model. Because they want to be involved in projects that succeed. They want to do things and achieve things and the US have the resources of USAID and their initiative behind the projects, they're not going to waste their money.[116]

This opinion may be expected from a senior USAID-funded contractor, but it was supported by the numerous criticisms of EU aid implementation from consultants who did not have an association with USAID. One UN official, however, was somewhat critical of the technical assistance model used by USAID in Pillar IV, suggesting that it was inflexible and risked producing inappropriate outputs:

> USAID had relatively short-term benchmarks. That was the major difference. The impact was that USAID people were chasing after these benchmarks ... Ultimately it had advantages because sometimes certain project goals were pushed harder. On other occasions, when you required a specific flexibility because the basic assumptions were wrong, or the circumstances had changed, there wasn't enough flexibility ... When it comes to legislative drafting, what counted was having the legislative draft ready no matter whether it fit in the landscape or not.[117]

The successive USAID projects in economic governance were notable for their size and comprehensiveness. Each of the consultancy contracts covered a very broad range of activities under the single overall objective of supporting private-sector-led recovery. A review of USAID activities in 2006 noted that the breadth of the issues covered by the projects was unusual,[118] although similar 'umbrella projects' have since been implemented in Afghanistan, Iraq and elsewhere. This model means the project has a large degree of flexibility: if progress stalls in one area of activity, resources can be easily redirected to other subjects without the delays of project development and procurement. It also means that project failures are less obvious. Non-performing consultants can be dismissed or replaced and component activities can be curtailed or expanded without renegotiating the overall contract. Poor results in one activity can be balanced by good results in others.

There was also a considerable degree of continuity in USAID funding. Tendering processes for each new USAID 'Task Order' were completed before the conclusion of the previous phase to ensure a smooth transition from one project to the next. In fact, although the name of the consulting firm engaged to deliver USAID economic governance projects changed over the years as a result of company restructuring, takeovers and mergers, the contracts were awarded to essentially the same organisation between 1999 and 2010.[119] Some individual advisers also remained in place for many years. Such comprehensive projects require large financial commitments. The USAID contracts for these activities ranged in value from $6 million to $26 million. At times USAID was spending around $1 million per month on its economic governance projects. In contrast, an average EAR project cost around that amount per year.

USAID officials in Pristina took a close interest in the day-to-day activities of advisers engaged by the contractor. There were detailed lists of benchmarks for each component of the project, and consultants were required to report on what they were doing week by week and to meet regularly with USAID officials to discuss progress. In general, however, USAID-funded technical advisers did not consider the reporting requirements arduous and felt they had scope to exercise judgement and adapt their work to changing circumstances:

> You had to report on what you did and how that related to what you were supposed to achieve and that sort of thing. Terms of Reference were in general terms and it's very much how you interpret that.[120]
>
> I prefer the American reporting system because it's simple. Every fortnight or every week you just explain to the company how you are going.[121]

It should be pointed out, though, that not everything USAID attempted under the heading of economic governance was successful. Considerable technical assistance effort was directed by both USAID and the EU to the privatisation of former socially owned enterprises, but the privatisation process was plagued with problems and has been widely criticised.[122] King and Mason note, for example, that 'the EU agency responsible for running public enterprises and privatising socialist ones proved that a small army of Western technocrats and consultants was just as able to preside over a dysfunctional mess as any socialist apparatchik.'[123]

US relations with other actors

The difficult relationship at the time between the US and the UN has been noted already. Relations between the US and other actors were also sometimes strained. The heavy involvement of USAID in Pillar IV, with US-funded consultants occupying positions which were formally under the authority of the EU, left both organisations with a serious 'principal-agent' problem.[124] This became more obvious later in the exercise, as reported by one adviser:

> When the contract started there was great common cause between USAID, or the US administration, and the EU and the British and so on, and there was a lot of concord about what was necessary for Kosovo. I think eventually things became a little difficult to manage shall we say. The ideological positions of the US and the EU in particular began to be more divergent in this area of government.[125]

USAID complained that there were areas where European and US philosophies and approaches diverged and that this had slowed progress in achieving USAID's objectives.[126] The consultants engaged by USAID to work with the EU Pillar sometimes found themselves caught up in disputes between the two:

> Where there were very strong differences of principle between the US dominant policy line and the European dominant policy line ... the US felt it had, through the [consulting firm] contract, a way of getting leverage on its policy preferences, whereas they were actually staffing something which the EU had nominal responsibility for and where the EU wanted to push its policy preferences.[127]

A difference of opinion over the speed of the transfer of functions from UNMIK to the PISG after 2002 was one source of friction,[128] and was particularly pronounced over the handling of the privatisation programme when 'it became clear that the Head of the Pillar could not command his troops and had to look on as key staff members followed the advice of USAID and its subcontractor'.[129]

Several international advisers suggested that, as a consequence of US political influence, USAID-funded consultants have had better access and more influence at higher levels of the government, particularly compared to EU representatives. An EU-funded adviser complained that 'The IMF and the Americans are the only people who have any weight around here. A lot of the other donors don't get so much respect. The UK gets some respect but nothing compared to the IMF and the Americans, and the EC are at the bottom of the pile.'[130] A Kosovar consultant agreed. 'If you are in a USAID project you will probably get an entry to the Ministry very easily ... in the EC, for example, [we] are EC-funded advisers but we don't have very much weight with the EC people. We can't push that much.'[131]

Although the US government expresses support for Kosovo's 'path to European integration' and claims to base its work on helping Kosovo to meet the standards required for EU membership, there have been accusations that the US is in fact pursuing its own political, military or commercial interests in Kosovo, to the detriment of the reform programmes supported by other donors.[132] Some advisers were also suspicious of the motives of USAID staff and USAID-funded technical advisers, seeing their involvement with senior levels of the administration as a strategy for maintaining US influence or achieving US government policy preferences. It was suggested, for example, that USAID advisers encouraged changes to the procurement law that did not accord with policies proposed by EU advisers working on the issue, and there has reportedly been conflict between EULEX and the US Embassy over how to deal with organised crime:

> If you were a European looking from a purist point of view you would say that the Americans seem to be happy to tolerate certain politicians who are deeply involved in organised crime because they are their politicians and they want them in place, and that's where the tension came from.[133]

The US is thus seen by some as a divisive presence and an impediment to the achievement of the goals of other actors. Given this background, the apparently high level of cooperation between US-funded consultants and EU staff within Pillar IV in the first years of the Mission is significant.

UK Department for International Development (DFID)

The UK government was not a major bilateral donor in Kosovo. Much of its assistance was channelled through broader EU programmes and the small bilateral programme managed by the UK aid agency, DFID, was initially classified as a sub-component of aid to FRY/Serbia. After 2003 DFID aid was counted as regional assistance to the Western Balkans. It is difficult, therefore, to isolate information on all DFID activities in Kosovo. However, DFID's involvement was significant because it had a strong focus on civil service development. The UK identified civil service issues as one of its spheres of comparative expertise. DFID's 2001 Kosovo Strategy Paper noted an urgent need to establish the basic elements of a functioning and politically neutral public service and to avoid the establishment of political power bases in ministries, issues that had, it was argued, not been addressed in drafting the Constitutional Framework. 'If Kosovo is to become a democratically run entity free of the political weaknesses and corruption of other countries in the region it is essential that the structure of an impartial, non-political public service is put in place. There is no tradition of such approaches in Kosovo.'[134]

DFID thus undertook to support the development of 'an accountable and professional Kosovo-led public service which delivers services effectively and equitably'.[135] However, the technical assistance projects funded by DFID in the field of public administration were quite small, in relative terms. Total funding for public administration over the period was around £9.6 million (approximately €13.4 million). The two largest DFID projects in public administration were the relatively successful Personnel Policies and Procedures (PPP) Project, implemented from 2002 to 2004, with a total funding commitment of £3 million, and a functional review of government ministries, implemented from 2008 to 2010 at a cost of £2.8 million. Smaller projects supported policy coordination and planning in the Office of the Prime Minister, EU integration and the 'Standards' process.[136]

DFID performance

DFID officials in Pristina identified flexibility and responsiveness as the strong points of DFID's approach to providing assistance to the government. This, they said, allowed it to deal with emerging issues. DFID has thus been able to provide small-scale assistance not necessarily reflected in its reporting on major projects. The larger DFID activities in public administration were described as 'design and implement' projects, which meant that consultants had considerable flexibility to formulate the details of the project around broad terms of reference. A DFID-funded consultant confirmed that he had felt relatively free to work without close supervision, unlike the detailed oversight and monitoring provided by EAR. However, the downside of this degree of flexibility and the delegation of project design to the implementing consultants was that, to some extent, DFID officials appeared to have little influence over how projects were implemented or what outputs they produced. A DFID official in Pristina also noted a lack of continuity in project activities due to procurement delays. A DFID evaluation of its programmes has also identified this as a problem.[137]

International financial institutions: The World Bank and the IMF

Under the terms of their respective Articles of Agreement, the World Bank and the IMF had no legal authority to be in Kosovo. Yugoslavia had ceased to be a member of the Bretton Woods institutions during the 1990s and Kosovo, as a non-sovereign territory, was not eligible to join. Nevertheless, the two international financial institutions were highly influential in setting the agenda for post-conflict reconstruction and guiding the public finance development programmes of other international actors. Both sent regular expert 'missions' to the territory to provide advice on the economic policies and systems that should be implemented, and technical advisers were generally ready to follow the policies proposed by IMF and World Bank experts.

World Bank assistance

The World Bank was keen to participate in post-conflict reconstruction in spite of the lack of a clear legal mandate to do so. As the Bank's Regional Director for South East Europe noted at a press conference in July 1999,

> the fact that Kosovo, being a province of Serbia, and Serbia itself being part of Yugoslavia, which is not a member of the WBG, nor is it a member of the IMF. Therefore, for us to be in Kosovo requires a certain amount of legal work for us to be able to say that we have the justification and the legal basis to get involved ... but we are confident that we can at least get involved in Kosovo and play our role.[138]

The World Bank found its justification for involvement in Kosovo in the clauses of UNSCR 1244 that urged UN agencies to assist the Mission. The World Bank qualified as a UN affiliated agency. However, because Kosovo was not a member, the funding the Bank could make available was limited. In particular, Kosovo was not in a position to accept World Bank loans. The Bank expected to be able to achieve its objectives, however, 'by using its comparative advantage in policy advice, institution building and aid coordination to help ensure the overall sustainability of the reconstruction and recovery effort'.[139] Between July and November 1999, the Bank produced, either alone or jointly with the IMF or the EU, a succession of detailed, although somewhat repetitive, analytical reports on the situation in Kosovo, which were intended to assist other bilateral and multilateral donors in developing their reconstruction programmes.[140] These were presented and discussed at donor conferences organised by the joint EU-World Bank Office for South East Europe in Brussels.

The World Bank also provided some financial assistance in the form of grants.[141] Around $25.5 million of total World Bank assistance was provided to support public finance development through several budget support grants and technical assistance projects. The World Bank is unusual among aid donors in that it provides public access on its website to appraisal, monitoring and completion reports for all its projects. These provide detailed information on the processes of project development and frank assessments of performance and impact. Similar comprehensive information is rarely available on the activities of other donors.

Four 'Economic Assistance Grants', each providing $5 million to the KCB as budget support, were intended to reinforce World Bank advice on public finance and economic development and to facilitate World Bank engagement in policy dialogue with UNMIK, the Kosovo government and other donors.[142] Given that the total forecast Kosovo Budget in 2000 was DM423 million, compared to a World Bank contribution equivalent to around DM9.5 million, or 2.2 per cent of the total, the actual persuasive value of the grant money may be questioned. The Bank considered, however, that even this relatively small amount was able to generate significant leverage over policy. In normal circumstances World Bank policy 'leverage' is applied to a national government and its officials. In this case, however, the grant conditions and policy prescriptions were being applied to UN officials in UNMIK and to donor-funded technical advisers working in Pillar IV who were particularly amenable to accepting World Bank advice. The World Bank's reputation and its influence with other donors thus carried far more weight than the actual amount of money proffered.

The World Bank began funding technical assistance for PFM after the PISG government had been established. In October 2004, the Bank proposed a $5.5 million Public Expenditure Management Technical Assistance Grant (PEMTAG) to the new government to be used for a variety of activities including assistance in budget formulation, budget execution, procurement and internal audit, as well as support to the health and transport ministries and the implementation of pay and grading reform in the civil service.[143] The internal audit and pay and grading activities had been deleted by the time the project was approved in June 2005, although the total grant amount remained at $5.5 million.[144] Of this, $2.4 million was allocated for assistance on budget formulation, cash management, book-keeping, accounting, financial reporting and procurement.

The history of the PEMTAG programme illustrates the complexities of the World Bank's project development processes and the long lead times often involved. The project was first officially proposed in late 2004 but did not commence until early 2007. As is usual with World Bank projects, the procurement of consulting services was undertaken by the local authorities, in this case the PISG through the Ministry of Public Services. Although the Bank provided a procurement adviser to assist with this task, the procurement process was delayed. The project's activities were completed in March 2009. The Bank considered PEMTAG to be a 'project at risk' for some time because of the slow rate of disbursement of funds. The final evaluation report also found that monitoring and evaluation had not been adequate and rated the quality of supervision by Bank staff as 'unsatisfactory'. In terms of project outcomes, the completion report judged that overall the project was 'moderately satisfactory'. There had been improvements in budget formulation and execution, and in procurement capacity, but in view of the significant levels of support for PFM from other donors it was not possible to attribute these improvements to PEMTAG alone. In addition, the value of the procurement mentoring activity had been compromised by the high turnover of procurement officers.[145] Given the small size of the World Bank's contributions relative to larger donors such as the EU and the US, the significant delays in implementing World Bank technical assistance and the qualified assessment of impacts, the value of World Bank financial assistance in this sector in Kosovo is questionable. The Bank's contributions have apparently been designed more to raise the Bank's profile and to give it a role in policy discussions than to have a significant impact on Kosovo's development.

PEMTAG was expected to be followed by a second project, the $8-million Public Sector Modernisation Project (PSMP), originally planned to start in 2010.[146] The

PSMP would continue work in budget formulation, budget execution and public procurement with additional activities in payroll management and human resource management in the civil service. This project was also considerably delayed. One reason for this was that, as Kosovo had become a World Bank member after independence, the project loan required Kosovo Assembly approval, which was held up by a 2010 constitutional crisis and subsequent elections. Procurement for the project eventually commenced in late 2011 and the project closing date was extended from 2013 to 2016.[147]

The IMF's role

The IMF did not engage consultants or implement technical assistance projects in the way that other international actors did, and it provided only minimal financial assistance before independence. Nevertheless, the IMF has had a significant impact. Staff from the IMF Fiscal Affairs Department played a major role in providing advice to Pillar IV officials and advisers on how to establish taxation and budget institutions and set up a banking and payments system, and on general macroeconomic policy issues. The IMF's impact in Kosovo was primarily the result of its reputation and its influence over other actors. According to an international adviser, 'They recommend which direction the organisation should go and the other donors take notice of that ... The IMF has the biggest say always, really, they always do. And generally it's a positive relationship.'[148]

The IMF took a particular interest in the early development of the BPK, which later became CBAK, and appointed the international Managing Director until the position was transferred to a Kosovar in March 2008. In 2005, when the Kosovo budget moved from surplus to deficit following the transfer of responsibility to the PISG government, the IMF was closely involved in formulating the joint PISG/UNMIK Memorandum and 'Letter of Intent' committing the government and the UN civil administration to a programme of IMF-approved fiscal policies. The role of the IMF has become even more significant since Kosovo was accepted as the Fund's 186th member in June 2009. The IMF is now in a position to impose its policies through conditions on financial assistance. In 2010, the Kosovo government negotiated a 'standby arrangement' to support the 2010 and 2011 budgets in exchange for adherence to IMF-approved policies. In early 2011, however, a government decision to grant large salary increases to civil servants breached the agreement with the IMF on budget restraint. The IMF programme and EU funding that had been linked to it were suspended pending Kosovo's fulfilment of a new set of conditions involving 'decisive steps towards fiscal sustainability and stronger budget management and execution'.[149] The Kosovo government complied with the IMF's recommendations and the IMF programme was restarted during 2012.[150]

The Kosovars

The people of Kosovo, of course, also played a role in the development of their future government institutions, although their presence as positive participants is often difficult to see in accounts written by foreigners. Many international donors and advisers did not have high expectations of their Kosovar counterparts and have been more than ready to identify their behaviour and attitudes as reasons for poor outcomes from institutional development, while claiming credit for themselves for any positive results. Kosovars, for their part, seem to have been surprisingly tolerant of the heavy international presence, although many have ambivalent attitudes towards the international actors and recent developments suggest growing resistance to external intervention.

International attitudes to Kosovars

Although in 1999 there were no reliable statistics on the size or ethnic composition of the Kosovo population most estimates suggested that more than 90 per cent were ethnic Albanian, with ethnic Serbs accounting for most of the remainder.[151] An official census conducted eventually by the Kosovo Statistics Office in 2011 recorded a population of 1.7 million, but was not able to collect reliable data in predominantly Serb areas leaving the exact size of the population, and the number of Serbs, unclear.[152] However, the very obvious disproportionate ratio of Albanians to Serbs in all population estimates made the actions of Serb and Yugoslav authorities towards Albanian citizens particularly inexcusable in the eyes of some international personnel and helped to convince many of the impossibility of a return to Serbian sovereignty.

This did not necessarily mean, however, that their attitudes to the Albanian Kosovar population were positive. Although the World Bank noted in one report that rapid rebuilding after the conflict gives 'testament to the industry of the population and its determination to make up for lost time',[153] similar positive comments about Kosovars by international observers are rare. Only one international adviser I spoke to spontaneously identified Kosovar staff as a factor in the success of institutional development. More often, official donor reports and comments by advisers and even some Kosovars paint a bleak picture of Kosovo society and culture, the people and their leaders, as well as conditions in the Balkans more generally. Descriptions of a traditional Albanian culture based on clans, patriarchal family relationships, blood feuds and illegality offer a ready explanation for the frustrations experienced by technical advisers. Cultural values and attitudes are thus frequently identified as factors contributing to deficiencies in the quality of government administration and to poor outcomes of development projects.

There is no shortage of examples of this in reports by almost all donors and international bodies. A DFID document argued that 'Kosovo has a long history of the exerting of influence by family networks and interference in the operation of judicial systems ... establishing impartial systems will require a major change of behaviour and attitudes.'[154] USAID suggested that Kosovars 'do not have positive expectations from government, a tradition of public participation or tolerance of minority groups'[155] and EAR identified 'existing alternative practices, less reliant on written communication, more on authoritarian structure and verbal negotiation, following another logic than modern, rational administrative culture' as a challenge to improvements in public administration.[156]

The Kosovar problem is sometimes also identified as a consequence of the bad habits engendered by socialism, or the effects of official discrimination against Albanians and the years of conflict. The ICG suggested that 'politicians who were raised in an environment of one-party rule apply the only methods they know to secure power and economic benefits'[157] and USAID argued that 'suppression under Milošević's totalitarian regime developed a tolerance among the majority of people to uncontrolled arbitrariness of the government and pessimism about the mission of government to serve in the public interest'.[158] Other comments identify the absence of 'modern management' behaviours such as forward planning, timekeeping, discipline, accountability and analytical thinking. UNDP reported that 'Most Kosovo citizens and municipal staff are inclined to short-term thinking. As one local official put it "anything going beyond three months is in the distant future for most people"'.[159] The fact that Kosovo is in 'The Balkans' is sometimes cited as sufficient explanation for the perceived deficiencies of Kosovar society and behaviour. 'This is the Balkans. Some things we consider corrupt might be considered quite normal in the Balkans, e.g. nepotism, finding jobs for friends and supporters.'[160] Another adviser described people of the region as suffering from an 'Eastern mentality' different from the 'shared values' of the rest of Europe.[161] Whatever the perceived cause, many people saw the Kosovars themselves as the main obstacle to improvements in their economic and political situation and to the achievement of donor objectives.

This portrayal of Kosovar, or Balkan, behaviour and attitudes is also found in some academic literature. Kanin, for example, identifies geography, economy and history as explanations for the presence of corruption and crime in the Balkans and in Kosovo in particular.[162] He argues that economic marginality and fragmentation, poor transport and isolation, and conquest and subjugation to foreign empires have all contributed to creating a tradition where corruption and crime are central aspects of society and will not easily disappear. Todorova, on the other hand, argues that statements such as those made by international advisers in relation to Albanian Kosovar society are consistent with a particular negative Western conception of 'The Balkans' which she describes as 'Balkanism'. Her argument that 'the Balkans have served as a repository of negative characteristics against which a positive and self-congratulatory image of the 'European' and the 'West' has been constructed'[163] certainly seems applicable to the attitudes of international, mainly Western, actors in Kosovo.

Negative statements that contrast European or Western values with local behaviours are not specific to the Balkans, however. Similar views tend to be expressed about almost any poor, underdeveloped country where foreign donors work, and are arguably a product of the concepts that underlie development assistance itself, particular those ideas that identify local attitudes and behaviours as the problem and propose capacity development by technical advisers from the West as the solution. People living in less successful economic areas are easily seen as 'flawed and failed human beings',[164] rather than as rational individuals responding to the situation in which they find themselves.

Kosovar attitudes to the international Mission

Although Albanian Kosovars clearly welcomed the international intervention, which had ended a decade of conflict, relations between Kosovo's political leaders and UNMIK were often difficult. There were ongoing tensions over the division of responsibility between internationals and Kosovars and the rate at which functions were transferred to local control. This was particularly evident after the establishment of the PISG in 2002 when the interpretation of the Constitutional Framework and the slow pace of the handover of administrative responsibilities to local institutions became major sources of disagreement. Kosovar politicians claimed that UNMIK had failed to prepare for the efficient functioning of the PISG and that international staff still controlled the main 'instruments of institutional establishment' and did not appear ready to hand them over, even when provided for in the Constitutional Framework.[165] Other complaints concerned the SRSG's slowness in promulgating laws after their approval by the Kosovo Assembly and UNMIK's failure to consult the government on important judicial appointments.[166] Government officials perceived a tendency for technical advisers to underestimate the capacity of Kosovars and resented the use of expensive foreign experts in roles that could have been performed by locals. Their perceptions of foreign advisers were summed up by a Kosovar consultant:

> People with different backgrounds, with different systems in mind, came in, offered different proposals, not always consistent. When you talk to people with no capacities in these fields they get confused. I'm not a specialist, I don't know anything, but I expect from you the specialist to teach me. You tell me one thing, and the next guy comes and tells me the other thing, and the third guy tells me the third thing, so where do I stand? I don't know anything, but apparently you also don't know anything.[167]

The views of the wider population were also at times antagonistic towards the international Mission. In early 2002 UNMIK's approval rating was only 27 per cent compared to 70 per cent approval of KFOR. This improved to 62 per cent later that year, but then reached a low of 20 per cent in 2004.[168] Public approval of UNMIK has tended to rise as its involvement in the administration of the territory has declined.

On the whole, however, the people of Kosovo and their leaders have shown remarkable patience with the intrusive international presence in their territory. More than fifteen years after the end of the conflict large numbers of international personnel continue to work in the country in various capacities and the government continues to listen to the advice of the IMF and the demands of the EU's enlargement machinery. There is some evidence, however, that their enthusiasm for this relationship is waning in the increasing support in recent years for Vetëvendosje (Self determination), a left-wing nationalist movement that opposes involvement by the UN and EU in Kosovo's affairs, rejects conciliation with Serbia, supports closer integration with Albania and proposes a larger government role in the economy, in direct opposition to the policies promoted by most international actors.[169] In the 2014 elections Vetëvendosje received more than 13 percent of the vote and is now the third-largest political party in the Assembly.[170] The strength of support for the Vetëvendosje political platform raises doubts about the long term sustainability of the policies that have been imposed by international actors.

The other Kosovars – Kosovo Serbs

The UN Security Council's aspiration, expressed in UNSCR 1244, was that Kosovo would be a multi-ethnic society and that there would be a role for Serbs and other non-Albanians in the new administration. For the Serb residents of Kosovo, however, this represented a major reversal of fortune. Before June 1999 they had been members of the majority population of the Federal Republic of Yugoslavia, fluent in the dominant language and with privileged access to jobs and opportunities. They now found themselves just one of several 'minority' groups in an Albanian-speaking majority, classified with Bosniaks, Turks and Roma. Although the provincial administration during the period of Kosovo's autonomy in the 1970s and 80s had also been dominated by Albanian Kosovars, Serbs at that time had comprised more than 18 per cent of the population, Kosovo's educated Albanians had spoken Serbo-Croatian and participated in Serb and Yugoslav politics, and Kosovo's communist government had looked to Belgrade for its authority and financial support.[171] Now these links with Serbia were severed. Moreover, in many official accounts of the situation in Kosovo, Serbia and the Serbs as a group were held responsible both for the conflict and for the current underdeveloped state of the Kosovo economy. In these circumstances their reluctance to accept with any enthusiasm the reality of their changed circumstances and to participate in the new administration is perhaps not surprising. The fact that ethnically motivated violence and harassment against Serb communities was rife immediately after the conflict and remained a threat provided a further powerful disincentive for peaceful coexistence. Donors' statements arguing for a complete break with the Yugoslav past, a new set of institutions and laws, and a new economic framework for an autonomous Kosovo could also be said to be inconsistent with calls for Serb participation in the administration. Some commentators were pessimistic from the start about the prospects of achieving the goal of ethnic harmony. In 1999 Samantha Power reported 'The United Nations remains nobly but anachronistically committed to the idea of getting Serbs and Albanians to live together even as each group still harbors hopes of pushing the other out of power – or out of Kosovo altogether.'[172] Later USAID noted 'Ethnic enmity makes the hope of a tolerant, multi-ethnic society a distant goal.'[173]

Thus, although equal opportunity, ethnic cooperation and bilingualism were official policies of UNMIK, the reality was that most of the day-to-day activities of the majority of international actors, particularly those involved in the civil administration, were almost entirely conducted with Albanian Kosovars. It proved difficult to recruit Serbs to public sector jobs, and few working documents were produced in both languages. While there have been some examples of Serb Kosovars participating in Kosovo politics, the estimated 120,000 Serbs who were still living in Kosovo, and in particular those concentrated in the northern border region of Mitrovica, in general refused to deal with the authorities in Pristina. The 'Ahtisaari plan' for supervised independence included proposals for decentralisation of government functions and the creation of new municipalities to represent the interests of ethnic enclaves, aimed at engaging Serbs in local government administration and EU-sponsored negotiations between Kosovo and Serbia have also had some success in increasing Serb participation in Kosovo's administrative structures.[174] During the initial post-conflict phase, however, the central institutions of public administration were almost entirely in the hands of Albanian Kosovars.

A difficult partnership

The various international organisations and donors engaged in the Kosovo reconstruction effort were meant to be partners. However, their different interests and priorities, as well as their different management and staffing arrangements, sometimes made this difficult. UNMIK's pillar structure did not succeed in eliminating conflict and disagreement between the lead participants and has itself been identified as a source of difficulty for the mission. Garton Ash, for example, commented on 'the complexity and chaos of the international presence itself, which matches and compounds the local Kosovar confusion ... all these international organisations have their own marked bureaucratic styles and political constraints. All compete with each other. All are subject to innumerable national pressures.'[175] King and Mason similarly argue that 'it became clear that some of UNMIK's problems were a result of structural deficiencies.'[176] Many functions were duplicated, which led to turf wars and confusion. Both the UN and OSCE, for example, initially had plans to establish an international police force.[177] Three of the four Pillars had been given a role to play in developing the public administration. Within Pillar IV, although there was on the whole a high level of cooperation between the various technical advisers and between the organisations that funded them, relations between them were also sometimes difficult. There was also a degree of confusion over who was the Mission's ultimate political master. The UN Security Council, which had authorised the Mission, the UN Departments of Peacekeeping Operations and Political Affairs, the 'Contact Group' of major Western powers and the European Commission all felt they had a significant part to play. 'All of these were offering advice to the mission and much of it was contradictory'.[178]

The national donors and international bodies who sought a role for themselves in the post-conflict reconstruction of Kosovo had similar overall objectives: they all intended to improve the welfare of the people who had been affected by the conflict. The particular form and scale of their involvement, however, were driven by national interest or organisational self-interest, their own assumptions about their purpose, mission and 'comparative advantage', and by competition between them for influence, authority and reputation. They each arrived with their own policy agendas and various different views about what achieving 'peace and a normal life' in Kosovo would entail. These differences sometimes generated disputes over the allocation of responsibilities, the objectives to be pursued, the policies to be implemented and the speed at which it all needed to be done, mostly conducted with limited reference to the wishes of the people of Kosovo. The following two chapters describe what happened when these diverse actors tried to work together to create a new set of public administration institutions on the 'green field' site of post-conflict Kosovo and how their differing objectives, resource levels and administrative capacities influenced the outcomes that, as a group, they were able to achieve.

Notes

1 A number of other organisations also provided financial assistance and technical advice over the period, including the US Treasury Department, the Canadian and Swedish aid bodies (CIDA and SIDA), the Norwegian government, the Support for Improvement in Governance and Management (SIGMA) programme of the OECD, and the UN Development Programme (UNDP), but their contributions were less significant.

2 M. Weller, *The Crisis in Kosovo 1989–1999: From the Dissolution of Yugoslavia to Rambouillet and the Outbreak of Hostilities. International Documents and Analysis* (Cambridge: University of Cambridge, Centre for International Studies, 1999).

3 Bellamy, *Kosovo and International Society*; Judah, *Kosovo: War and Revenge.*

4 http://peacemaker.un.org/kosovo-rambouilletagreement99 and www.alb-net.com/kcc/interim.htm, accessed 22 January 2016.

5 ICG, *Kosovo: Let's learn from Bosnia* 7.
6 M. Albright, *Madam Secretary: A Memoir* (London: Macmillan, 2003) 385.
7 M. Hirsh, 'The fall guy: Washington's self-defeating assault on the UN', *Foreign Affairs* 78: 6 (1999) 2–8 5; B. D. Jones, 'The Challenges of Strategic Coordination' in S. J. Stedman, D. Rothchild and E. M. Cousens (eds), *Ending Civil Wars: The Implementation of Peace Agreements* (Boulder, CO; London: Lynne Reiner, 2002) 89–115, 103.
8 ICG, *The New Kosovo Protectorate,* Balkans Report N° 69 (Sarajevo: International Crisis Group, 1999) 1.
9 J. Dobbins, 'The UN's role in nation-building: From the Belgian Congo to Iraq', *Survival* 46: 4 (2004) 81–102.
10 Hirsh and Terzieff, 'Holbrooke's Ultimatum: Perform or Perish' 27.
11 ICG, *Kosovo: Let's learn from Bosnia*, i.
12 ICG, *The New Kosovo Protectorate* 4.
13 DANIDA, *Evaluation: Humanitarian and Rehabilitation Assistance to Kosovo, 1999–2003* (Copenhagen: Ministry of Foreign Affairs, 2004) 71; Jones, 'The Challenges of Strategic Coordination' 103.
14 UN General Assembly, *Financing of the United Nations Interim Administration Mission in Kosovo: Report of the Secretary General, 22 October 1999* (New York: United Nations General Assembly, 1999).
15 Dobbins, 'The UN's role in nation-building' 100.
16 King and Mason, *Peace at any Price* 55.
17 ICG, *Kosovo Report Card*, Balkans Report No. 100 (Pristina: International Crisis Group, 2000) 3.
18 Magalachvili, 'Kosovo: A critique of a failed mission' 122.
19 Holohan, *Networks of Democracy* 128.
20 R. Wedgwood and H. K. Jacobson, 'Symposium: State reconstruction after civil conflict: Foreword', *American Journal of International Law* 95: 1 (2001) 1–6, 2.
21 Cohen, 'Kosovo: "Nobody's country"'; Y. Hysa, 'Kosovo: a permanent international protectorate?' in E. Newman and R. Rich (eds), *The UN Role in Promoting Democracy: Between Ideals and Reality* (Tokyo; New York: UN University Press, 2004) 282–301; Pula, 'The UN in Kosova'; A. Yannis, 'The UN as Government in Kosovo', *Global Governance* 10 (2004) 67–81.
22 Dobbins, 'The UN's role in nation-building' 83.
23 Dobbins, 'The UN's role in nation-building' 96; J.-P. Klein, 'The United Nations and administration of territory: Lessons from the front line: The United Nations Transitional Administration in Eastern Slavonia (UNTAES)', *ASIL Proceedings* (2003) 205–9.
24 Albright, *Madam Secretary: A Memoir* 424.
25 ICG, *The New Kosovo Protectorate* 5.
26 UNSC, *Report of the Secretary-General pursuant to paragraph 10 of Security Council Resolution 1244 (1999) 12 June 1999*, 3.
27 TAFKO, *Monthly summary of Task Force activities: July-August 1999* (Pristina: European Commission Task Force Kosovo, 1999) 2.
28 UNSC, *Report of the Secretary General on the United Nations Interim Administration Mission in Kosovo, 12 July 1999*, 4.
29 International UNMIK Official (IU3).
30 UN General Assembly, *Performance report on the budget of the United Nations Interim Administration Mission in Kosovo for the period from 1 July 2005 to 30 June 2006, Report of the Secretary-General* (New York: United Nations General Assembly, 2006); UNSC, *Report of*

the Security Council Mission to Kosovo and Belgrade, 14–17 December 2002 (New York: United Nations Security Council, 2002) para 8.

31 UN General Assembly, *Budget for the United Nations Interim Administration Mission in Kosovo for the period from 1 July 2006 to 30 June 2007, Report of the Secretary-General* (New York: United Nations General Assembly, 2006).

32 UNSC, *Report of the Secretary-General on the United Nations Interim Administration Mission in Kosovo, 24 November 2008.*

33 International USAID public finance adviser (IA16).

34 International public finance adviser, USAID Pillar IV (IA1).

35 UN General Assembly, *Report of the Panel on United Nations Peace Operations (Brahimi Report)* (New York: United Nations General Assembly, 2000) 21–2.

36 International civil service adviser, DFID and EU (IA9).

37 International USAID public finance adviser (IA16).

38 International audit adviser, USAID and EU (IA7).

39 Garton Ash, *History of the Present* 454.

40 Cohen, 'Kosovo: "Nobody's country"' 123.

41 International UNMIK Official (IU3).

42 Hirsh, 'The fall guy' 3.

43 UNMIK/European Union, *The 10 Key Achievements: End of Mission Report 1999–2008* (Pristina: EU Pillar IV, 2008) 6.

44 International USAID public finance adviser (IA1).

45 USAID, *Strategy for Kosovo 2001–2003* 6; USAID, *Kosovo: Results Review and Resource Request* 5; USAID, *USAID/Kosovo Annual Report 2002* (Washington, DC: United States Agency for International Development, 2002) 5.

46 IMF, *Kosovo: Progress in Institution-Building and the Economic Policy Challenges Ahead* 17.

47 A. J. Miller, 'UNMIK: Lessons from the Early Institution Building Phase', *New England Law Review* 39: 9 (2004) 9–24, 16.

48 http://ec.europa.eu/enlargement/policy/conditions-membership/index_en.htm, accessed 3 June 2015.

49 W. Koeth, 'State building without a state: the EU's dilemma in defining its relations with Kosovo', *European Foreign Affairs Review* 15: 2 (2010) 227–47; D. Papadimitriou, 'The EU's strategy in the post-communist Balkans', *Southeast European and Black Sea Studies* 1: 3 (2001) 69–94; A. J. K. Shepherd, '"A milestone in the history of the EU": Kosovo and the EU's international role', *International Affairs* 85: 3 (2009) 513–30; K. M. Torbiorn, *Destination Europe: The Political and Economic Growth of a Continent* (Manchester; New York: Manchester University Press, 2003) 174.

50 This amount includes funding provided through the Community Assistance for Reconstruction, Development and Stabilisation programme (CARDS), the Instrument for Pre-Accession Assistance (IPA), which replaced CARDS, the cost of UNMIK Pillar IV, the first years of EULEX and early humanitarian assistance (European Commission, *Instrument for Pre-Accession Assistance (IPA) Multi-annual Indicative Planning Document for Kosovo 2008–2010* (2008)).

51 Torbiorn, *Destination Europe.*

52 European Commission, 'Conditions for Membership' web page http://ec.europa.eu/enlargement/policy/conditions-membership/index_en.htm accessed 12 July 2013.

53 A. Dimitrova, 'Enlargement, institution-building and the EU's administrative capacity requirement', *West European Politics* 25: 4 (2002) 171–90, 178.

54 G. Knaus and M. Cox, 'The "Helsinki Moment" in Southeastern Europe', *Journal of Democracy* 16: 1 (2005) 39–53. The Czech Republic, Estonia, Latvia, Lithuania, Hungary, Poland, Slovakia and Slovenia all joined the EU in 2004 and Romania and Bulgaria joined in 2007.

55 O. Anastasakis, 'The Europeanization of the Balkans', *Brown Journal of World Affairs* 12: 1 (2005) 77–88, 84; Balkan Insight, *European Leaders Greet EU's Green Light to Serbia* (Balkan Investigative Reporting Network, 23 April 2013); European Commission, *Joint Report to the European Parliament and the Council on Serbia's progress in achieving the necessary degree of compliance with the membership criteria and notably the key priority of taking steps towards a visible and sustainable improvement of relations with Kosovo* (Brussels: High Representative of the European Union for Foreign Affairs and Security Policy, 2013) 4–5.

56 M. Klasnja, 'The EU and Kosovo: Time to Rethink the Enlargement and Integration Policy?' *Problems of Post Communism* 54: 4 (2007) 15–32; Knaus and Cox, 'The "Helsinki Moment" in Southeastern Europe'.

57 Anastasakis, 'The Europeanization of the Balkans'; Dimitrova, 'Enlargement, institution-building and the EU's administrative capacity requirement'.

58 D. Papadimitriou, P. Petrov and L. GreiÇivci, 'To build a state: Europeanization, EU actorness and state-building in Kosovo', *European Foreign Affairs Review* 12 (2007) 219–38.

59 European Commission, *IPA: Interim Evaluation and Meta-evaluation of IPA Assistance – Country Report Kosovo*, EuropeAid/131184/C/SER/Multi (Brussels: European Commission, 2013) 24.

60 K. H. Goetz, 'Making sense of post communist central administration: Modernization, Europeanization or Latinization?' *Journal of European Public Policy* 8: 6 (2001) 1032–51, 1037.

61 DFID, *Kosovo: Strategy Paper 2001–2004*, 3.

62 S. Keukeleire, A. Kalaja and A. Çollaku, *The EU and Kosovo: Structural Diplomacy in Action – but on the Basis of One-sided Paradigms?*, Policy Paper 4, The Diplomatic System of the European Union (Loughborough: Loughborough University, 2011).

63 European Commission, *Kosovo – Fulfilling its European Perspective* (Brussels: European Commission, 2009) 7.

64 European Commission, *Proposal for a Regulation of the European Parliament and of the Council on the Instrument for Pre-accession Assistance (IPA II)* (Brussels: European Commission, 2011) 3–4.

65 Council of the European Union, *Council Regulation (EC) No 1085/2006 of 17 July 2006 establishing an Instrument for Pre-Accession Assistance (IPA)* (Brussels: Official Journal of the European Union 2006) Article 2.

66 GHK/Technopolis, *Evaluation to Support the Preparation of Pre-accession Financial Instruments beyond 2013: Final Report* (Brussels: European Policy Evaluation Consortium (EPEC), 2011) 2–3.

67 A. Wittkowsky, 'Squaring the circle: A short history of UNMIK's European Union Pillar, 1999–2008', *Sudosteuropa Mitteilungen* 49: 1 (2009) 16–35, 18.

68 UNSC, *Report of the Secretary-General pursuant to paragraph 10 of Security Council Resolution 1244 (1999) 12 June 1999*, 4.

69 Ibid. 3.

70 Dixon, *Pillar IV's Role within UNMIK* paras 21–4.

71 S. Fidler, 'Albright irked by Kosovo funds delay', *Financial Times* (28 January 2000); Torbiorn, *Destination Europe* 133.

72 King and Mason, *Peace at any Price* 89; USAID, 'Results of Kosova Economic Sector Assessment, July 15 to July 29' (unpublished document, copy held by author, 1999) 8; Wittkowsky, 'Squaring the circle' 19.

73 International USAID public finance adviser (IA1).
74 King and Mason, *Peace at any Price* 89.
75 UNMIK/European Union, *EU Pillar Annual Report 2005* (Pristina: Pillar IV, 2006) 5; Wittkowsky, 'Squaring the circle' 19.
76 TAFKO, *Monthly Summary of Task Force Activities: July–August 1999*.
77 Wittkowsky, 'Squaring the circle'.
78 UNMIK/European Union, *The 10 Key Achievements: End of Mission Report 1999–2008*.
79 European Commission, *Commission Decision of 15 December 1999 Establishing a Programme for the Agency for the Reconstruction of Kosovo* (Brussels: European Commission, 1999).
80 TAFKO, *Monthly Summary of Task Force Activities: July–August 1999*.
81 European Agency for Reconstruction, *EAR Annual Report 2000* (Thessaloniki: European Agency for Reconstruction, 2001).
82 European Agency for Reconstruction, *Kosovo 1999 Action Programme* 5 (Thessaloniki: European Agency for Reconstruction, 1999); European Agency for Reconstruction, *Kosovo 2000 Action Programme* (Thessaloniki: European Agency for Reconstruction, 2000).
83 European Agency for Reconstruction, *Institutional Capacity Building Support (Kosovo) Executive Summary*.
84 International EU education adviser (IA5).
85 Ibid.
86 Ibid.
87 International EU audit adviser (IA7).
88 International EU customs adviser (IA10).
89 European Agency for Reconstruction, *Evaluation of the Implementation of Council Regulation 2667/2000 on the European Agency for Reconstruction, Synthesis Report Volume I Part C – Main Evaluation Report* (Brussels: Development Researchers' Network Consortium, 2004) 3.
90 International EU education adviser (IA5).
91 Kosovar EU public finance adviser (KA1).
92 European Agency for Reconstruction, *Institutional Capacity Building Support (Kosovo) Executive Summary* 3–4.
93 European Commission, *Retrospective Evaluation of the CARDS Programmes: Kosovo, Final Evaluation Report* (Brussels: Enlargement Directorate-General, 2009) i–iii.
94 GHK/Technopolis, *Evaluation to Support the Preparation of Pre-accession Financial Instruments beyond 2013: Final Report*, 28–31.
95 European Commission, *IPA: Interim Evaluation and Meta-evaluation of IPA Assistance – Country Report Kosovo* 52.
96 European Commission, *2009 Annual Report on the Implementation of the Instrument for Pre-Accession Assistance (IPA)* (Brussels: European Commission, 2010) 2; European Commission, *Proposal for a Regulation of the European Parliament and of the Council on the Instrument for Pre-accession Assistance (IPA II)*.
97 European Commission, *2013 Annual Report on Financial Assistance for Enlargement* (Brussels: European Commission, 2014).
98 USAID, *Budget Justification, Fiscal Year 2001: Annex III, Europe and Eurasia* (Washington, DC: United States Agency for International Development, 2000) 4.
99 USAID, *Foreign Aid in the National Interest: Promoting Freedom, Security, and Opportunity* (Washington, DC: United States Agency for International Development, 2002).
100 Torbiorn, *Destination Europe* 182.

101 International EU audit adviser (IA7).
102 King and Mason, *Peace at any Price* 84.
103 Kosovar EU technical adviser (KA3).
104 ICG, *Kosovo's First Month*, Europe Briefing No 47 (Pristina; Belgrade; Brussels: International Crisis Group, 2008) 4; ICG, *Kosovo's Fragile Transition*, Europe Report No. 196 (Pristina; Brussels: International Crisis Group, 2008) 20.
105 Congressional Research Service, *Kosovo: Reconstruction and Development Assistance*, RL30453 (Washington, DC: US Library of Congress, 2001) 1–2.
106 European Commission/World Bank, *Donor Polling for Kosovo (Under UNSCR 1244)*.
107 R. J. Muscat, *Selected Lessons from Evaluations of Responses to Complex Humanitarian Emergencies: Implications for the Kosovo Crisis* (Washington, DC: USAID Bureau for Europe and the New Independent States/USAID Mission to Yugoslavia, 1999) 5; USAID, 'Results of Kosova Economic Sector Assessment, July 15 to July 29'; USAID, *Strategy for the Federal Republic of Yugoslavia (Serbia, Montenegro, Kosovo) 1999–2000* (Washington, DC: United States Agency for International Development, 1999) 30.
108 International USAID public finance adviser (IA1).
109 Center for Public Integrity, *U.S. Official Says Government Wasted $6–8 Billion in Iraq Reconstruction* (Washington, DC: Centre for Public Integrity, 2012).
110 Barents Group, 'Government Infrastructure Support, United Nations Mission in Kosovo, Pillar IV' – Weekly Reports 1999 (Pristina: unpublished reports in possession of author, 1999).
111 USAID, USAID Kosovo Economic Growth Office, Presentation Slides (unpublished material provided by USAID staff, Pristina, 2010).
112 USAID, *USAID Assistance in Fiscal Reform: The Kosovo Economic Reconstruction Project* (Washington, DC: United States Agency for International Development, 2006) 4.
113 USAID, *USAID/Kosovo Annual Report FY 2004* (Pristina: United States Agency for International Development, 2004); USAID, *USAID Assistance in Fiscal Reform: The Kosovo Economic Reconstruction Project* 4.
114 USAID, *Mid-Term Performance Evaluation of the Kosovo Growth and Fiscal Stability Initiative (GFSI) – Final Report* (Washington, DC: United States Agency for International Development, 2012).
115 USAID, *Kosovo Country Development Cooperation Strategy 2014–2018* (Washington, DC: United States Agency for International Development, 2013).
116 International USAID public finance adviser (IA13).
117 International UNMIK official (IU2).
118 USAID, *USAID Assistance in Fiscal Reform: The Kosovo Economic Reconstruction Project*, 3.
119 The initial contract in 1999 was with the Barents Group, which was subsequently acquired by KPMG consulting, which then changed its name to BearingPoint. In 2009 BearingPoint went into receivership and its public services business, which was responsible for the work in Kosovo, was acquired by Deloitte.
120 International USAID accounting adviser (IA15).
121 International EU audit adviser (IA7).
122 King and Mason, *Peace at any Price* 139; R. A. Knudsen, *Privatization in Kosovo: The International Project 1999–2008* (Oslo: Norwegian Institute of International Affairs, 2010).
123 King and Mason, *Peace at any Price* 139.
124 Wittkowsky, 'Squaring the circle' 19.
125 International USAID public finance adviser (IA16).

126 USAID, *Kosovo: Results Review and Resource Request* 4.
127 International USAID public finance adviser (IA16).
128 International EU public finance adviser (IA14).
129 Wittkowsky, 'Squaring the circle' 19.
130 International EU public finance adviser (IA14).
131 Kosovar EU technical adviser (KA1).
132 A. Capussela, 'Road to ruin: An unnecessary highway in Kosovo could bankrupt Europe's poorest state', *Transitions Online* (13 January 2012); Skendaj, *Creating Kosovo: Intenational Oversight and the Making of Ethical Institutions* 87.
133 International customs adviser (IA17).
134 DFID, *Kosovo: Strategy Paper 2001–2004*, 5.
135 Ibid. 18.
136 Data on DFID projects and funding in Kosovo was formerly available on the DFID website and is still available through the UK government web archive http://webarchive.nationalarchives.gov.uk/*/http://projects.dfid.gov.uk/SearchResults.asp?countrySelect=KO-Kosovo. The information in this section was downloaded by the author from the DFID website in 2008 and 2010.
137 DFID, *Regional Program Evaluation: Western Balkans, Evaluation Report EV693* (London: UK Department for International Development, 2008).
138 World Bank/European Commission, *Rebuilding Kosovo: A Complicated Challenge for the International Community, Press Conference, Brussels, 12 July* (Brussels: Joint Office for South East Europe, 1999) para 4.
139 World Bank, *World Bank Group Transitional Support Strategy for Kosovo* 9.
140 IMF/World Bank, *Update on Economic Policy Issues and Institutional Development, First Donors' Conference,* Statement of the IMF and World Bank staff at the Informal Donor Meeting for Kosovo, Brussels, 28 July 1999 (Brussels: Joint Office for South East Europe, 1999); World Bank, *Kosovo: Building Peace through Sustained Growth*; World Bank, *Strategic Directions for the Economic Recovery of Kosovo*; World Bank/European Commission, *Rebuilding Kosovo: A Complicated Challenge for the International Community*; World Bank/European Commission, *Towards Stability and Prosperity*.
141 World Bank, *IDA/IFC Interim Strategy Note for Republic of Kosovo for the Period FY10-FY11* (Washington, DC: World Bank; International Finance Corporation, 2009) 17.
142 World Bank, *Implementation Completion Report on Two Grants to the United Nations Interim Administration in Kosovo for the Benefit of Kosovo* (Washington, DC: World Bank, 2001); World Bank, *Kosovo: Economic Assistance Grant IV – Project Information Document* (Washington, DC: World Bank, 2002); World Bank, *Program Document: Proposed Fourth Economic Assistance Grant to the United Nations Interim Administration Mission in Kosovo* (Washington, DC: World Bank, 2003); World Bank, *Implementation Completion Report: Economic Assistance Grant IV Kosovo* (Washington, DC: World Bank, 2004).
143 World Bank, *Economic Policy/Public Expenditure Management, Project Information Document (PID)* (Washington, DC: World Bank, 2004).
144 World Bank, *Public Expenditure Management Technical Assistance Project (PEMTAG), Project Appraisal Document* (Washington, DC: World Bank, 2005).
145 World Bank, *Public Expenditure Management Technical Assistance Project, Implementation Completion and Results Report* (Washington, DC: World Bank, 2009).
146 World Bank, *Public Sector Modernization Project, Project Appraisal Document (PAD)* (Washington, DC: World Bank, 2009).

147 World Bank, *Public Sector Modernization Project (P101614) Implementation Status & Results Report* (Washington, DC: World Bank, 2015).
148 International USAID taxation adviser (IA8).
149 IMF, *Republic of Kosovo: First Assessment Under the Staff-Monitored Program*, IMF Country Report No. 11/374 (Washington, DC: International Monetary Fund, 2011).
150 IMF, *IMF Mission to Kosovo Assesses Performance under the Staff-Monitored Program and Reaches Staff-Level Agreement on a Stand-By Arrangement*, Press Release No 12/65 (Washington DC: International Monetary Fund, 2012); IMF, *IMF Executive Board Completes Fifth Review under the SBA with Kosovo; Approves €4.8 Million Disbursement*, Press Release No 13/537 (Washington, DC: International Monetary Fund, 2013).
151 ICG, *Kosovo Spring* (Pristina;Sarajevo: International Crisis Group, 1998) 3.
152 Statistics Office of Kosovo, *Population and Housing Census in Kosovo Preliminary Results – June 2011* (Pristina: Republic of Kosovo, 2011).
153 World Bank, *Transitional Support Strategy for Kosovo: Progress Report* (Washington, DC: World Bank, 2000) 3.
154 DFID, *Kosovo: Strategy Paper 2001–2004*, 4.
155 USAID, *Strategy for Kosovo 2001–2003*, 4.
156 European Agency for Reconstruction, *Institutional Capacity Building Support (Kosovo) Executive Summary* 3.
157 ICG, *Kosovo: A Strategy for Economic Development*, Balkans Report No. 123 (Pristina; Brussels: International Crisis Group, 2001) 4.
158 USAID, *Corruption in Kosovo: Observations and Implications for USAID* (Washington, DC: United States Agency for International Development, 2003) 3.
159 UNDP, *Assessment of Administrative Capacity in Kosovo* (Prepared for the United Nations Development Programme by the Kosovo Capacity Assessment Project (KCAP) Team 2005) 78.
160 International EULEX customs adviser (IA6).
161 International EU audit adviser (IA3).
162 D. B. Kanin, 'Big men, corruption, and crime', *International Politics* 40 (2003) 491–526.
163 M. Todorova, *Imagining the Balkans* (New York; Oxford: Oxford University Press, 1997) 188.
164 Weinstein, 'Developing inequality' 9.
165 Early Warning Report, *Kosovo Early Warning Report No. 1, May–August 2002* (Pristina: UNDP/Riinvest, 2002) 11–12.
166 Early Warning Report, *Kosovo Early Warning Report No. 2, Sept–Dec 2002* (Pristina: UNDP/Riinvest, 2002) 16; Early Warning Report, *Kosovo Early Warning Report No. 3, January–April 2003* (Pristina: UNDP/Riinvest, 2003) 15; Early Warning Report, *Kosovo Early Warning Report No. 4, May–August 2003* (Pristina: UNDP/Riinvest, 2003) 4.
167 Kosovar technical adviser (KA3).
168 Early Warning Report, *Kosovo Early Warning Report No. 1, May–August 2002*, 5; Early Warning Report, *Kosovo Early Warning Report No. 5, September–December 2003* (Pristina: UNDP/Riinvest, 2003) 4; Early Warning Report, *Kosovo Early Warning Report No. 9, January–March 2005* (Pristina: USAID/UNDP/Riinvest, 2005) 4.
169 www.vetevendosje.org/en/, accessed 16 June 2015.
170 Republic of Kosovo, *Zgjedhjet për Kuvendin e Kosovës 2014: Rezultatet për Kosovë* (Pristina: Republic of Kosovo, 2014).
171 Judah, *Kosovo: War and Revenge*.

172 S. Power, 'Kosovo dispatch: Breathing room', *The New Republic* (9 August 1999) 18–20, 20.
173 USAID, *Strategy for Kosovo 2001–2003*, 9.
174 C. Ashton, *Statement by EU High Representative Catherine Ashton Following Today's Meeting in the Framework of the EU-facilitated Dialogue* (Brussels: European Union External Action, 2014).
175 Garton Ash, *History of the Present* 452.
176 King and Mason, *Peace at any Price* 126.
177 UNSC, *Security Council minutes, 4011th meeting, Thursday 10 June 1999 (Resumption 1)* (New York: United Nations Security Council, 1999) 4.
178 King and Mason, *Peace at any Price* 126.

3

Public finance management

Donors, public finance and 'liberal peace'

There is a high level of agreement between most donor organisations on the centrality of public finance management (PFM) for effective government and economic stability, and broad concurrence on the policies and systems that constitute good management of public finances. Although the 'neo-liberal' philosophies that inform donor policies in this area tend to favour a reduced role for government, the sound management of public resources, effective tax collection and the right kind of fiscal policy are regarded as essential and unavoidable functions of government. The standard fiscal policy agenda promoted by the IMF and other international organisations in all countries emphasises balanced budgets through low taxes and low public expenditure, tight controls on public sector pay and employment levels, limited social welfare, minimal private sector subsidies, and a rapid reduction in the need for donor support. In war-torn countries, therefore, almost as soon as the conflict ends, citizens are expected to start paying a raft of donor-recommended taxes to finance the new peacetime government. At the same time, however, the collection of unauthorised payments by former combatants and putative alternative governments may not have ceased, and the new regime may have limited capacity to actually deliver the services the taxes are intended to pay for.

Much of the work of PFM development is seen as largely technical, involving the application of well-established rules of accounting and reporting, standard software and uniform classification systems. Other aspects of PFM are, however, highly political and contested. The macroeconomic and fiscal objectives of the finance ministry are often in conflict with political aspirations to provide economic stimulation, social welfare and employment, or to win votes. The nature of the political system itself can also have implications for the processes of budget formulation and control. In particular, proportional representation and coalition governments, often proposed in post-conflict countries to encourage cooperation between political opponents, may produce suboptimal fiscal policies and 'pork barrel' projects, while the strong, centralised Ministry of Finance considered necessary to ensure fiscal discipline may be regarded as a threat to political harmony.[1] The idea of a representative government making rational and equitable decisions on the distribution of economic benefits among the population, on which Western public finance models are based, may also be at odds with the cultural systems and political realities in many developing countries.

Aid donors have been criticised for imposing donor-defined PFM 'blueprints' and best practice models regardless of the context.[2] Bodies such as the World Bank, the IMF and the OECD have produced numerous manuals, guidelines, textbooks and assessment frameworks that establish the standards that countries are expected to apply in the management of public revenues and budgets.[3] The EU also has defined 'blueprints' for the development of customs and taxation procedures and detailed 'directives' to be applied by member countries and aspiring members. However, to a significant extent what public finance experts aim to transfer to developing countries is a set of objectives and principles rather than any particular system for achieving them. These principles include, for example, transparency and credibility in budget preparation, central control of government funds in a single account, effective control of the use of public funds, timely reporting and auditing of payments and payroll, and transparent, non-corrupt procurement of government supplies. There is often limited room for variation in these principles, and it is therefore considered that there is a limited requirement for consultation or adaptation. Ownership in this context generally means ensuring local understanding of the recommended procedures rather than involvement in developing them.

Agreement on the principles of good practice does not extend to all fields of financial management in government. There are differences of view, for example, on the best way to organise government procurement, the mechanisms for audit and financial control, the value or otherwise of 'performance budgeting' and the benefits of decentralisation in the management of resources. Donor assistance for PFM development also sometimes suffers as a result of the pursuit of 'best practices' and ideal models of financial administration that fail to appreciate the deficit in education and experience available to operate complex systems in these environments. But exactly where the boundary lies between the 'basics' of manual accounting in ledger books and the unnecessary sophistication of multi-million-dollar computer systems is difficult to define.[4]

Setting up new public finance arrangements in post-conflict countries thus generates complex policy issues and there is potential for international actors to disagree over objectives and priorities, the systems and procedures that should be adopted and the balance between pragmatic short-term solutions and achieving long-term objectives. This chapter documents the process of establishing the main public finance functions under UN interim administration and transforming them into institutions of the Kosovo government. It examines developments in revenue collection, expenditure management, public procurement, and audit and financial control, and describes the actions of the main international actors in these fields and the challenges they faced. In some areas there was considerable cooperation and agreement between donors on what should be done and a significant investment of effort. In others delayed action, disagreements over policy, changes in donor responsibility or inadequate resources undermined international efforts. Nevertheless, the overall impact of the combined efforts of the lead actors is generally judged to have been successful and has contributed to the creation of a relatively effective PFM function in Kosovo.

PFM development in Kosovo

Developing Kosovo's revenue and expenditure management institutions was high on the list of reform and transformation initiatives planned by donors in the lead up to the post-conflict intervention. It was also an important issue for UNMIK for very practical reasons. Public administration in Kosovo had previously been financed by the Republic of Serbia, but this source of funding had ceased months earlier. The Security Council had given the Mission responsibility for interim civil administration but had not provided the funds to pay for it. The 2,700 UN civil administration staff proposed in the UNMIK budget would not be sufficient to deliver the health, education or refuse collection services required for a population of around two million people. Kosovo was thus in urgent need of money to support public service operations. Four weeks after the passage of UNSCR 1244, the Secretary General was appealing for emergency funds to cover the cost of essential services,[5] but donors, as always, were reluctant to pay for the normal ongoing activities of government. Re-establishing local revenue collection and setting up systems to manage expenditure was a necessity.

The most significant providers of technical assistance in PFM in the initial period of the Mission were the EU and USAID in Pillar IV, supported by IMF and World Bank advisory missions. EAR started funding technical assistance projects in this field in 2002, and World Bank technical assistance in public finance did not begin in earnest until 2007. In the first few years of the post-conflict period, EU and USAID-funded personnel were much more than simply technical advisers. Many were appointed to executive positions equivalent to Ministers or Permanent Secretaries, exercising legal authorities under UN regulations and responsible for establishing the structure of new organisations, recruiting and training their future staff, developing policies and drafting legislation. This gave international actors a significant degree of control over Kosovo's newly established institutions. What they did with this authority was an important factor in the outcomes achieved. After the creation of the PISG in 2002, advisers and officials continued to play a significant role in PFM but moved to a more conventional technical assistance model, providing policy and operational advice to Kosovar officials.

UNSCR 1244 did not provide clear guidance to the interim administration on economic policy issues, objectives or strategies, but a broad interpretation of the meaning of 'substantial autonomy' was considered to provide scope for basic budget and finance operations.[6] International experts soon decided that the previous Yugoslav system of financial administration could not, and should not, be revived, nor would the parallel system established by Albanian Kosovars during the 1990s be a suitable foundation to build on. The parallel system had been funded by contributions from Albanian emigrant workers in Europe and America, kept largely as cash, and it was unclear how much money had been collected, or exactly what happened to it. In the splintered political environment of the time there were allegations of misappropriation and large losses from investments in pyramid schemes in Albania.[7] These financial administration arrangements would certainly not have met World Bank or IMF standards of transparency and accountability. It was understood, therefore, that it would be necessary to create PFM institutions 'from scratch'. At the first donors' conference, the head of Pillar IV, Joly Dixon, set out a concise but comprehensive list of the steps that would be taken to establish a functioning economy and institutions for managing public finances.[8] His plan said, in many fewer words, more or less what the World Bank and the IMF had already set out in their lengthier reports for the conference.

Revenue agencies

Given the urgency of identifying revenues to support the interim administration, establishing a Customs Service was one of the earliest steps in public finance development. The creation of a Tax Administration to collect internal revenues followed very soon after. Both functions developed rapidly in a very short period through the passage of numerous new laws and the recruitment and training of local staff. Although primary responsibility for the two functions fell to different international bodies, their methods and outcomes were similar.

The Customs Service

The EU played the lead role in establishing the customs function by extending the customs development programmes it was already operating in other countries in the region. The initial intention of the UN had been to operate an UNMIK Customs Service on the same basis as the UNMIK Police, using a large number of seconded international officials for an extended period. The EU, however, elected to develop a local customs service from the start to ensure sustainability once the international presence was withdrawn.[9] This illustrates quite clearly the differences in thinking between these two arms of the Mission about both the purpose of the international presence and the future of the Kosovo administration. Within the first few weeks the EU established the Kosovo Customs Assistance Mission (CAM-K), comprising ten customs officials seconded by EU member states, and began recruiting and training a local Customs Service.[10]

By the July donors' conference, the Head of Pillar IV was able to announce that a number of Kosovars who had previously worked in the FRY customs organisation had already been identified and would start work shortly.[11] This approach was supported by the IMF, which claimed that the customs administration 'was a rare service in that Kosovar Albanians continued to be employed in responsible positions' and these individuals seemed to possess the requisite skills and a strong willingness to return to their duties.[12] By the end of August, thirty-eight former FRY customs officers had been appointed to the Kosovo Customs Service. The positive assessment of these Yugoslav-era officials was apparently short lived, however. International advisers expressed concern that these staff from the 'stagnant' Yugoslav service were unfamiliar with modern techniques.[13] Recruitment of further staff focused on attracting younger recruits with no previous customs experience and, according to one Pillar IV adviser, the former FRY officials were gradually phased out of the service.[14] By 2008 only two of the original employees remained.[15]

In early August, approximately six weeks after the start of the post-conflict mission, the new UNMIK Customs Service commenced work controlling the border crossings with Albania and Macedonia. The rate of customs duties to be applied had yet to be agreed, however. Import duties and fees are a readily identifiable and easy-to-collect source of government revenue, but at the same time the level of tariffs may have an impact on the economy and on the development of trade. The World Bank and the IMF decided that, on these criteria, the previous FRY customs code was unacceptable and proposed in its place a flat *ad valorum* tax on all items. This was a radical reshaping of the previous trade and customs regime and the World Bank argued that it demonstrated that UNMIK was taking a pragmatic approach to the sovereignty/autonomy issue.[16] On 3 September 1999, the Customs Service began collecting revenue.

The recruitment of further local staff for the Customs Service was tightly controlled by international advisers. More than 1,100 applications were received for the advertised positions in the first recruitment round and 270 applicants were shortlisted for interview. By March 2000 around fifty people, nearly 30 per cent of them women, had been appointed and trained. In the absence of a formal public sector employment policy at that time, employment conditions and salary rates were decided by Pillar IV in negotiation with the recruited staff. Attempts were made to involve the already recruited staff in conducting interviews, but they were reportedly reluctant to participate because of the pressure being put on them from outside the service to influence appointments.[17]

Although the EU took the lead in the customs field, multiple other actors were also involved in the initial phase. Until early 2000, UNMIK's Pillar II had formal policy responsibility for customs matters and the post of Director of Customs was held by a succession of Pillar II officials. A USAID-funded adviser in Pillar IV was also working on customs issues in cooperation with CAM-K.[18] In early 2000 a full-time international Director General of Customs and several other senior customs managers were seconded from the UK Customs Service to exercise executive authority in the Customs Service. This arrangement with UK Customs continued until the eventual transfer of the organisation to the Kosovo government in 2008. A number of people, not all of them British, suggested that the consistent use of British advisers in senior positions in the Customs Service over the period was a significant advantage both because it provided a single, consistent approach, and because of the perceived status of the British customs service.

Tax administration

While the EU took the lead in establishing the Customs Service, USAID-funded advisers in Pillar IV played the primary role in setting up the tax administration. While this may appear inconsistent with the image of the US as pro-small government and anti-tax, the aims of tax administration development were to eliminate the need for donors to fund the Kosovo government as quickly as possible, and to influence the types and rates of the taxes levied. As in customs, the previous Yugoslav system of taxation was rejected, for both practical and ideological reasons. 'The locals wouldn't accept it, they wouldn't use it. That meant we had to get our own taxation system. Secondly, we weren't looking at a socialist, soviet-type taxation system. We were looking at a democratic, Western, market-based system.'[19] Tax collections began in January 2000 with taxes that were simple and easy to implement: an excise tax and a 15 per cent sales tax on imported goods, both of which could be assessed and collected at border posts along with customs duties. A regulation imposing a tax on the larger hotels and restaurants came into effect in February 2000. This targeted a relatively small number of clearly identifiable businesses which, at the time, derived most of their profits from the international community in Pristina. Because of its simplicity, collecting the Hotel, Food and Beverage Tax was seen as a good training exercise for Kosovar tax inspectors, but it attracted criticism from UN staff, who saw it as a direct imposition on them as the main users of the affected establishments.[20]

Taxes were collected by the newly established Kosovo Tax Administration. This organisation was also, like Customs, almost entirely staffed by Kosovars. Recruitment of tax inspectors started in November 1999 and the first 34, selected from 700 applicants and including one Serb, started work in January 2000 after completing a short training programme. The majority had no previous experience in tax administration activities. International advisers controlled the recruitment process and selected candidates on the basis of merit, as they defined it, which meant future potential more than existing qualifications or experience. The exclusion of Albanian Kosovars from employment and education during the previous decade had meant that verifiable qualifications and relevant experience were in short supply. Several of the new recruits were designated as team leaders, but executive decision-making authority for taxation administration was exercised by a USAID-funded international adviser performing the role of Director of Taxation.

The tax system developed rapidly during 2000. Six pieces of tax legislation were approved by the SRSG between January and May.[21] The Hotel, Food and Beverage tax was expanded to more establishments, and a 'Presumptive Tax', which applied a fixed tax to businesses based on their size and was similar to the small business tax used in neighbouring Albania, was also introduced. This was followed in May 2001 by a Value Added Tax (VAT). The hotel tax and the presumptive tax were subsequently replaced in 2002 by a more conventional Profits Tax and Personal Income Tax. The recruitment of further Tax Administration staff also proceeded rapidly throughout 2000. A process for evaluating the work performance of all employees every six months was developed, and in March disciplinary action was taken against two of the new tax inspectors for misconduct.[22] By October 2001, when a Kosovar Co-Director of Tax Administration was appointed, virtually all day-to-day operational work was being performed by Kosovars on civil service salaries. The Tax Administration's performance in terms of revenue collection improved steadily over the next few years and in the 2002 Kosovo Budget, 93 per cent of recurrent expenditure of the Kosovo administration was expected to be funded by local revenue from customs and taxation.[23]

Challenges in revenue collection

Collecting revenue in post-conflict Kosovo was not an easy task. There was a high level of non-compliance, which only began to improve after the first enforcement action was taken for non-payment of the Hotel, Food and Beverage Tax in June 2000. A senior Kosovar tax official explained:

> The taxpayers' mentality at that time was that, for some years we don't need to pay taxes because they were somehow frustrated from the war, and they were thinking that this past war time could last longer and they don't need to pay taxes. So that's why we had to go step by step slowly to try to change the approach and to say to them that, since you were ready to give your life for this country, then you have to pay taxes ... before, during the Serbia time, they had presented that as patriotism not to pay taxes to the Serbian government and that had built up in their mind so it was difficult to change it. And then they have inherited the logic and the skill to make the tax evasion.[24]

In some instances, objections to paying taxes and import duties led to threats, intimidation and physical violence against local officials. In October 1999, for example, a Customs officer was beaten and hospitalised, and in 2001 the Kosovar Co-Head of Customs received death threats related to the removal of staff believed to be involved in corruption.[25] These dangers did not affect international officials and advisers to the same extent, although a senior CFA adviser reported receiving regular threatening phone calls related to requests for tax exemptions, and one USAID tax adviser left the country abruptly in response to perceived threats. Official tax collections also had to compete in some places with illegal 'parallel' taxes collected by local bodies or by extortionists. Evidence of the continued operation of parallel business taxes continued into 2000, in spite of the JIAS agreement to disband the parallel administrative structures of Kosovo's political factions.[26]

Despite the rapid progress in passing new tax legislation, revenue advisers in Pillar IV frequently expressed frustration with the UN, and in particular with UN officials in Pillar II, who were considered to be obstructing their work. There was concern, for example, that UNMIK's apparent inability to deal with unauthorised parallel taxes would undermine the authority of the Tax Administration[27] and frustration over delays in opening a customs post on the administrative boundary line with Montenegro, which allowed importers to avoid customs and tax payments and resulted in lower-than-forecast revenue collections.[28] The time taken by UN lawyers to review draft tax legislation was also a source of frustration. One USAID adviser claimed that UN legal staff 'had a pronounced anti-tax bias', a surprising statement given the low tax regime favoured by USAID.[29] Implementing the Presumptive Tax, once it was approved by the UN, was also delayed by the failure of the Kosovo Statistical Agency in Pillar II to complete the registration of local businesses on time. The absence of an official gazette to make tax regulations available to the public was another problem attributed to inaction by the UN. In mid-2000 the Tax Administration eventually published its own Tax Gazette.

There was also a major stand-off between Pillar IV and the UN over the expansion of the tax regime to include personal income taxes. The draft income tax law prepared by USAID advisers in February 2000 was clear that the tax would not apply to any international staff working in Kosovo, but the UN insisted that its local employees should also be exempt. UN salaries for local secretaries, cleaners, drivers and security guards were considerably higher than those paid to civil servants or private sector workers and would have provided an estimated 35 per cent of income tax revenue. Pillar IV advisers felt strongly that it would be politically unacceptable to exempt them. 'If you had someone who was earning DM 1500 a month not paying tax because he works for the UN, while someone earning 300 DM a month is paying tax because he works for the government, you would have riots.'[30]

The UN's position was based on the provisions of the long-standing 'Convention on Privileges and Immunities of the United Nations'.[31] The originators of these employment policies presumably never envisaged that the UN would ever be the largest employer in an economy. Subjecting UN employees in Kosovo to income tax would set precedents for other governments to impose similar taxes, which the UN would then need to reimburse to its staff. The UN ultimately won this battle, but the dispute over the issue significantly delayed the introduction of the tax.

Kosovarisation of revenue agencies

Control of the Customs Service remained a 'reserved function' of the SRSG under the Constitutional Framework for Self Government, which came into effect at the start of 2002, although by this time almost all senior positions were held by

Kosovars. Full responsibility for the Customs Service was not formally transferred to the Kosovo government until after independence, however the Kosovar official who then became Director-General had, according to several customs advisers, effectively been performing that role for much of the pre-independence period.

The Tax Administration, on the other hand, became a responsibility of the elected Kosovo government quite soon after the formation of the PISG. During the first year of the PISG government, a USAID-funded adviser continued to share the role of Director of Taxation with a Kosovar counterpart, but in 2003 the Tax Administration became a responsibility of the new Ministry for Finance and Economy (MFE) and full authority was handed to the Kosovar Director. A new team of USAID experts arrived to work simply as advisers to the Kosovar staff rather than in executive roles. Opinions differ on whether the timing of the transfer of responsibility was appropriate. An international adviser working in the Tax Administration in 2010 believed the handover at that time had been justified. 'You had a group of people at the management level who had been in their jobs for three or four years, they had received some sort of training from previous advisers, and they were doing a reasonable job.[32] Interestingly, it was the Kosovar head of the Tax Administration who suggested the transfer had been premature. 'I am thinking that probably the transfer of responsibilities to the local Director, if that had happened two years later, in 2005, that would probably have been better.'[33] Skendaj has also argued that the early transfer of responsibility for the Tax Administration has undermined the performance of the tax collection function.[34] One of the consequences of handing the Tax Administration to local control, for example, was a higher turnover of senior and middle management staff compared to the relatively stable staffing in the Customs Service. In the years after the PISG assumed responsibility there were several changes of Director-General of Taxation, and a number of management staff were appointed who had no previous experience in taxation but who were believed to be political allies of the minister of the day.[35] The Tax Administration has therefore been more exposed to political influence, at least in its staffing and possibly in its day-to-day operations, and this appears to have adversely affected its performance relative to the Customs Service.

Europeanisation of the tax system

Up until 2002, US-funded advisers had taken the lead in formulating taxation policy, with considerable input from the IMF. After the creation of the PISG, however, the need to align Kosovo's customs and taxation regimes with the EU *acquis communautaire* was increasingly raised as an issue in documents produced by EU agencies. In 2001, the EU carried out an analysis of the customs and taxation systems, comparing them to the EU 'blueprints' used in other pre-accession countries, and developed proposals for the comprehensive modernisation of these services. The use of the term 'modernisation' in relation to Kosovo's Customs Service and Tax

Administration is somewhat perplexing given that both institutions had been in existence for only a few years and had been established by international customs and taxation specialists, so presumably should have already been quite 'modern'. The issue, however, was the need to develop these services 'along European lines' using 'EU best practice'.[36]

The scope of EU involvement, through CAFAO, in the revenue function was thus expanded to include the Tax Administration, and the VAT legislation was redrafted to align it with the EU's sixth VAT directive.[37] However, USAID also continued to fund a team of taxation advisers, including a Senior Adviser to the Director-General, and it is generally agreed, by both USAID and EU advisers, that CAFAO's impact in the Tax Administration was less than intended. These advisers differ, however, on the reasons for this. A former senior customs adviser suggested that CAFAO assistance was not welcomed by the Tax Administration because 'to be brutally frank, it was not in the interests of certain vested interests for Tax Administration to develop in the same way as Customs.'[38] A USAID adviser, however, argued that the fault was more with the CAFAO approach to providing assistance:

> 'they weren't working in the tax office. They were working in their own CAFAO building and they were visiting the tax office on an occasional basis and I believe that's one of the reasons why, traditionally, EU projects have not been that successful in the tax office ... the USAID projects have always been based in the tax office, working alongside the counterparts.[39]

An EU assessment of its customs and taxation activities in 2008 agreed that the use of short- and medium-term technical advisers with frequent turnover and gaps in assistance had been less effective than the USAID approach of placing long-term, full-time advisers in the Tax Administration.[40] This was not the first EU report to argue that long-term assistance would have been more effective than short-term or intermittent adviser inputs. Successive evaluations of EAR projects had made the same point.

Revenue issues after independence

Both the Kosovo Customs Service and the Tax Administration continued to receive a significant amount of assistance from donors after the government's declaration of independence in 2008. In fact, in 2010 both services seemed to have more external advisers than at any time since their creation. EULEX had a large customs assistance component with around seventy international staff, although the majority of these were engaged in operational duties in the Serb-dominated northern areas where Kosovo government officials were unable to operate. ECLO also funded a small 'EU Customs and Taxation Technical Assistance' project and USAID continued to be actively involved in the Tax Administration. Under the terms of the

Ahtisaari plan for supervised independence, both the Customs Service and the Tax Administration were subject to international monitoring by the ICO, including final approval over appointments to the Director-General posts in both organisations. This arrangement was formally ended in September 2012. Both functions, therefore, in spite of being transferred to local political control, remained under some degree of international supervision for an extended period. To some extent this scrutiny continues through both the annual EU reporting process, and the IMF's regular reviews of fiscal performance.

Budget, treasury and payments

Immediately after the conflict Kosovo lacked all normal financial infrastructure: there were no functioning banks, no secure arrangements for transferring funds into the territory and limited supplies of any kind of currency in the required denominations. The first official public expenditures by the international administration were 'stipend' payments to a number of judges and health workers in early August, funded from a UN Trust Fund. The payments were made by UN staff in cash. This procedure was criticised by the World Bank, which expressed concern that the spending 'has been organized in an *ad hoc* fashion outside the context of an overall fiscal framework and budget planning process'.[41] Kosovo's administration therefore needed not only sources of revenue but also an agreed budget, a mechanism for making payments and reliable accounting for expenditure.

At this point, however, it was not yet clear which component of the Mission should have responsibility for these functions, with both Pillar II and Pillar IV making a claim. This unclear division of responsibility for finance issues in the early stages, and confusion within UNMIK about how the budget process should work, made donors reluctant to release budget support funds.[42] The matter was eventually decided, on the basis of World Bank and IMF advice, in favour of Pillar IV, and by September the first US-funded public finance advisers were working with a small group of EU Pillar IV staff to set up the basic processes and functions of the budget office and treasury.[43]

Central Fiscal Authority

The first step was to establish a Central Fiscal Authority (CFA) as a legal entity with authority to perform financial management tasks such as opening bank accounts, preparing the budget and making payments. In September, a simple financial management regulation and associated administrative directions were drafted and submitted to UNMIK for approval. This generated another conflict between Pillar IV and the UN over the slow response to the draft regulation in New York. A Pillar IV adviser doubted the capacity of UN lawyers to deal with the legislation. 'They had no idea. They had never dealt with a legal situation that was trying to set up a government. They had no precedent to work to.'[44] Pillar IV refused to process payments from the foreign bank accounts that held donor contributions to the Kosovo budget until there was an UNMIK regulation in place to authorise them to do so. Reportedly, the IMF wrote directly to the UN Secretary General requesting him to intervene to have the legislation finalised. The regulation was eventually promulgated by the SRSG on 6 November 1999. The Kosovo budget for the last months of 1999 was approved at the same time.[45]

The most important aspect of the three-page regulation setting up the CFA was the clause that established a Kosovo Consolidated Budget (KCB) separate from the UNMIK budget controlled by the UN General Assembly. This was one of the first decisive steps towards an autonomous administration in Kosovo. The government in Belgrade protested to the UN Security Council about the decision to create a separate budget authority for Kosovo, arguing that it constituted a violation of UNSCR 1244.[46] The creation of a Kosovo budget outside UNMIK was also, initially, a matter of concern at UN headquarters. Budget advisers in Pillar IV considered it important, however, to differentiate between the domestic Kosovo budget, used for the normal operations of public administration, and funding for activities related to humanitarian assistance and international administration. This would allow the cost of maintaining services in the long term, without donor assistance, to be clearly identified. One of the rules established to do this, for example, was to ensure that no salaries of foreign staff were paid from the KCB.[47] It also had the benefit that Kosovo's financial management procedures could be separated from the UN's complex procurement and finance processes. As more USAID technical advisers arrived, Pillar IV developed detailed budget and treasury procedures, accounting and payment forms, and a chart of accounts. They then began providing training to the people who would need to use them, which at that stage largely meant international UNMIK staff in Pillar II departments and in municipal and regional administrations.

As in the revenue agencies, developing local capability to manage public finance tasks was identified as a primary objective that should be pursued as soon as possible. When it had been a province of Serbia, Kosovo had had limited budget, treasury or revenue functions, which had been largely controlled from Belgrade.[48] When the CFA was created, therefore, there were no existing staff waiting to be re-employed. A former Pillar IV adviser noted that 'there wasn't anyone at all in that category from either the banking or finance side so we had to go out and hire everybody'.[49]

Recruitment of CFA staff started in November 1999. Advisers reported that the quality of applicants was not strong, but they managed to identify a number of qualified candidates who were appointed in February 2000. The work required of the Kosovar staff was initially quite basic. They managed the paperwork involved in processing payments for the expenses of the civil administration and reconciling CFA bank accounts. 'It was simple. At three o'clock you go to the bank, you check this, you write it down on an Excel spreadsheet, you tick them off, you check the bank balance against the cash book, and you teach them that sort of basic stuff and they learn that.'[50] From such simple beginnings some of the staff recruited and trained by the international advisers at that time have risen through the organisation to now hold senior management positions at Permanent Secretary, Division or Department Head level.

Banking and payments

By September 1999, the Customs Service had begun collecting revenue but there was, at the time, nowhere to deposit it. Cash was held in safes in UNMIK offices, and funds provided by donors were deposited in accounts with foreign banks outside Kosovo.[51] Establishing banking and payment arrangements for the Kosovo budget had been identified as an urgent task by the World Bank in its initial report in July 1999 but it proved to be one of the more complex PFM issues to resolve. Immediately after the end of the conflict the PDK-led 'provisional government' had set up its own central bank, with 135 staff, and had intended to take over and operate the former Yugoslav payments bureau, the Social Accounting Service (SDK). It had also established an expert task force, which prepared several draft laws on banking and payments. This was a major source of conflict for a while between international actors and the provisional government, described by one observer as a 'train wreck'.[52] It was eventually resolved in October by an UNMIK decree authorising the facilities of the SDK to be administered by UNMIK, and setting up a supervisory board to manage the funds of public institutions.[53] In November, a more detailed UNMIK regulation set up the Banking and Payments Authority of Kosovo (BPK), with responsibility for the facilities of both the SDK and the former National Bank of Kosovo.[54] The IMF appointed an international Managing Director and USAID-funded consultants filled several Deputy Managing Director posts. The BPK began taking deposits from the Customs Service and a few weeks later started making payments on behalf of the CFA Treasury as well as UNMIK's ongoing stipend payments to civil service staff.

The technical details of how the BPK should operate also took some time to resolve. USAID had initially planned to purchase a new computer system to manage the payments process. The World Bank, however, suggested reactivating the SDK in order to provide an operational system within a short timeframe.[55] This raised both practical and political issues. The SDK, which was set up to operate as an integral part of the payments system of the FRY, had become inoperative during the conflict and its computers were considered obsolete. Reviving it, including converting it to manage a different currency and ensuring 'Y2K' compliance in the final months of 1999, was not considered viable.[56] There was concern among some international advisers, however, that cutting the link between the SDK system in Kosovo and Belgrade would have political implications in relation to the distinction between 'substantial autonomy' and Yugoslav sovereignty.[57] Eventually, in early 2000, a new computer system using software donated by the Norwegian government was installed to replace the SDK.

The BPK took over not only the buildings but also the staff of the former payments bureau. More than 400 former SDK personnel in the central and regional offices were employed on six-month contracts to enable the new organisation to commence operations without needing to interview and train new staff. They were put to work in 'first line' jobs, under close supervision, and without access to safes.[58] The BPK did not, however, absorb the staff of the National Bank. In January 2000, former Bank employees protested that UNMIK had violated their right to work by failing to recruit them to the new organisation. Pillar IV declared, however, that there was no commitment to employ former staff and that recruitment to positions in both the BPK and CFA would follow employment practices based on the principles of fairness and transparency.[59] The transferred SDK staff were therefore subjected to a detailed skills assessment process, conducted by the IMF, and all positions in the proposed organisation structure, which had been developed by the IMF, were advertised in early 2000. At least one of the USAID consultants working in the BPK, however, initially resisted the requirement to advertise the positions, considering that the incumbent SDK staff were adequately capable, and that the limited international staff resources would be overstretched by the process.[60] They also noted that very few of the 57,000 Kosovar civil servants who were by then on the official payroll in the UN-managed departments had been subject to a recruitment process. However, the EU Head of Pillar IV, the IMF-appointed Managing Director, and the USAID advisers in the CFA all insisted on a process of open recruitment and merit selection.[61] After the available positions had been filled, a large number of staff were found to be surplus to requirements. A process to determine 'realistic and appropriate' staffing levels was initiated in consultation with the Kosovar branch managers, who proved to be resistant to the idea of staff reductions. In May, ninety-four staff were declared redundant and paid three months' worth of stipends in compensation. The surplus staff protested about their loss of employment at the BPK headquarters building in Pristina for several weeks. The retained staff, in spite of the competitive selection process and their previous experience, were provided with a considerable amount of training over the next few years, including courses in 'basic accounting'.

One of the more contentious early decisions of UNMIK, which was seen as a clear challenge to Yugoslav sovereignty, was to authorise the use of foreign currencies for financial transactions in addition to the volatile Yugoslav Dinar. Both the international organisations and Kosovars, many with relatives working in Germany, rapidly adopted the German Deutsche Mark as their preferred currency. There was, however, a shortage of notes and coins of the needed denominations within Kosovo's borders. Neither the UN nor the BPK were keen to take on the risks involved in transporting large amounts of cash, but Pillar II, nevertheless, expected BPK to take responsibility for distributing its welfare and stipend payments throughout the territory. The advisers working in BPK were concerned about security, insurance and the potential personal liability of advisers. Security was certainly a serious issue. In February 2000 a Kosovar BPK sub-branch manager was murdered in his office, and there were two major robberies. It was unclear whether UN insurance policies would apply to BPK operations and whether members of the Board of Governors would be held liable for any losses. A CFA adviser reported having to use various ad hoc and risky arrangements involving KFOR military transport and private security firms to meet urgent cash requirements. BPK advisers complained about these 'cowboy banking' cash transport practices used by the CFA, while CFA advisers in turn were highly critical of the inability of the BPK to offer an alternative:

> [the consulting firm] brought in some sophisticated bankers and their issues were to set up a world class banking authority in a situation in which all we wanted, really, was money ... They had three people who were more interested in writing the banking law and regulatory framework but they had no money in the bank and they had no idea how to get it.[62]

It should be noted that these heated disputes over the payment system, staffing policy and cash transport were often conducted between advisers who all worked for the same company on the same project and for the same donor. By mid-July 2000, the establishment of a private bank in Kosovo and the development of private secure cash transport services reduced the significance of the cash management problem.

In 2006, BPK became CBAK, an independent public body.[63] By this time all department manager positions were held by Kosovars[64] and the appointment of a Kosovar Managing Director after independence marked the full Kosovarisation of the institution. Pillar IV's final report praised the achievements of the banking authority, including the development of a large and very competitive commercial banking sector, given the previous distrust of banks in Kosovo.[65]

Budget planning and expenditure policy

Reducing reliance on donor support had been identified by donors and by Pillar IV as a priority, and this meant both raising revenue and keeping public expenditure low. The forecast Kosovo Budget for the 2000 fiscal year anticipated that donors would only need to meet one-third of the recurrent cost of the Kosovo administration, even though at this stage the Customs Service had only been in operation a few months and internal tax revenue collection had not yet begun.[66] The IMF noted that the proposed expenditure levels in the first annual Kosovo budget were 'not excessive' in comparison with other low-income countries, given the considerable social and economic needs.[67]

The main problem faced by the budget formulation process at this time was the limited ability of the international staff in UNMIK's civil administration departments to develop budget plans or to estimate expenditure requirements. UN staff were often on relatively short-term secondments, and the IMF expressed concern that many had limited understanding of government finance processes.[68] Pillar IV staff found it difficult to identify the relevant Pillar II officials responsible for budget issues and there were delays in the submission of budget requests. In March 2000 seven Kosovar staff were recruited to the Budget Office and over subsequent years gradually assumed responsibility for dealing with the budget process. They were hampered in their work, however, by the fact that, even after the commencement of the PISG government in 2002, most of the people they were required to deal with in government departments were still non-Albanian-speaking international staff rather than Kosovars.[69]

Transfer of financial management functions to the PISG

The unanimity that had existed between the lead actors in public finance started to break down around the time of the creation of the PISG and the emergence of a new actor in the form of an elected Kosovo government. Until early 2002, fiscal policy decisions had been almost entirely in the hands of international officials and advisers. Under the terms of the Constitutional Framework for Self Government, responsibility for most economic policy and budget issues was to be transferred to the PISG.[70] However, the process of moving funding, staff and responsibilities to the PISG was far more complex and slow than the Constitutional Framework implied and was one of the major sources of conflict between UNMIK and the new government. It also generated disputes between some of the international actors involved.

As Kosovo approached the first Assembly elections in 2001, there was considerable concern about the future direction of fiscal policy under a local government. An IMF analysis identified the key expenditure policy issues for the new government in terms consistent with its usual fiscal policy framework: maintaining a lean public sector and avoiding pay increases, preventing the budget 'becoming a magnet for industrial subsidies', keeping state enterprises at arm's length and avoiding commitments on public pensions.[71] The World Bank gave similar advice on the need for fiscal discipline:

> Economic viability clearly depends greatly on tailoring the aspirations of the populace to the resources available over the short and medium terms and ensuring that public expenditures and welfare programs fall within these constraints of resource availability.[72]

UNMIK Regulation 2001/19 established a Ministry for Finance and Economy (MFE) with an extensive list of public finance functions.[73] A Minister of Finance was appointed by the PISG coalition government in April 2002. However, the 2002 Kosovo budget provided the MFE with funding for only fifty-one civil service staff, and the CFA, although not mentioned in the Constitutional Framework, continued to exist in the budget as a 'reserved power' and retained the bulk of its staff and most of its former functions.[74] The UN Secretary General reported that the CFA would work alongside the MFE to be responsible for fiscal and financial issues not yet transferred to the government.[75]

The retention of the CFA separate from the MFE generated criticism from a number of UNMIK's international partners, in particular USAID, which pushed for a quicker transfer of responsibility. An adviser described the situation as USAID saw it:

> The UN didn't want to release any important functions ... UNMIK wanted to retain the budget, treasury, tax all under their guidance for some time. So there was a fight that emanated because USAID decided that they're here to support governments and they moved all their advisers across to the Ministry of Finance, or most of them anyway ... So unfortunately we had parallel institutions which was what we were all trying to avoid at the time. And it took a couple of years to eradicate.[76]

Because the CFA continued to be a Pillar IV responsibility, under EU authority, this difference of view on the transfer of functions implied a change in the previously cooperative relations between the EU and USAID.

Difficulties between the MFE and UNMIK escalated towards the end of 2002, mainly over the process for approval of the 2003 budget. The Assembly of Kosovo refused to endorse the budget that had been approved by the SRSG and complained about the way the budget process had been handled.[77] By late 2002 UNMIK acknowledged that the situation was unsatisfactory and in the following year the size and functions of the MFE were significantly increased with the transfer of treasury, budget, economic policy, internal audit and donor coordination functions.[78]

Tensions between the MFE and UNMIK continued, however. A new Public Financial Management and Accountability law, drafted by international advisers to replace the original 1999 regulation and approved by the Kosovo Assembly in January 2003, was amended by the SRSG to specify that budget appropriations proposed by the Kosovo Assembly would first be reviewed by the SRSG and, if necessary, changes would be effected.[79] It became clear that this was by no means simply a matter of the SRSG rubber-stamping budget decisions made by the Kosovo Assembly. Significant changes in policy and expenditure amounts were sometimes made by UNMIK after the government had concluded its deliberations. A well-organised, transparent and timely budget process is one of the central tenets of good public finance practice so international public finance experts working with the MFE were also affronted by the SRSG's involvement. One complained that 'Some budgetary decisions were made by the SRSG ... overnight ... and took millions out of the Kosovo budget ... It was really complicated. Sometimes at the end of the process ... which actually unravelled the whole process.'[80] Another claimed that 'the budget could be created by the PISG ... then basically the SRSG would come in and change it as he saw fit'.[81] The World Bank expressed concern about the division of budget responsibilities between UNMIK and the PISG noting that the SRSG constituted a 'court of appeal' over the government.[82] The IMF was also critical, arguing that 'unhealthy competition between reserved and transferred power agencies' had impeded the development of a clear fiscal strategy.[83] A USAID report in 2005 argued that the 'bifurcation' of the government budget into separate UNMIK and PISG spending agencies made it difficult to establish a clear and sustainable medium-term fiscal strategy.[84]

UNMIK officials, for their part, criticised the performance of the MFE. The SRSG's report to the Security Council in April 2004, for example, complained that 'Owing to a lack of preparation by the MFE' critical budgetary discussions and processes had been delayed, including monthly fiscal reports to UNMIK and launching the annual budget process.[85] Given that the MFE at that time was still fairly reliant on USAID-funded technical advisers it is difficult to know whether these criticism were aimed mainly at local officials or at their foreign advisers.

The change of SRSG in mid-2004 following the March riots, and the more constructive attitude towards the Kosovo government adopted by UNMIK from that point, appears to have had a positive effect on UNMIK's relations with the MFE and from 2005 all financial management functions were progressively transferred to the government. By 2010, in spite of the continuing presence of some international advisers, observers considered that Kosovars were fully in control of the MFE. 'There's no question about that. I don't think I'd say there are a lot of advisers. It's what you'd see anywhere when you have a World Bank project or a USAID project.'[86]

Fiscal policy under the PISG

In 2004 and 2005 international actors' initial concerns about management of the Kosovo budget by the PISG seemed to be justified. Under CFA administration, the KCB had accumulated a large surplus, equal at the end of 2003 to around 25 per cent of Kosovo's GDP. This was largely due to the inability of the UN-managed administrative departments to either accurately forecast or implement their spending plans. While most governments are delighted if they achieve a budget surplus, in Kosovo it was seen as a problem. Local observers argued that it justified an increase in spending, suggesting that the surplus indicated a 'worrying disconnection between budget policy and the economic realities of Kosovo',[87] while US government officials reportedly argued it meant taxes should be lower.

This surplus did not last long after the handover to the PISG. The level of public expenditure rapidly increased to support the new government institutions, and political leaders were under pressure to increase spending before the 2004 Kosovo Assembly election. Expenditure in 2004 reached levels that were considered unsustainable and the budget ended the year in deficit. The accumulated surplus from previous years covered the shortfall, but if the trend continued this source of financing would soon be exhausted. Kosovo's political status under international administration meant that the government had no capacity to borrow to finance a deficit. The

World Bank warned the government to 'resist pressure to spend on unsustainable recurrent costs and ill conceived capital projects',[88] and the IMF proposed reductions in wage expenditure and decreases in the number of employees.[89] The Kosovar authors of the Early Warning Report argued that this would raise social tensions and instead suggested reductions in goods and services spending and increased taxation.[90] The IMF's preferred policies prevailed, however.

In late 2005, the Kosovo government and UNMIK signed a joint Memorandum on Economic and Financial Policies and a formal 'Letter of Intent' which, although addressed to donors, was identical to the agreements normally negotiated between a national government and the IMF.[91] The Memorandum committed the government to a fiscal programme developed by the IMF, including an agreement to maintain a low tax regime, strict targeting of welfare payments and limited increases in benefits, reducing the size of the civil service by 10 per cent by 2008, holding civil service wages down and achieving savings in civil service allowances and benefits. This IMF agreement is considered to have been successful, at the time, in imposing fiscal discipline on the PISG government.[92] Thus, although Kosovo was not formally a member of the IMF, the Fund had considerable influence on fiscal policy in the territory as a result of the willingness of other international bodies, and the Kosovo government, to follow its advice.

Public procurement

In the creation of revenue and expenditure management agencies there was a high level of cooperation and agreement between the lead players over the content of legislation and the policies to be pursued. In contrast, the development of public procurement policy has, at times, generated heated disagreement between the main actors. This, together with the high exposure of this sector to political interference, has led to disappointing outcomes. Public procurement is a relatively complex topic and an area of government operations where there are competing policy objectives. The primary goal is to make the most cost-effective use of public resources through transparency and competition in the purchase of goods and services. But the state's expenditure on goods and services also has potential economic impacts, so governments sometimes structure procurement rules to favour local suppliers or industries. Public procurement is also an area where inefficiency, conflict of interest and outright corruption easily flourish without adequate regulation and monitoring. At the same time, however, a system that is excessively strict may be inefficient and costly, impeding the delivery of public services.

The procurement system therefore needs to find an acceptable compromise between maximising competition and achieving local economic benefits, and between centralised supervision and efficiency. Disagreement over the best way to achieve this has been a major cause of delay and confusion in government procurement policy in Kosovo. The development of a public procurement system was further complicated, as elsewhere in Eastern Europe, by the fact that concepts of competition, equal treatment of suppliers and transparency were new ideas in a former socialist economy. Market competition was not well developed and there were a limited number of local providers for many items. Over the years since the start of the international Mission there have been repeated efforts to develop an agreed and workable legal framework for government procurement that would address all these issues satisfactorily. Six procurement laws or regulations were promulgated between 1999 and 2014, but many more draft laws were prepared and debated during this time in an effort to achieve a model that was acceptable to all interest groups.

Financial Administrative Instruction No 2 1999

Procurement rules for the Kosovo administration were first established by USAID-funded advisers as part of the exercise of setting up expenditure processes for the Kosovo budget.[93] Finance Administrative Instruction (FAI) No 2 1999, 'Public Procurement Using KCB Funds' was based on the procurement regime previously adopted by most Central and South East European countries in transition, which had in turn been based on World Bank and United Nations Commission on International Trade Law (UNCITRAL) models. At the time, most large-scale procurement activity was implemented by donors using their own rules and procedures, and the civil administration's local purchasing requirements were relatively limited. Complex rules were therefore not considered necessary.

The FAI set up a Public Procurement Regulatory Body (PPRB) within the CFA, but actual responsibility for procurement operations was devolved to each UNMIK administrative department. In parallel, however, the UN's civil administration in Pillar II established a Central Procurement Entity (CPE) to provide assistance to UNMIK entities in implementing procurement processes and to manage complex or high-value procurements. The CPE's role was not clearly specified in the FAI. The approaches to procurement policy and to practical implementation issues taken by the PPRB, in Pillar IV, and the CPE, in Pillar II, were often different and neither of the two procurement bodies was adequately resourced to carry out its functions, with each having only two staff; one international and one local. As most international UN staff in the civil administration had limited prior experience in public procurement activities and tended to be on relatively short-term contracts, much of the work of the PPRB involved providing training in how to conduct procurements. Lack of resources also meant there were significant delays in preparing the detailed rules, procedures and forms needed to implement the legislation, and some of this was never completed in full. Standard bidding documents were initially available only in English, later being translated into Albanian and, later again, Serbian. Even when translated, however, the legal and technical language was difficult for local suppliers to understand so they were at a disadvantage relative to international bidders.

The FAI addressed an immediate need for simple guidance on how to administer KCB funds, but its simplicity was its major defect. It gave procuring entities considerable freedom in selecting the procurement method, so single source and 'emergency' procurement methods were used frequently. There was concern among USAID advisers that procurement rules were being ignored or abused in the JIAS departments, primarily by international staff.[94] A senior Pillar IV adviser claimed that the CPE, in Pillar II, had been associated with a number of 'procedurally poor and unsuccessful' procurements and that throughout the system there was evidence of poor procedure, high risk of compromise, poor asset management and considerable waste.[95]

The 2004 PISG Procurement Law

It had initially been expected that the simple FAI would be in place for about a year until a more complete document could be issued. In fact it remained in operation for more than four years while procurement experts and donors debated what should replace it. Two attempts were made between 1999 and 2003 to develop new legislation but both stalled due to disagreement between donors about how Kosovo's procurement laws should be formulated. The World Bank proposed an approach that had been used previously in other Balkan countries, including Montenegro, Albania and Bosnia. These procurement arrangements had been developed before the EU started to formulate clear procurement directives and at a time when membership of the EU was not an immediate prospect for the region. From the early 2000s, however, Balkan countries with aspirations towards EU membership were expected to align their laws with new EU directives. Consistent with the idea of an internal EU market these directives prohibit discrimination on the grounds of nationality.[96] In early 2002 several competing draft procurement laws, prepared by international experts working with either the PPRB, in Pillar IV, or the CPE, in Pillar II, were under consideration. A PFM adviser who was involved at the time identified one of the major points of contention between the various experts:

> They were over-complexifying the thing. They were putting far too many process checks in on the basis of accountability, basically reproducing one of the most complex and time consuming procurement systems in the world, to no good benefit. Although I don't have any problems with the basic principles that underlie it, it was a question of how you would make it actually work in a country like that.[97]

It was eventually agreed to develop a compromise version that would comply with EU requirements. In the meantime, responsibility for this policy issue had been transferred to the PISG and the Kosovo Assembly. In June 2003 a draft law was presented to the Assembly, debated, eventually passed, with numerous amendments, and subsequently signed and promulgated by the SRSG in February 2004.[98] This new law, at ninety-one pages, was considerably more detailed than the previous FAI. It addressed many of the flaws in the prior legislation, established open tendering as the main procedure for awarding public contracts, made abuses of procurement procedures more difficult and improved transparency in decision making.[99] USAID announced that the essential benchmark for its involvement in the procurement field, contributing to the draft law, had been achieved and so its work was complete.[100] EAR assumed primary responsibility for providing further technical assistance in this area.

The new law envisaged a four-month transition period, but by the deadline of June 2004 the new procurement institutions it created had not been established, mainly due to delays by the Assembly in nominating members. The previous bodies and rules therefore continued to operate. It was not until a year after the passage of the law, in February 2005, that the new Public Procurement Regulatory Commission started work. The Public Procurement Agency (PPA) officially began operating another year later, in March 2006. The first phase of EAR assistance to public procurement, intended to draft the necessary secondary legislation, was also considerably delayed and this in turn delayed training of procurement officers on the new procedures. The new secondary legislation eventually entered into force in January 2006, two years after the primary legislation was approved.[101]

2007 amendments to the law on public procurement

If the 1999 FAI had been too simple and incomplete, the main problem with the 2004 law was that it was too complex. All donors and external commentators broadly agreed on this point. The concerns that had been expressed by some advisers during its preparation appeared to be validated. A UNDP assessment in 2005, for example, observed that 'Kosovo has gone from a position of having no or little procurement law to a position of having a full and comprehensive procurement law extending to over 90 pages. Given the existing procurement capacity in Kosovo and the novelty of this law, users have difficulty in applying it.'[102] The World Bank also expressed concern over the complexity of the law[103] and the European Commission progress report noted that there had been serious difficulties in its application: 'Instead of simplifying public procurement processes and making them more transparent, the procurement law proved too complicated to apply properly in the Kosovo context and led to delays and higher costs to the Kosovo Consolidated Budget.'[104]

The law was thus under revision well before it had been fully implemented. EAR-funded technical advisers developed another draft law during 2005 but the next year the EU adopted a new procurement directive requiring additional revisions to the Kosovo law. EAR assistance therefore focused on both simplifying the 2004 legislation and implementing the new EU directive. However, according to a Kosovar familiar with the EAR project, World Bank and USAID advisers were also involved in providing advice to the government on procurement and, as before, there were differences of opinion between international donors.

A draft amended law was eventually agreed between them and was provided to the government in May 2006. The debate in the Kosovo Assembly was protracted and once again many amendments were made. The version that was finally approved by the Assembly in February 2007 and submitted, as required under the Constitutional Framework, to the SRSG for endorsement, was not considered by EAR to sufficiently reflect the requirements of the EU and the advice of their consultants. In response to approaches from EU representatives, UNMIK lawyers prepared a new version, which was approved and published by the SRSG, without further reference to the Assembly.[105] The amended law came into force in June 2007. A further EAR technical assistance project was initiated to train and certify procurement officers and to develop secondary legislation, which was eventually completed in January 2009.[106]

The 2010 Republic of Kosovo Procurement Law

The first post-independence report by the European Commission on Kosovo's progress towards 'European Standards' gave the procurement arrangements, as expressed in the 2007 legislation, a reasonably positive assessment.[107] A year later, however, the September 2009 report was much more critical. It found fault with the activities of all three procurement regulatory bodies, considered training and certification of procurement officers insufficient, and noted a high turnover of procurement officers and that a high proportion of tenders were cancelled on the grounds of non-compliance with legal requirements. Procurement officers were considered to be vulnerable to interference and intimidation.[108] A Kosovo government official expressed surprise that public procurement appeared to have become so much worse in one year.[109] An EU adviser, however, claimed that the more negative 2009 report was a response to complaints from international advisers that the previous assessment had been too generous: 'The World Bank, the UN, the EU, up to a year ago, had used a tick box. Do we have a law? Yes. Do we have secondary legislation? Yes. Are there institutions in place and functioning? Yes. But that's not the same as it's functioning OK.'[110]

In response to the EU report the Kosovo government decided to prepare a new law, which was finalised in four months and submitted to the Assembly in late 2010.[111] This was significantly faster than the passage of any previous procurement legislation. Although the process was, as in the past, supported by international technical advisers, there was reportedly significant input from Kosovar procurement officers and the government's central procurement body.

The 2011 Procurement Law

EU procurement advisers considered that the draft submitted to the Assembly in 2010 would address their concerns about the law. However, in the final stages of the debate in the Assembly, a large number of changes were made and the version that was eventually approved was, again, significantly different from the draft that had been proposed by the foreign technical advisers and accepted by the executive government. According to the European Commission's 2011 Progress Report, the gazetted law not only diverged from EU public procurement directives but also exposed procurement officers to political interference and provided opportunities for corruption.[112] This 'hijacking' of the law[113] generated several months of conflict between the EU Office in Kosovo and the government. In early 2011, EU-funded technical experts prepared yet another version of the legislation. Its acceptance by the government and safe passage through the Assembly was achieved in August 2011.[114] A full set of secondary legislation supporting the new law was also completed and enacted. Assessments by SIGMA and the European Commission considered that the new legislation met most EU legal requirements.[115]

The 2014 amendments to the law

The battle over procurement law was not over, however. In March 2014 the Kosovo Assembly amended the 2011 law.[116] The revised law deviated from the *acquis* by giving preference to domestic bidders. The Assembly had also disregarded the recommendations of an independent selection panel when it appointed members to the Procurement Review Board.[117]

It is difficult for someone who is not an expert in the complexities of public procurement to understand, or sometimes even to identify, the differences between the various versions of the legislation. Procurement experts were also unable, or unwilling, to say exactly why the Kosovo Assembly has repeatedly failed to pass the legislation in the form recommended by the EU. The inclusion of preferences for local firms in the 2014 amendments suggests nationalistic motives, but international observers are inclined to suspect self-interest objectives on the part of Kosovo's politicians. Other explanations attribute the ongoing debates over procurement policy either to US government meddling or resistance to the imposition of the EU model.

Although the US has not formally provided technical assistance in this field since 2003, USAID advisers continue to have an interest in all PFM matters and there were suggestions that the US government and USAID-funded consultants have been involved in behind-the-scenes lobbying in support of non-EU-compliant policies. Other sources go further and suggest that US firms have benefited from weaknesses in Kosovo's procurement practices.[118] Disputes over procurement law may also be motivated, however, by concerns about the complexity and appropriateness of the EU legislative model for Kosovo's public administration environment. EU procurement directives have been developed in a different institutional context with objectives that may not be immediately relevant for Kosovo and some people are not convinced of the benefits of aligning Kosovo's legislation with the EU model, as reflected in comments by a USAID adviser:

> Every time a procurement project comes in here, all they want to do is rewrite the law, because everyone has a different perspective on how procurement should work. And everyone asks me is procurement complex here and I say, the law is EU compliant so what do you think? It is complex. It has to be just from that very definition.[119]

Accounting, audit and financial control

An important aspect of financial management, in government or in the private sector, is ensuring that funds are used as intended, without fraud, theft or waste, through the application of effective accounting rules and systems, clear delegation of authority, separation of duties, regular reporting and internal and external audit processes. However, the institutional arrangements for public sector financial control vary markedly between countries. There are, for example, significant differences between the 'inspection and control' approach of communist governments, the 'Anglo-Saxon' audit tradition, which is concerned with identifying systems to prevent errors or fraud, and the more legalistic Francophone model based on a Court of Audit. More recently 'new public management' ideas about devolved managerial responsibility have added to the options available for implementing financial control functions. The development of public accounting arrangements, financial controls and audit in Kosovo since 1999 is another example of the way different views among international actors on the most appropriate model to apply and changes in the policy approach may have delayed the development of effective institutions.

Internal audit: Pillar IV and USAID 1999–2003

The communist system of financial management, which Kosovo inherited from FRY, was highly centralised and incorporated the concept of financial inspection; a process of checking all transactions for compliance and punishing mistakes. Kosovars who had worked in the FRY administration prior to 1999 would be oriented towards this concept of financial control. The expenditure and accounting system initially established by accounting advisers working in Pillar IV was also very centralised, largely due to the absence of accounting and financial management skills and systems among either local civil servants or the UN staff in UNMIK. Pillar IV set up an automated Financial Management Information System in the CFA and issued instructions on basic procedures for the use of public funds. All expenditure commitments and payments from the KCB were approved and processed centrally by the Treasury Department in the CFA.

An Internal Audit Unit was established in the CFA in mid-2000 and several local staff were recruited, including a Kosovar Director of Internal Audit. The Internal

Audit Unit was somewhat misnamed, and consequently misunderstood, as it was responsible for auditing any transactions from the Kosovo budget and was thus, at the time, effectively performing the role of an external auditor in relation to other civil administration agencies. The longer-term plan was that each ministry and municipality would have its own internal audit function and in 2002 USAID advisers began establishing audit units in the PISG ministries.[120] The CFA Internal Audit Unit was transferred to the MFE in 2002 and draft legislation to establish an independent Office of the Auditor General was approved in October 2002.[121] A year later an international auditor was appointed to the position of Auditor General.

A USAID report praised its achievements in the internal audit function, reporting that all benchmarks had been consistently met or exceeded. Local staff were judged capable of developing and managing a basic audit plan, and the unit had carried out a number of significant audits.[122] Another evaluation of USAID's activities concluded that internal audit was operating at the level of a mature and efficient institution, demonstrated by the fact that it was administered and operated entirely by Kosovars, unlike most other institutions at that time. On the basis that the Internal Audit Unit in MFE was fully sustainable without continuing adviser involvement, USAID decided in 2003 to discontinue its support.[123]

The EU and public internal financial control

A review conducted by the Netherlands Supreme Audit Institution the following year, in 2004, found that, contrary to USAID's positive assessment, internal audit did not meet requirements and there was a need to develop the legislation and further strengthen capacity.[124] A year later, in 2005, EAR initiated a two-year programme of technical assistance to support internal audit, providing training to a large number of internal audit staff in ministries and municipalities and conducting thirty pilot audits.[125] As in other PFM functions, ensuring that Kosovo's systems complied with EU best practice became a primary objective and this meant the introduction of the concept of public internal financial control (PIFC). EU standards for PIFC have been established since 1999 specifically for candidates for EU membership that have had limited experience of Western-style financial management and auditing. One of the objectives of the policy is to protect EU interests in relation to the administration of EU funds. Countries seeking EU membership are required to reform their public finance systems to incorporate PIFC best practice.[126] A European Commission booklet on PIFC explains the concept and sets out the processes to be followed by governments wishing to implement it, including a 'conceptualisation' phase, drafting a policy paper and an action plan, the establishment of a Central Harmonisation Unit for PIFC, the passage of new legislation and a comprehensive training programme for senior managers.[127] However, PIFC, as such, is not a concept that exists in older EU member states or in any other developed economies. As a PIFC expert explained it, 'Financial management and control is what, in most of the developed world, would just be regarded as good management … None of the developed EU countries have a Central Harmonisation Unit. You wouldn't find one anywhere. There's no special procedures around financial management and control because it's just good management.'[128]

PIFC has a wider focus than financial audit and encompasses the modern administrative concept of 'managerial accountability'. PIFC therefore raises broader issues about the approach to public administration. It represents a fundamental change in focus from traditional practices of central, hierarchical control towards delegation of budgets and spending decisions to lower level managers, who are then to be held accountable for results. Managers are expected to prepare strategic plans, set objectives and assess risks, and then develop control systems to address and mitigate risks, all of which are to be set out in written form. This concept is quite different from the centralised control systems of the socialist era, and the personalised and heirarchical management style favoured by many of Kosovo's government ministers.[129] It is also different from the more centralised accounting strategy implemented initially by advisers in the CFA. An EU PIFC adviser was highly critical of the approach taken by previous technical assistance projects. 'The problem was that internal audit came first. Absolutely wrong! Financial management and control, which is the developing of management capacity, should have come first and then internal audit should come afterwards … They re-created the communist system which had the central bureau and everything and that was what was recreated.'[130]

The EAR office, however, was reportedly initially reluctant to support PIFC because it was considered premature and too complex for Kosovo. In the opinion of a former EAR employee,

> In Kosovo, internal audit as such is a new concept completely. It is completely different from what was before and people don't understand it. So you need to start from that. If you have some basic rules in place that would be sufficient for the initial phases. And then you develop. But you cannot start with perfect systems with people who have no clue about it.[131]

Nevertheless, in 2005, EAR-funded advisers assisted the MFE to develop a PIFC policy paper and an action plan, which were adopted by the government.[132] New legislation on internal audit was also drafted, approved by the Kosovo Assembly in November 2006, and submitted to the SRSG for ratification. However, a new group of EAR-funded PIFC experts subsequently reviewed the yet-to-be-enacted legislation and proposed amendments in areas where they considered it departed from best practice.[133] These changes were incorporated into the legislation, without further debate in the Assembly, before it was eventually promulgated by the SRSG in 2007.[134] Further implementation of the PIFC framework followed with the approval of a 'Strategy for the Internal Audit Function', adoption of a revised PIFC policy paper, and establishment of a Central Harmonisation Unit for Internal

Audit within the Treasury in MFE.[135] Another EC-funded PIFC project, a few years later, extended the scope of activity to encompass an array of modern management concepts such as risk assessment and monitoring, and performance management. The existing laws were reviewed, again, amendments were proposed to the law on Public Financial Management and Accountability, and another new PIFC policy paper and action plan were developed and ratified by the government in April 2011. The project advisers also prepared a new financial management procedures manual and organised a training programme for ministers and high-level public managers to improve their awareness of public management, public governance, control and accountability.[136]

In spite of the level of activity and apparent progress made in implementing the elements of a PIFC framework, a number of observers expressed reservations about the appropriateness of the PIFC model in Kosovo. One portrayed it as an invention of EU officials in Brussels which is being imposed on non-EU countries.[137] However, the main practical concern about the approach relates to the decentralisation of financial responsibilities to lower levels of management. PIFC significantly increases the responsibilities and obligations of managers in government agencies in an environment where civil servants generally have low or inappropriate educational attainment, limited experience, relatively low pay and are more than likely to be political appointees. As one technical adviser in the field commented, 'It's a big ask'.[138] The decentralisation of internal control functions also requires the establishment of internal audit units in all government agencies and municipalities, some of which would necessarily be very small, possibly limiting the quality of their work.[139] In addition, despite the number of policy papers and legislative changes, the process of implementing the new framework at management level has been very slow and the actual level of government commitment to the policy is questionable. An EC strategy paper noted that, after EU technical assistance ended in 2011, coordination from the Ministry of Finance stopped and, although Kosovo has developed the basic legal framework for PIFC, 'substantial efforts are still required to implement the concept of decentralised managerial accountability'.[140]

PFM outcomes

Evidence of the long-term results of these efforts to develop PFM institutions in Kosovo can be drawn from donors' own assessments, official reviews and evaluations, comments by independent observers and the opinions of international advisers and Kosovars. These all suggest that PFM is widely regarded as a success of the international intervention. The Customs Service, the MFE, the Central Bank and, to a lesser extent, the Tax Administration are, in particular, considered to be relatively competent, well-functioning institutions. However, not all components of PFM are rated well. Functions that are adversely affected by the lack of capacity of the wider civil service or exposed to influence by Kosovo's politicians perform poorly. These include budget planning in spending ministries and fiscal policy decisions by ministers, as well as internal audit and public procurement.

Successes

Good performance in customs, taxation, budget, treasury and central banking is frequently cited by donors as evidence of the overall success of their own activities. The major international participants all claim responsibility for this success. USAID's 2001 report to Congress, for example, claimed that 'Progress toward the achievement of projected results in economic and fiscal reform has far outpaced expectations'[141] and in 2005 USAID argued that the Law on Financial Management and Accountability, drafted by its consultants, was 'very likely the best law of its kind in the Balkans' and was being well implemented. The Treasury system developed by the USAID project was also described as 'state of the art'.[142] An independent performance evaluation commissioned by USAID in 2012 concurred:

> Key GOK economic institutions such as the Ministry of Finance and Economy and the Central Bank of Kosovo were created from scratch and by 2009 were perceived to be functioning at a level of proficiency generally consistent with what one typically finds in neighboring or other low-middle income countries.[143]

However, the EU's 'end of mission' report on Pillar IV also noted, and claimed credit for, the same achievements including the tax system, banking and insurance supervision, and the Customs Service,[144] while the World Bank considered that its budget support operations had contributed to a satisfactory outcome in the sector,[145] and the IMF commended its own efforts.[146]

Kosovo's PFM systems also rate reasonably well in objective assessment exercises. Several Public Expenditure and Financial Accountability (PEFA) reports have produced positive and steadily improving results.[147] The 2007 report identified MFE's Treasury system and centralised budget processing as the greatest strength of the PFM arrangements. The operation of the Customs Service was also praised.[148] However, the assessment found problems in long-term budget planning, weak internal audit capacity in ministries, poor performance in public procurement and major weaknesses in payroll management. Further analysis, in 2009 and 2013, produced even better results, although similar weaknesses were identified in procurement, payroll controls, tax collection and multi-year budgeting.[149] A similar IMF assessment in 2012 found that Kosovo's PFM practices were no worse than any of its neighbours, and considerably better than some. Kosovo scored well on the quality of fiscal reporting, medium-term budget planning and budget execution, but relatively poorly on parliamentary approval processes.[150]

Annual EU progress assessments focus on compliance with 'European Standards' and their purpose is to identify problem areas and priorities for further work. The fact that, over the years, the reports have raised relatively few concerns about most matters of PFM performance can be taken to indicate relative success in this field. The significant exceptions relate to budget planning and the political processes of budget formulation, audit and financial control, and the public procurement system. The EU reports have also been less positive about the performance of the Tax Administration, noting weaknesses and inefficiencies in tax collection, administration and compliance with EU standards, although steady improvement on these issues is also noted year on year.[151]

A SIGMA assessment of public administration in 2013 found that the legal and institutional framework for budget management is in place and does not require significant change, the budget execution system is resilient, and the PFM framework provides the potential for a coherent, well-coordinated approach to planning and implementing the budget.[152] The DFID-funded 'FRIDOM' review of the MFE and the horizontal review of public expenditure management both commented positively on the competence of the MFE and its agencies.[153] However, the reviews found problems in the execution of financial management functions elsewhere in the administration, limited understanding of public expenditure management at the political level and low administrative capacity across the government.

The positive view of the work done to develop central PFM institutions is shared by many independent commentators. King and Mason, for example, praise the economic advances made in the first years of the mission:

> The CFA provided an effective fiscal backbone to Kosovo's rapidly burgeoning government services. It managed to handle very large sums of money without any scandals or inefficiencies ... By 2002 the CFA had transformed Kosovo's budget from being totally donor-driven to being almost entirely domestically funded. This process was faster and smoother than much else that went on at the time.[154]

Blair *et al.* suggest: 'Perhaps UNMIK's greatest success was in ensuring a fiscally autonomous and sustainable state' and that creating the CFA and the Customs Service and achieving a self-funding budget within a few years was 'a remarkable achievement'.[155] In 2005, the Eide review of conditions in Kosovo, prepared for the UN, praised the establishment of economic structures and legislation and in particular mentioned the 'well functioning Ministry of Finance and Economy' and its achievements in establishing the framework for economic management.[156]

Most technical advisers and donor representatives in Kosovo, as well as many Kosovars, also agree that, in most areas of public finance, the international effort has been a success. This was true even among international personnel who had no direct involvement in public finance issues. The Kosovo Customs Service, in particular, received almost universal praise from both foreign advisers and Kosovars. The majority of advisers also rated the MFE as one of the more successful Kosovo government institutions. One, for example, described the Ministry of Finance as 'a functioning institution conducting its normal business in a fairly professional way and sometimes better than others, certainly better than other agencies, and maybe even compared to the region, and I think that at the moment it will be sustainable.'[157] Another declared, 'We would be more advanced than any country in the Balkans. Without a doubt. The Treasury system here, even the World Bank, I can quote them, they believe it is the best implementation of a Treasury system in any like situation in the world.'[158] The Tax Administration is also well regarded within Kosovo, although its performance is rated below that of Customs. Several people noted, for example, that the Kosovo tax office does not generate the amount of revenue that would be expected based on the level of economic activity, suggesting deficiencies in tax collection activities. However, a World Bank 'Doing Business' assessment rated Kosovo ahead of most other European and Central Asian countries in terms of 'ease of paying taxes', and well above neighbouring Albania and Bosnia.[159]

Failures

Most assessments also agree on the areas of weakness in PFM. A World Bank report noted, for example, that the strengths of the system are offset by limited professional and technical capacity and gaps in implementation, in particular in relation to budget planning and preparation, capital investment management, internal financial control and audit, and procurement.[160] In most cases these deficiencies stem from poor administrative capacity across government and an apparent lack of interest by politicians in implementing the reforms proposed by donors. Despite a considerable amount of technical assistance on strategic planning, public investment planning and medium-term expenditure forecasting provided to ministries over the years by the EU and the World Bank, the budget preparation process continues to be undermined by weak strategic policy direction.[161] Government organisations do not develop their annual budget proposals on the basis of existing plans or government policies, nor comply with MFE budget instructions.[162] Developing and implementing a credible economic strategy has been identified as a major challenge for the administration.[163]

Auditing and financial control in ministries and municipalities is also frequently found to be deficient. EU progress reports note that there is a poor understanding of the concepts of managerial accountability for internal control and the legal framework is only partly applied in most government agencies.[164] The Kosovo Auditor General's 2013 report on government finances is highly critical of the slow progress and lack of compliance in this area.[165] Technical advisers and Kosovar officials agree that internal audit and financial control capacity remains weak:

> if we want to say how effective or efficient they are, I must say they are not that effective, either internal audit or internal control ... The main problem is the role of senior managers who don't understand the importance of internal control of finances. They

> are persistent in trying to accomplish political goals and who knows what other interests they are trying to protect. They are not interested in implementing these regulations.[166]

One adviser commented that there also appeared to be limitations on the willingness of trained Kosovar staff to apply their skills, largely due to the political environment:

> At the end of the day the locals were very superficial about anything they did, and I thought it was fairly deliberate. In my view there is still a bit of fear there of looking too deep and looking for something. Because it's their future. They'll lose their job. And I'm sure there are a lot of things have gone on that they should have found but they didn't.[167]

Public procurement, however, is the area that receives the most negative comments in reports, evaluations and interviews. During the decade-long process of negotiating the content of the procurement law, the actual practice of public procurement by individual budget agencies has been very poor, with frequent accusations of irregularities, mismanagement and corruption. Auditor General reports identify procurement as one of the main challenges in the public finance system and list numerous shortcomings.[168] All EU progress reports are particularly critical of the public procurement system. Government entities ignore instructions and procedures and procurement officers are subject to intimidation.[169] Government procurement is perceived by the public to be prone to favouritism, nepotism and corruption,[170] a perception confirmed by an international procurement consultant:

> What we have found out is that corruption is just massive. It is all over the place. The poor procurement officers are leaned upon, intimidated, and are even corrupt themselves sometimes, but they are really in a bad spot. They are signing contracts and everybody else says they didn't sign it, so you're guilty.[171]

Getting the basics right

This detailed account of the creation of basic PFM institutions reveals, if nothing else, exactly how complex the process was. Simple statements about the need to establish a modern revenue system, a competent Ministry of Finance, a well-regulated annual budget process, a functioning cash management and payments system, and reliable government accounting, immediately unleashed a multiplicity of complex and contested issues beginning with who should do it, the speed at which it should be done and the form and content of the new institutions. The physical and political challenges of the post-conflict environment added to the complexity. Institutional development 'from scratch' in a war-ravaged territory is not something that should be taken on lightly.

In spite of this there is evidence of success in many aspects of PFM development. The early efforts of technical advisers in this field put in place the basic frameworks and procedures needed for effective financial management. It is generally agreed that the MFE, CBAK and the Customs Service are well-functioning institutions, given the circumstances in which they operate, and that the Tax Administration, while not as highly regarded or as effective as Customs, is considerably better run and less corrupt than many equivalent institutions in other countries. These organisations have made considerable progress since 1999 and are now able to deal with advanced economic and fiscal policy issues. International actors continue to be involved in monitoring and advising on Kosovo's management of public finances, as they do in most developing economies, but day-to-day responsibility now rests with Kosovar managers, many of whom were recruited and trained by international advisers in the early post-conflict years. Although the EU's annual progress reports quibble about the need for further PFM 'reform', their complaints are marginal when viewed against the situation in 1999 and the serious defects in other parts of the administration.

Reasons for success in PFM

The experience of PFM development in Kosovo suggests that donors achieved the results they sought when there was strong agreement on policy and a willingness to invest significant effort. Early attention to the development of local staff capacity, while at the same time limiting the influence of the local political culture, was also important. In areas where these conditions could not be readily achieved the outcomes were less satisfactory.

Donor unity

A striking feature of accounts of the development of public finance functions in Kosovo in the years immediately after the conflict is the level of agreement between the lead actors on what needed to be done, and the high level and quality of resources and effort they directed to achieving their shared goals as rapidly as possible. Within Pillar IV, EU officials, USAID advisers and visiting IMF and World Bank staff largely agreed on the policy directions that should be pursued. These actors were clear that the objective of their intervention was to create modern, Western, market-oriented institutions in a self-governing Kosovo. Their interpretation of the wording of UNSCR 1244 allowed maximum reorganisation of the local economy and its legislative framework and institutions. The decision to hand responsibility for managing public finances to Pillar IV also meant that these like-minded actors were able to maintain control over the size and distribution of the Kosovo budget, at least until the function was handed to the PISG, and so were able to implement their preferred fiscal policies and to resist demands for higher public sector wages, expanded employment and more generous social welfare.

Agreement on the objective and the need to achieve immediate progress apparently overcame potential sources of conflict between the lead participants in Pillar IV and took precedence over institutional rivalry, as noted by one USAID-funded technical adviser:

> We got agreement with them [USAID], and I think reluctantly, that we would implement and propose policies that we thought were best for Kosovo, and in some instances it could be conceivable that it may not be what the US government would prefer. Because we all had different agendas and there was some concern there that some of the policies we might implement, particularly on tax and privatisation, may not be the policies that the US government would want supported. They had to accept it I think.[172]

Strong agreement on objectives and principles did not rule out differences of opinion and debate over details such as the staffing of BPK or the arrangements for a new payments system, but these debates were short lived and did not significantly delay the broader programme. In those areas where there have been extended disagreements over the policy direction, however, such as in public procurement, or changes of direction, as in financial control and audit, the outcomes have not been as positive, although other factors may also have contributed to these failures.

The lead actors in PFM had little hesitation in rejecting the pre-existing FRY systems, which were seen as inefficient, socialist and inconsistent with current best practice. They were supported in this by the lack of cooperation from Serbia. In general, the concepts of consultation and 'ownership' in this field largely meant achieving local buy-in and cooperation with donor intentions, rather than seeking input or direction.

Resources and effort

The positive outcomes achieved in the development of PFM institutions in Kosovo, particularly in the early years, can also be attributed to the energy and urgency with which the leading players addressed the task and the resources provided. The development of public finance institutions moved remarkably quickly. The Customs Service was established within a few weeks of the arrival of the UN Mission and the Tax Administration and budgeting, banking and accounting functions were in place not long after. The high priority given to PFM by the lead actors also translated to a significant commitment of resources, with an estimated €255 million spent by the major organisations over a ten-year period.[173]

The number of international technical experts engaged in the exercise was also significant. A very large contingent of specialists in financial management issues was deployed by USAID to work in Pillar IV within months of the end of the conflict, chosen for their professional expertise and, in most cases, their prior experience of similar assignments. Numbers increased during 2000, and USAID soon had around seventy technical advisers working in various capacities in Pillar IV, most of them on long-term contracts.[174] The EU also, eventually, recruited more than 130 specialist international staff to work in Pillar IV, although the majority were engaged on privatisation issues rather than PFM.[175] The intensity of the technical assistance and capacity development effort was commented on by both internationals and Kosovars. A USAID contractor, for example, observed that 'MFE, from the beginning, has had very, very heavy donor assistance and engagement. Look at our project. We were basically in all core departments of the Ministry, very integrated, sitting down day to day ... Also the policy side was led by internationals, plus the IMF, the World Bank ...'[176] This could perhaps be described as the bulldozer approach to post-conflict re-engineering. According to another adviser involved at the time 'The CFA was one of the two or three institution-building components of building government in Kosovo which was ahead of just about everybody else. It was dragging a lot of the rest of government with it.'[177]

Early Kosovarisation based on merit

Another important factor in the ongoing performance of these institutions was international control of the selection, training and management of local staff. Building the expertise of Kosovars was one of Pillar IV's explicit goals, and a major difference between the EU Pillar and the UN.[178] There was an early start to the recruitment of Kosovars, a strong focus on merit and performance as the criteria for employment, and a willingness to transfer day-to-day responsibility quite quickly, while nevertheless maintaining international control of the organisation as a whole. Throughout Pillar IV, a clean slate and transparent recruitment were insisted on, even sometimes, as in BPK, against the wishes of some technical advisers, and in the face of complaints from previous employees. International advisers managed the recruitment of staff, and fought off efforts by local politicians to appoint friends and supporters. When management responsibility was eventually transferred, it was generally handed to counterparts who had been selected and trained by the international experts. Through these strategies, international actors managed to keep the adverse influences of Kosovo's patronage-based political environment at bay, at least for a while.

The 'blank slate' factor

The post-conflict environment posed many challenges for donors, but it also had benefits. The lack of existing functioning PFM institutions facilitated the work of external actors by allowing them to set up new organisations and recruit and train new staff. To a significant extent, however, these actors created their own 'blank slate' by choosing to employ younger, promising but inexperienced staff through open recruitment, and by resisting proposals to re-employ former personnel or to attempt to re-establish defunct institutions. This approach was opposed at the time by many former public sector employees, who felt they should be given preference, and by the Serb government who objected to the creation of new government structures.

The post-conflict context also enabled the international community to provide the Kosovo administration with an extended period of tutelage. The absence of a local government in the first few years gave advisers and EU officials executive authority over public finance functions for a considerable period. The advisers were in a position, unprecedented in normal aid projects, to implement their preferred policies with limited local consultation and to identify and dismiss corrupt or poor performing staff. Exactly how long this period of tutelage should be, however, and how soon real responsibility should be transferred to local control, was a matter of disagreement between the international partners. Both the MFE and the Tax Administration were transferred to the Kosovo government relatively early. The Customs Service remained under international oversight for a longer period and it has been argued that this explains its superior performance relative to the Tax Administration. It is unlikely, however, that a lengthier period of international control of all central government functions would have been feasible.

Insulation and professionalisation

It could be argued that the small size of some of the PFM institutions and their relative isolation from the wider public administration also helped to achieve good outcomes. The CFA, for example, was a rather small entity with a large number of USAID and EU international staff who were able to dominate the organisation during its establishment. The highly centralised nature of the budget and treasury functions at the time also made it possible to separate the organisation from both the Kosovar political environment and the UN bureaucracy. Merit recruitment and intensive training provided staff with a sense of professionalism, which was reflected, a decade later, in a much lower rate of staff turnover than had been anticipated.[179]

The same conditions did not apply as clearly, however, to either the Customs Service or the Tax Administration. Both organisations are relatively large and many of their staff work in decentralised locations across the country at border posts and in regional tax offices. They are therefore more exposed to external influence and pressure. The fact that even in these circumstances the Customs Service has managed to maintain a good reputation for effective performance is surprising. This is explained, at least in part, by the intense and focused efforts of the EU's development of the Customs Service. 'They put in place quite rigorous procedures and good forms of legislative basis and regulatory basis … Recruitment was done on a very assiduous basis, training was done on an assiduous basis, and there was a hell of a lot of training on values and anti-corruption and that sort of thing.'[180] International actors thus succeeded in establishing a professional identity and unity of purpose in the Customs Service that motivates good performance.[181]

Staff engaged in the decentralised procurement and financial control functions, on the other hand, are located within and report to their individual ministries and agencies. In spite of the extensive external training provided and efforts to establish a professional status for these staff through independent certification processes, their dispersal throughout the administration means they do not have the separate identity or independence of the MFE, Customs or Tax Administration. Within each ministry these staff are vulnerable to corruption and politicisation and their performance is influenced by the level of inefficiency and mismanagement in their home organisations. This serves to undermine the training and supervision provided by the relevant central coordination agencies. In the absence of a strong civil service ethic and an effective system of legal controls and sanctions there is limited scope for donor projects to have influence in these areas.

An 'island of excellence'

Donors have been successful in establishing efficient operational and technical procedures in PFM, creating an island of relative good performance in Kosovo's administrative landscape. But the technical achievements in PFM have not been able to alter the wider social context and it is primarily where these intersect that international engagement in PFM has been less successful. The major weaknesses in the public finance systems are found, on the whole, in functions devolved to line ministries, such as budget planning, financial audit and control, and public procurement. These deficiencies are largely a consequence of the low capacity of the public sector more broadly, an issue discussed in the following chapter, as well as the realities of Kosovo's politics. However, failures by international actors in these areas have also played a role. Disagreements over the correct policy direction, changes in the lead donor, inconsistent technical adviser support, and the EU's apparent obsession with refining legislation, arguably at the expense of practical implementation and compliance, have hampered the development of a workable procurement regime and the effective implementation of internal financial controls.

Notes

1 A. Alesina and R. Perotti, *Budget Deficits and Budget Institutions*, NBER Working Paper No. 5556 (Cambridge, MA.: National Bureau of Economic Research, 1996).

2 M. Andrews, 'The logical limits of best practice administrative solutions in developing countries', *Public Administration and Development* 32 (2012) 137–53; L. Pritchett and M. Woolcock, *Solutions when the Solution is the Problem: Arraying the Disarray in Development*, Working Paper No. 10 (Washington, DC: Center for Global Development, 2002).

3 IMF, *Manual on Fiscal Transparency* (Washington, DC: International Monetary Fund, 2007); OECD, *Managing Public Expenditure: A Reference Book for Transition Countries*

(Paris: Organisation for Economic Cooperation and Development, 2001); PEFA, *Public Financial Management Performance Measurement Framework* (Washington, DC: World Bank, 2011); A. Premchand, *Public Expenditure Management* (Washington, DC: International Monetary Fund, 1993); A. Schick, *A Contemporary Approach to Public Expenditure Management* (Washington, DC: World Bank Institute, 1998); World Bank, *Public Expenditure Management Handbook* (Washington, DC: World Bank, 1998).

4 Andrews, 'The logical limits of best practice administrative solutions in developing countries'; A. Schick, 'Why most developing countries should not try New Zealand's reforms', *World Bank Research Observer* 13: 1 (1998) 123–31.

5 UNSC, *Report of the Secretary General on the United Nations Interim Administration Mission in Kosovo, 12 July 1999*, 21.

6 L. C. Seale, 'Establishing financial management in the Kosovo interim administration' (unpublished report in possession of author, 2000) 2.

7 Judah, *Kosovo: War and Revenge* 69.

8 Dixon, *Pillar IV's Role within UNMIK*, paras 21–4.

9 Former international Director General of Customs.

10 TAFKO, *Monthly Summary of Task Force Activities: July-August 1999*, 4.

11 Dixon, *Speech at first donor's conference for Kosovo, Brussels, July 28.*

12 IMF/World Bank, *Update on Economic Policy Issues and Institutional Development, First Donors' Conference* para 5.

13 European Commission, *Annual Programme 2002 for Kosovo* (Brussels: European Commission, 2002) 8.

14 International USAID public finance adviser (IA16).

15 Skendaj, *Creating Kosovo: Intenational Oversight and the Making of Ethical Institutions* 125.

16 World Bank, *Kosovo: Building Peace through Sustained Growth* 3.

17 Barents Group, Government infrastructure support, United Nations Mission in Kosovo, Pillar IV – Monthly and weekly reports 2000 (Pristina: unpublished reports in possession of author, 2000) June.

18 Barents Group, Government infrastructure support, United Nations Mission in Kosovo, Pillar IV – Weekly reports 1999; Barents Group, Government infrastructure support, United Nations Mission in Kosovo, Pillar IV – Monthly and weekly reports 2000.

19 International USAID public finance adviser (IA1).

20 International USAID public finance advisers (IA1, IA16).

21 www.unmikonline.org/regulations/unmikgazette/02english/Econtents.htm#, accessed 23 June 2015.

22 Barents Group, Government infrastructure support, United Nations Mission in Kosovo, Pillar IV – Monthly and weekly reports 2000, March.

23 UNMIK, *The New Kosovo Government 2002 Budget* (Pristina: Central Fiscal Authority, United Nations Mission in Kosovo, 2002) 2.

24 Senior Kosovar tax official (KG2).

25 ICG, *Kosovo: A Strategy for Economic Development* 8.

26 Ibid. 7; IMF, *Kosovo: Macroeconomic Issues and Fiscal Sustainability* 12.

27 Barents Group, Government infrastructure support, United Nations Mission in Kosovo, Pillar IV – Monthly and weekly reports 2000, March.

28 World Bank, *Kosovo, Economic and Social Reforms for Peace and Reconciliation, Volume I* (Washington, DC: World Bank, 2001) 16.

29 Barents Group, Government infrastructure support, United Nations Mission in Kosovo, Pillar IV – Monthly and weekly reports 2000, 19 February.

30 International USAID public finance adviser (IA1).
31 UN, *Convention on Privileges and Immunities of the United Nations* (New York: United Nations, 1946).
32 International USAID taxation adviser (IA8).
33 Senior Kosovar tax official (KG2).
34 Skendaj, *Creating Kosovo: Intenational Oversight and the Making of Ethical Institutions* 126.
35 International USAID taxation adviser (IA8).
36 European Commission, *Annual Programme 2002 for Kosovo* 8–9.
37 European Commission, *Cooperation in the Field of Customs and Taxation: The European Union and the Western Balkans* (Brussels: Directorate General for Enlargement, 2005) 11.
38 Former international Director General of Customs.
39 International USAID taxation adviser (IA8).
40 European Commission, *2008 Project Fiche Kosovo– IPA centralised programmes, Support to Customs and Taxation Administrations* (Brussels: European Commission, 2008) para 3.8.
41 World Bank, *Kosovo: Building Peace through Sustained Growth* 21.
42 del Castillo, *Rebuilding War-Torn States* 162.
43 Seale, 'Establishing financial management in the Kosovo interim administration' 1.
44 International USAID public finance adviser (IA1).
45 UNMIK/REG/1999/16, 6 November 1999; UNMIK/REG/1999/17, 6 November 1999.
46 Xinhua News Agency, 'Belgrade protests UN decision to set up budget authority for Kosovo', *People's Daily Online* (17 November 1999).
47 Seale, 'Establishing financial management in the Kosovo interim administration'.
48 S. Lewarne and D. Snelbecker, *Economic Governance in War Torn Economies: Lessons Learned from the Marshall Plan to the Reconstruction of Iraq* (Washington, DC: United States Agency for International Development, 2004).
49 International USAID public finance adviser (IA1).
50 International USAID treasury adviser (IA15).
51 Seale, 'Establishing financial management in the Kosovo interim administration' 4.
52 USAID, 'Results of Kosova economic sector assessment, July 15 to July 29' 8–9.
53 UNMIK Reg. 1999/11, 13 October 1999.
54 UNMIK Reg. 1999/20, 15 November 1999.
55 World Bank, *Kosovo: Building Peace through Sustained Growth* 21.
56 IMF/World Bank, *Update on Economic Policy Issues and Institutional Development, First Donors' Conference* para 2.
57 Barents Group, Government infrastructure support, United Nations Mission in Kosovo, Pillar IV – Weekly reports 1999, 26 November.
58 Ibid. 11 December.
59 UNMIK, *UNMIK News Archive 2000* (Pristina: United Nations Mission in Kosovo, 2000) January.
60 Barents Group, Government infrastructure support, United Nations Mission in Kosovo, Pillar IV – Monthly and weekly reports 2000, February.
61 Ibid. January.
62 International USAID public finance adviser (IA1).
63 UNMIK Reg. 2006/47, 24 August 2006.
64 USAID, *USAID/Kosovo Operational Plan FY 2006* (Washington, DC: United States Agency for International Development, 2006).
65 UNMIK/European Union, *The 10 Key Achievements: End of Mission Report 1999–2008*, 15–16.

66 UNMIK/REG/1999/27, 22 December 1999.
67 World Bank/European Commission, *Kosovo Donors' Meeting Feb 25–26, 2001, Pristina – Statements* (Brussels: Joint Office for South East Europe, 2001).
68 S. Symansky, *Donor Funding and Public Finance Management Reform in Post Conflict Countries: Recommendations Derived from Personal Observations* (London: Centre for Aid and Public Expenditure, Overseas Development Institute, 2010) 2; UNMIK, *Partnership in Kosovo: Reconstruction 1999–2000*, 7.
69 Barents Group, Government infrastructure support, United Nations Mission in Kosovo – Monthly reports 2002 (Pristina: unpublished reports in possession of author, 2002) January.
70 UNMIK Regulation 2001/9, 15 May 2001.
71 IMF, *Kosovo: Macroeconomic Issues and Fiscal Sustainability* 15–16.
72 World Bank, *Kosovo, Economic and Social Reforms for Peace and Reconciliation, Volume I*, 10.
73 UNMIK/REG/2001/19, 13 September 2001 Annex II.
74 UNMIK, *The New Kosovo Government 2002 Budget* 22.
75 UNSC, *Report of the Secretary General on the United Nations Interim Administration Mission in Kosovo, 15 January 2002* (New York: United Nations Security Council, 2002) 4.
76 International USAID public finance adviser (IA13).
77 Early Warning Report, *Kosovo Early Warning Report No. 2, Sept–Dec 2002*, 17.
78 UNMIK, *Kosovo: UNMIK-Government report for the Donor Coordination Meeting for Kosovo, Brussels, 5 November 2002* (Pristina: United Nations Mission in Kosovo, 2002) 47.
79 UNMIK/REG/2003/17, 12 May 2003.
80 International USAID public finance adviser (IA12).
81 International EU public finance adviser (IA14).
82 World Bank, *Public Expenditure Management Technical Assistance Project (PEMTAG), Project Appraisal Document* 19.
83 IMF, *Kosovo: Gearing Policies Toward Growth and Development* (Washington, DC: International Monetary Fund, 2005) 2.
84 USAID, *USAID Assistance in Fiscal Reform: The Kosovo Economic Reconstruction Project* 5.
85 UNSC, *Report of the Secretary-General on the United Nations Interim Administration Mission in Kosovo, 30 April 2004* (New York: United Nations Security Council, 2004) 14.
86 International USAID public finance adviser (IA1).
87 Early Warning Report, *Kosovo Early Warning Report No. 5*, 18.
88 World Bank, *Kosovo Economic Memorandum* (Washington, DC: World Bank, 2004) iv.
89 IMF, *Kosovo: Gearing Policies Toward Growth and Development* 24–5.
90 Early Warning Report, *Kosovo Early Warning Report No. 9*, 19.
91 UNMIK/PISG, *Letter of Intent Between UNMIK and PISG to International Donor Community: Kosovo Memorandum of Economic and Financial Policies, 2 November 2005* (Pristina: United Nations Mission in Kosovo; Provisional Institutions of Self Government, 2005).
92 Kosovar World Bank representative.
93 Unless otherwise indicated, information on the early phase of public procurement development is based on I. Q. Duli, *Public Procurement in Kosovo* (Pristina: UBT Publications, 2008) and E. Piselli, 'The establishment and development of a public procurement system for Kosovo' in S. Arrowsmith and M. Trybus (eds), *Public Procurement: The Continuing Revolution* (The Hague; London; New York: Kluwer Law International, 2003) 47–59.
94 Barents Group, Government infrastructure support, United Nations Mission in Kosovo – Monthly reports 2001 (Pristina: unpublished reports in possession of author, 2001) January.

95 KPMG Consulting Group, Kosovo Project, Central Fiscal Authority Exit Report, 4 March 2000 to 28 February 2002 (Pristina: unpublished document, copy held by author, 2002) 7.
96 M. Trybus, 'The reform of public procurement law in the Western Balkans' in G. Piga and K. V. Thai (eds), *Advancing Public Procurement: Experiences, Innovation and Knowledge Sharing* (Boca Raton: PrAcademics Press, 2006) 392–412.
97 International USAID public finance adviser (IA16).
98 Assembly of Kosovo Law No 2003/17, 11 September 2003; UNMIK/REG/2004/3, 9 February 2004. Duli, *Public Procurement in Kosovo* 45.
99 World Bank, *Public Expenditure Management Technical Assistance Project (PEMTAG), Project Appraisal Document*, 19–20.
100 USAID, *Evaluation of the USAID/Kosovo Economic Reconstruction Project* (Washington, DC: United States Agency for International Development, 2003) 12.
101 Duli, *Public Procurement in Kosovo*.
102 UNDP, *Assessment of Administrative Capacity in Kosovo* 24.
103 World Bank, *Public Expenditure Management Technical Assistance Project (PEMTAG), Project Appraisal Document* 20.
104 European Commission, *Kosovo 2005 Progress Report*, (Brussels: European Commission, 2005) 41.
105 UNMIK/REG/2007/20, 6 June 2007.
106 European Commission, *2007 Project Fiche Kosovo, IPA centralised programme, Meeting EU Standards in Public Procurement* (Brussels: European Commission, 2007) para 3.1; European Commission, *Kosovo 2009 Progress Report* (Brussels: European Commission, 2009) 31.
107 European Commission, *Kosovo 2008 Progress Report* (Brussels,: European Commission, 2008) 37.
108 European Commission, *Kosovo 2009 Progress Report* 31.
109 Senior Kosovar procurement official (KG7).
110 International EU procurement adviser (IA2).
111 Republic of Kosova, Law No.03/L–241, 30 September 2010.
112 European Commission, *Kosovo 2011 Progress Report* (Brussels: European Commission, 2011) 37.
113 SIGMA, *Assessment: Kosovo 2012* (Paris: OECD, Support for Improvement in Governance and Management, 2012) 23.
114 Republic of Kosova, Law No. 04/L-042, 29 August 2011.
115 European Commission, *Kosovo 2011 Progress Report*, 37–8; SIGMA, *Assessment: Kosovo 2012*, 23–7.
116 Republic of Kosova, Law No. 04/L-237, 20 March 2014.
117 European Commission, *Kosovo 2014 Progress Report* 34.
118 Capussela, 'Road to ruin'; F. Strazzari and B. Kamphuis, 'Hybrid economies and statebuilding: On the resilience of the extralegal', *Global Governance* 18 (2012) 57–72.
119 International USAID public finance adviser (IA13).
120 KPMG Consulting Group, *Kosovo Project, Central Fiscal Authority Exit Report, 4 March 2000 to 28 February 2002*.
121 UNMIK/REG/2002/18, 4 October 2002.
122 KPMG Consulting Group, *Kosovo Project, Central Fiscal Authority Exit Report, 4 March 2000 to 28 February 2002*, 7.
123 USAID, *Evaluation of the USAID/Kosovo Economic Reconstruction Project* 18.

124 European Agency for Reconstruction, *Kosovo Annual Action Programme 2006: Sector Fiche 2.3 Strengthening Public Administration Reform and EU Integration at Central and Municipal Levels* (Thessaloniki: European Agency for Reconstruction, 2006).
125 European Agency for Reconstruction, *EAR Annual Report 2005* (Thessaloniki: European Agency for Reconstruction, 2006) 86.
126 FRIDOM, *Horizontal Review of Internal Audit Function*, Functional Review and Institutional Design of Ministries (Pristina: Ministry of Public Administration, 2009) 8–9.
127 European Commission, *Welcome to the World of Public Internal Financial Control (PIFC)* (Brussels: Directorate-General for Budget, 2006).
128 International EU audit adviser (IA3).
129 C. Iles, *Implementing Financial Management and Governance in Transitional States: Reflections on Introducing Western Normative Models of Public Internal Financial Control in the new Republic of Kosovo* (London: Middlesex University, 2012).
130 International EU audit adviser (IA3).
131 Kosovar technical adviser (KA3).
132 European Agency for Reconstruction, *EAR Annual Report 2005*, 86; European Commission, *Kosovo 2005 Progress Report* 51; SIGMA, *Kosovo Public Internal Financial Control (PIFC) Assessment 2007* (Paris: OECD, Support for Improvement in Governance and Management, 2007).
133 Iles, *Implementing Financial Management and Governance in Transitional States.*
134 UNMIK/REG/2007/19, 6 June 2007.
135 Iles, *Implementing Financial Management and Governance in Transitional States*; SIGMA, *Kosovo Public Internal Financial Control (PIFC) Assessment 2007.*
136 European Commission, *2008 Project Fiche Kosovo IPA centralised programme: Public Finance* (Brussels: European Commission, 2008); Iles, *Implementing Financial Management and Governance in Transitional States.*
137 Kosovar technical adviser (KA3).
138 International audit adviser (IA7).
139 SIGMA, *Kosovo Public Internal Financial Control (PIFC) Assessment 2007*, 3.
140 European Commission, *Instrument For Pre-Accession Assistance (IPA:II): Indicative Strategy Paper for Kosovo (2014–2020)* (Brussels: European Commission, 2014) 17; SIGMA, *Assessment: Kosovo 2012*, 17–19.
141 USAID, *Kosovo: Results Review and Resource Request* 1.
142 USAID, *USAID/Kosovo Annual Report FY 2005* (Washington: United States Agency for International Development, 2005) 6.
143 USAID, *Mid-Term Performance Evaluation of the Kosovo Growth and Fiscal Stability Initiative (GFSI) – Final Report* 1.
144 UNMIK/European Union, *The 10 Key Achievements: End of Mission Report 1999–2008*, 3.
145 World Bank, *Implementation Completion Report: Economic Assistance Grant IV Kosovo* 3.
146 IMF, *Technical Assistance Evaluation Program: Findings of Evaluations and Updated Program* (Washington, DC: International Monetary Fund, 2006) 19.
147 The widely used PEFA evaluation framework comprises twenty-eight PFM performance indicators and applies scores ranging from A plus to D minus (www.pefa.org/en, accessed 9 September 2012).
148 MFE, *Public Expenditure and Financial Accountability (PEFA) Assessment Report* (Pristina: Government of Kosovo, 2007).

149 MFE, *Public Expenditure and Financial Accountability (PEFA) Public Financial Management Assessment* (Pristina: Republic of Kosovo, 2009); MFE, *Public Expenditure and Financial Accountability (PEFA) Public Financial Management Assessment* (Pristina: Republic of Kosovo, 2013).

150 B. Olden, D. Last, S. Ylaoutinen and C. Sateriale, *Fiscal Consolidation in Southeastern European Countries: The Role of Budget Institutions*, IMF Working Paper WP/12/113 (Washington, DC: International Monetary Fund, 2012).

151 European Commission, *Kosovo 2013 Progress Report* 31.

152 SIGMA, *Assessment Kosovo 2013* (Paris: OECD, Support for Improvement in Governance and Management, 2013) 21.

153 FRIDOM, *Functional Review of Public Expenditure Management Systems*, Functional Review and Institutional Design of Ministries (Pristina: Ministry of Public Administration, 2010); FRIDOM, *Functional Review of the Ministry of Finance and Economy*, Functional Review and Institutional Design of Ministries (Pristina: Ministry of Public Administration, 2010).

154 King and Mason, *Peace at any Price* 135.

155 S. A. Blair, D. Eyre, B. Salome and J. Wasserstrom, 'Forging a viable peace: Developing a legitimate political economy' in J. Covey, M. J. Dziedzic and L. Hawley (eds), *The Quest for Viable Peace: International Intervention and Strategies for Conflict Transformation* (Washington, DC; Arlington, VA: United States Institute of Peace Press; Association of the United States Army, 2005) 205–43, 237.

156 UNSC, *A Comprehensive Review of the Situation in Kosovo (Eide Report)* 11.

157 International USAID public finance adviser (IA12).

158 International USAID public finance adviser (IA13).

159 World Bank, *Doing Business 2015: Economy Profile Kosovo* (Washington, DC: World Bank, 2014).

160 World Bank, *Kosovo Country Fiduciary Assessment* (Washington, DC: World Bank, 2012) 43.

161 H. Tavakoli and S. Saneja, *Public Financial Management Reforms in Fragile States: The Case of Kosovo* (London: Overseas Development Institute, 2012) vi.

162 World Bank, *Kosovo Country Fiduciary Assessment* 44.

163 European Commission, *Kosovo 2011 Progress Report* 24.

164 European Commission, *Kosovo 2013 Progress Report* 44; European Commission, *Kosovo 2014 Progress Report* 11.

165 Office of the Auditor General, *Annual Audit Report 2013* (Pristina: Office of the Auditor General, 2014) 26.

166 Kosovar government audit official (KG3).

167 International audit adviser (IA7).

168 Office of the Auditor General, *Annual Audit Report on the Financial Year 2010*, (Pristina: Republic of Kosova, 2011) ii; Office of the Auditor General, *Annual Audit Report 2013*, 32.

169 European Commission, *Kosovo 2010 Progress Report* (Brussels: European Commission, 2010) 34–5.

170 SIGMA, *Assessment: Kosovo 2012*; SIGMA, *Assessment Kosovo 2013*.

171 International procurement adviser (IA2).

172 International USAID public finance adviser (IA1).

173 Estimated total funding for PFM-related activities comprised EU funding for Pillar IV (€136 million), USAID economic governance projects (€88.8 million), the World Bank's PEMTAG project (€4.7 million) and EAR and ECLO projects in public finance

(€25.9 million). (Sources: European Commission, Instrument for Pre-Accession Assistance (IPA) *Multi-annual Indicative Planning Document for Kosovo 2008–2010*; USAID Office, Pristina; http://ec.europa.eu/enlargement/archives/ear/agency/28-ContractListWeb/kos/kos.htm; www.delprn.ec.europa.eu/?cid=2,94; and www.worldbank.org/projects). The exact amounts spent by donors and international bodies on PFM are difficult to assess, however, due to the different approaches used to classify projects.

174 Barents Group, 'In-country list' (Pristina: unpublished document held by author, October 24, 2000).

175 UNMIK/European Union, *EU Pillar Annual Report 2005*.

176 International USAID public finance adviser (IA12).

177 International USAID public finance adviser (IA16).

178 Wittkowsky, 'Squaring the circle' 23.

179 International USAID public finance adviser (IA13).

180 International USAID public finance adviser (IA16).

181 Skendaj, *Creating Kosovo: Intenational Oversight and the Making of Ethical Institutions.*

4

The civil service

While Kosovo's public finance institutions are generally judged to perform well, opinions about the wider civil service are much less positive. The civil service in Kosovo means the staff in central and municipal administrations who deliver services to the public in areas as diverse as road maintenance and refuse collection, urban planning, vehicle licensing, business regulation, health care, education and social welfare. They are the ones who develop and implement government policies and regulations, who file papers and answer queries from the public, who stand at counters issuing licences and permits, and who manage and pay other civil servants who do these things. To perform these tasks well a government needs its staff to be competent and well motivated.

Weber, bureaucracy and development

The concept of an efficient, apolitical civil service bureaucracy is a product of the industrial revolution and is closely associated with ideas about modernisation and economic progress. Rational, impersonal, rule-based administration is considered essential for delivering optimal and equitable outcomes for society.[1] The essential characteristics of modern government administration, described in Max Weber's essay on bureaucracy in the early twentieth century, are still largely applicable to civil service systems in developed countries today. They include fixed official jurisdictions, government by rules, hierarchy and graded authority, management based on documents, specialised technical skills, security of office, a regular salary based on rank and career progression based on seniority or exams.[2] The civil service is also expected to be impersonal and apolitical. It is sometimes conceived of as a machine that operates reliably and predictably regardless of the political changes and disruption outside the bureaucracy. This type of administration is viewed as a vast improvement on inefficient patrimonial and nepotistic alternatives, and a potentially powerful tool for increasing social welfare. Public bureaucracies have also been criticised, however, for excessive regulation, excessive power, slowness, inflexibility and mediocrity. Balzac, for example, described bureaucracy as 'a gigantic power set in motion by dwarfs'.[3]

Early observers saw a clear connection between the emergence of bureaucratic public administration and the increased wealth and power of European states. Weber, for example, argued that the great modern state is absolutely dependent on bureaucracy.[4] More recently, the 'developmental state' literature also identifies a strong government bureaucracy in countries such as Japan, Taiwan, South Korea and Singapore as one of the essential elements of their economic successes.[5] An effective civil service has thus come to be seen as necessary for economic improvement and social welfare in developing countries and an appropriate target for donor-funded development projects. The EU also now applies a 'bureaucracy criterion', measuring the administrative capacity to apply EU laws and standards as one of the conditions for accession. Much EU assistance to potential members is therefore directed towards public administration reform.[6] The size of the civil service and rates of civil service pay also have an impact on government expenditure giving the Ministry of Finance and PFM experts an interest in civil service policy. Both the World Bank and the OECD have developed guidelines and measurement frameworks for assessing the quality and competence of public administration, setting out criteria for good performance in policy coordination, service delivery, efficiency, human resource management and ethics.[7]

There are, however, significant national differences in public attitudes to government bureaucracy and in the relationship between the civil service and the elected government. In the Westminster system, for example, senior civil servants generally remain in their posts regardless of election outcomes. In many other countries, including the US, senior positions at many levels are appointed by each incoming executive government. Popular attitudes to the value of the civil service also vary between countries, as do ideas about the appropriate size and scope of government administration, with some countries accepting an expansive role for the public sector and others pursuing the idea of 'small government'. The issue has become more complex as some Western countries have experimented with reforms intended to address the perceived inflexibilities and inefficiencies of the public sector. Sometimes referred to as 'new public management', these reforms include using mechanisms such as performance contracts, competition and decentralised management, and reducing the security and predictability of civil service salaries and conditions in efforts to stimulate improved public sector performance.[8] Western concepts of separation of state powers and merit-based bureaucracy were not, however, features of the previous socialist system of public administration in the former Yugoslavia: the party political bureaucracy had been closely intertwined with state administration, party directives often took precedence over legal rules, and public employment had been party controlled and highly politicised.[9] Many of the processes and behavioural norms introduced by international actors were therefore unfamiliar to Kosovars.

Ensuring a competent and effective civil administration in Kosovo was identified as one of the priority tasks in early discussions among donors,[10] but it generally received less attention than fiscal policies and institutions and most responsibility for achieving it was assigned to UNMIK's civil administration component. This chapter describes the main activities of the Mission in establishing the Kosovo civil service beyond the realm of the public finance institutions. It is organised in more or less chronological order and describes developments in public sector employment and management from the start of the Mission, through the formation of the JIAS Departments and the PISG, to the early years of independence. Responsibility for the civil service rested, initially, with the UNMIK Department of Administration and Support in Pillar II. This soon became the JIAS Department of Public Services (DPS), then the PISG Ministry of Public Services (MPS), and eventually the Ministry of Public Administration (MPA) of the Republic of Kosovo. Several donors, in particular DFID and EAR, provided technical assistance on public administration reform over the period, but initial policy development and implementation was largely in the hands of UN staff. The final section of the chapter reviews a number of measures of the outcomes of civil service development, the most important being the assessments of Kosovo's own citizens.

The Kosovo civil service in 1999

The fact that most Serbian government employees had left the province at the end of the conflict did not mean that Kosovo had no public sector workers. Within days of the end of hostilities, Albanian Kosovars started to reclaim the positions they had held in government departments, public enterprises and utilities ten years earlier, before the mass dismissal of Albanian staff by the Serb authorities. The Albanian-run parallel health and education services also prepared to restart their activities. International officials saw this return to work as an important step in reconstruction and UNMIK soon formally authorised thousands of pre-1989 government workers to resume their jobs, while at the same time trying to encourage Serb employees to stay. In July 1999, the UN Secretary General reported that UNMIK would make maximum use of skilled former or current public employees of any ethnicity who would be integrated into the interim civil administrative structure and would be selected on the basis of capability, the level of local confidence enjoyed by the individuals, their efficiency and integrity.[11] In fact, however, UNMIK had little opportunity to apply any kind of process for selecting public sector staff. In mid-July municipal employees officially returned to work in Pristina, and at the beginning of August, 400 former post and telecommunications employees were welcomed back to their jobs by newly arrived SRSG Kouchner. At the municipal and regional levels, UNMIK international administrators were working with self-identified 'local authorities' to provide water, electricity and health services. UNMIK's Civil Affairs Office soon found itself responsible for large numbers of workers.[12] In effect, the

UNMIK policy meant that everyone who had ever been employed in the government was offered a job.[13]

UNMIK's rationale for this expansive public employment policy was based on its peacekeeping objective and was intended as a temporary measure. According to one UNMIK official,

> Allowing the number of civil servants to grow rapidly initially ... was a conscious choice and based on the need to build peace. The UN's first priority was to get people into jobs in order to support the economy and to build peace. Efficiency could come later. The immediate issue was to prevent the derailment of the country. Derailment didn't happen, so it worked.[14]

While this policy may have helped to secure peace it also created an opportunity for politicisation of government employment, as noted by another UN official: 'Having been out of the system for ten or more years, the people who then occupied the positions were not qualified ... basically they were the KLA fighters and they just started taking over the institutions, like the socially owned enterprises, the factories and all those things ...'[15] An EU observer made a similar assessment: 'This huge body of thousands of people was created nearly from zero, so this was an excellent opportunity for occupation of power within the civil service, a political opportunity.'[16]

While this was happening, international bodies and donors were still debating how a local administration should be established. It was generally agreed that the informal parallel administration operated by Albanian Kosovars from 1989 to 1999 would not be a suitable basis for new institutions, while the previous administration during the period of Kosovo's autonomy, from 1974 to 1989, had been characterised by a lack of representation, an unaccountable bureaucracy and a lack of civil society engagement.[17] By this stage, however, in most areas of public service delivery, particularly health, education and the municipalities, it was too late. The parallel system had reconstituted itself and there appeared to be no practical alternative.[18]

Creating a civil service for Kosovo was not an immediate priority for UNMIK in part because it was busy recruiting its own local staff. In its first year UNMIK employed more than 3,000 Kosovar clerks, interpreters, administrative assistants, drivers and messengers, including around 2,000 to work in the Civil Administration, on UN rates of pay and conditions of employment. Salary levels for UN local staff were set by the International Civil Service Commission based on the 'Fleming Principle' that the UN should mirror the best prevailing conditions among other employers in the location. A local salary survey was conducted in Kosovo by the UN Secretariat in 1999 and arrived at salaries ranging from DM1,000 to DM3,000 per month.[19] It is not clear, however, how much reliable data on comparable employers in Kosovo was available at the time. Other donors, international organisations and NGOs also recruited local staff for their newly established offices and usually took the lead from the UN in setting salary levels. It has been estimated that by the second year of the Mission donors had employed around 18,000 local personnel.[20]

The distorting effect of donor and NGO employment on the civil service in developing countries is a frequent complaint in the literature on development. The impact is even greater in post-conflict environments where there are few other employment options and very large numbers of international organisations competing for the limited supply of educated, experienced and English-speaking staff. In Kosovo, the UN recruited not only senior staff and interpreters but also large numbers of unskilled and semi-skilled cleaners, guards and drivers on generous salaries. The first President of the Kosovo Assembly, Nexhet Daci, once complained that an UNMIK cleaner earned five times the amount paid to a teacher, and a security guard earned as much as a government minister.[21] The presence of the UN Mission itself, and its employment policies, thus presented an obstacle to successful formation of a competent civil service bureaucracy.

Civil service pay

Unlike the Kosovars fortunate enough to secure a job with the UN Mission, most of the self-selected public sector employees were initially working largely without an official salary. In August, however, UNMIK started paying ad hoc stipends to a handful of judges, prosecutors and customs officials using money from a UN Trust Fund. Further payments were subsequently made to teachers, health workers and fire fighters. Three pay rates were decided for the stipends: DM100 for support staff, DM200 for professionals and DM300 for executive positions. The recipients were reported to be very dissatisfied with these rates, no doubt based on comparison with UN wages which were ten times these amounts, often for similar work. The stipends were paid in cash but arrangements for delivering payments to individuals were at that time rudimentary given the absence of banking facilities and identity cards. UN officials faced the challenge of unambiguously identifying beneficiaries, establishing authorising procedures, and physically transferring cash throughout the province under NATO protection.[22] Rigorous controls were impossible.

> With the news that the UN would pay stipends, schools and hospitals were filled with people supposedly working there. There was no way of knowing who was employed and who was not since records had disappeared. In any case, since the main objective was to restore security and move the political transition forward, everyone present received the small stipend – whether they were entitled to it or not.[23]

A UN official who was involved in this task noted that 'When it came to paying stipends there was a difficulty knowing who is who and who is working where. We just had to trust the people.'[24]

The Kosovo Consolidated Budget for the 2000 financial year provided for a transition from stipends to a regular salary system. The civil service salary scale was issued in the form of a memo which identified seven standard job titles with a single salary level for each job. It was a simple system, intended as an interim measure, but in fact this rudimentary arrangement remained in operation for more than a decade. The UN's expansive public sector employment policy had raised fears that an excessively large civil service was being created. This did not, however, appear to be demonstrated by the data provided in the budget. This document, produced by Pillar IV, committed Kosovo to having 'a lean and productive public sector workforce' and provided funding for around 57,000 staff.[25] This was many fewer than the Serb government had employed under their administration,[26] and the World Bank suggested that it was very lean by the standards of the region, representing only about 2.5 per cent of the population.[27] However, the influx of donor money and international staff had produced price inflation and distortions in the cost of living. Pre-conflict salary levels were not considered adequate and demands for higher public sector wages meant that civil service salaries in Kosovo were well above those paid in neighbouring countries.[28]

Employment terms and conditions

Under UNMIK Regulation 1, issued in July 1999, the SRSG had the power to appoint any person to perform functions in the civil administration, and to remove them.[29] For a considerable time this was effectively the only legislation governing public sector employment. A Civil Service and Personnel Section was established within UNMIK's Department of Administration and Support to manage the future Kosovo civil service. The unit was expected to have two staff to address policy and institutional issues and three to develop civil service remuneration schemes.[30] In November 1999, however, an adviser working with Pillar IV made inquiries to determine who in Pillar II was handling local hiring and employment issues for the Kosovo budget and concluded 'It appears no one is'.[31] A UN official confirmed that there was very little guidance provided on civil service recruitment during the first phase of the mission. 'My understanding was that there was no standardised process of recruitment. We had this 2001 regulation on the civil service but until that time … there was a very *ad hoc* system of employment.'[32]

In the absence of policy direction from Pillar II, responsibility for appointments and conditions of service was, for all practical purposes, devolved to each of the employing agencies within UNMIK. Brief references to staff recruitment and personnel policies were included in early UNMIK regulations, but the focus was largely on the need for equitable ethnic representation. The regulation establishing the CFA, for example, simply stated that the head of the CFA 'shall implement non-discriminatory personnel policies designed to ensure that the composition of the staff of the CFA reflects the multi-ethnic character of communities of Kosovo', but made no reference to terms of employment, remuneration or performance.[33] The international authorities in charge of each of the new agencies, including the Customs Service and Taxation Administration, as well as the Kosovo Police Service and the Kosovo Protection Corps, drafted their own contracts of employment for staff.

Public administration under the JIAS

Beginning a Kosovar-led administration

The creation of the JIAS at the start of 2000 was intended to begin the process of forming a Kosovar-led administration. Twenty administrative departments were set up to manage public services, each under joint international and Kosovar leadership. The first task of the new IAC was to allocate responsibility for the various departments between the Albanian political factions represented on the Council. The political parties then nominated their own candidates to the Kosovar Co-Head positions in their departments. There was an intense process of negotiation over the number and importance of the departments each party would head.[34] Four Co-Head positions were reserved for representatives of minority communities and were allocated by the SRSG. A series of UNMIK Regulations were issued to formalise the establishment of each department and they contained a brief section on employment policy, which emphasised non-discrimination and ethnic representation, gender balance, professional qualifications, competence and merit, in that order. Formation of the civil service was discussed by the IAC in February 2000 and the Council reportedly adopted a set of guidelines for 'an objective and transparent recruitment policy aimed at hiring the best experts in the field',[35] but the guidelines were not formally promulgated in UNMIK documents or regulations.

The process of creating new JIAS departments out of the existing UNMIK departments was quite slow and there was considerable criticism of the UN's performance in this task.[36] The first to be staffed and operational were the Central Fiscal Authority, in Pillar IV, which had already commenced a programme of merit-based recruitment, and the Departments of Health and Education, which were largely based on the previous parallel institutions. In August 2000 the ICG reported that some departments still appeared to exist primarily on paper, and all were said to suffer from 'insufficient staff and resources, policy neglect at the top, lack of coordination between departments and lack of transparency between international and local Co-Heads'.[37]

The UNMIK Department of Administration and Support Services became the JIAS Department of Public Services (DPS). Although the UN staff of the Department nominally now shared responsibility with a Kosovar Co-Head, in effect, as in other JIAS departments, UN officials continued to play the lead roles. The Department assumed responsibility for the overall strategy on public services and for developing regulations on recruitment and terms of employment of civil servants, their rights and obligations, salaries, benefits, pensions and disciplinary procedures.[38] It would be more than eighteen months, however, before any of the envisaged regulations were issued and every subsequent step in the process of establishing the elements of civil service management, including procedures for senior appointments and independent oversight of public sector employment, was equally delayed.

UNMIK Civil Service Regulation 2001/36

The question of civil service employment conditions became urgent in 2001 with the development of the Constitutional Framework and the imminent transfer of responsibility for most public administration functions to an elected Kosovo government. Several UNMIK regulations on civil service issues were promulgated at this time, but they provided only part of the necessary legal framework. Regulation 2001/19, on arrangements for the Executive Branch of the PISG, was issued in September, shortly before the first Assembly elections. It set out the broad terms for administering the provisional government ministries, including defining the position of Permanent Secretary in each ministry, establishing a Senior Public Appointments Committee to coordinate recruitment to these posts, and creating an Independent Oversight Board (IOB) to deal with complaints from civil servants against their employing ministry.[39]

The British aid agency DFID, which regarded civil service matters as one of its core areas of expertise, became involved at this time. A draft basic Kosovo Civil Service Law (KCSL) had been prepared by a DFID-funded consultant and DFID expected it would be issued as an UNMIK regulation before the election of the Kosovo Assembly.[40] The law was eventually signed by the SRSG in December 2001 and issued as UNMIK Regulation 2001/36, after the election but before the composition of the executive government had been decided.[41] At the time, DFID considered passage of the civil service legislation before the election of a government important. It was hoped that this would ensure that the essential principles of sound civil service management would be enshrined in law before the civil service was handed over to local politicians, and thus the chance that elected representatives would reject the principles of the law would be reduced.[42] In subsequent reports, however, DFID officials had second thoughts about this strategy and noted that 'the KCSL was adopted before the current Government took office and therefore inevitably does not have the same degree of local ownership as later policies … the law has been felt by some senior politicians to have been 'imposed' with insufficient local discussion.'[43]

The Civil Service Law defined who would be classified as a civil servant, listed governing principles for the civil service and attached a civil service code of conduct. It still did not provide much detail, however, about the terms and conditions of employment of civil servants. These were to be set out in a further document, a separate Administrative Direction, which had also been drafted by DFID consultants, and was expected to be issued as soon as the Civil Service Law was approved. This did not happen until much later, however.

Public administration under the PISG

The transfer of most functions of the JIAS departments to an elected Kosovo government under the terms of the Constitutional Framework meant that in many areas of the administration there was a need to implement a rapid 'Kosovarisation' of the positions that were still in the hands of UN officials. In April 2001, UNMIK departments were instructed to appoint Kosovars to all senior and middle-level posts and to transfer substantive responsibility and authority to them before the November 2001 election.[44] It was not clear, however, where suitable senior and middle-level managers were to come from. Although there was a high level of unemployment, Kosovo's education system had produced few people with advanced qualifications and even fewer of these would have had the necessary experience or been available to step into management roles, particularly at the salaries on offer. There was also concern in some quarters that the selection criteria for the new positions placed too much emphasis on the need for candidates to have had previous experience in public administration. Given the events of the previous decade this tended to favour older people who had worked in the Yugoslav administration prior to 1989 and exclude most younger applicants.[45] It may also have biased civil service recruitment towards LDK supporters, who tended to be older than the followers of other political factions.

The transfer to local control was thus not as rapid as official statements anticipated, largely because of the difficulty of finding candidates to fill the vacant positions at middle management levels and jobs requiring particular skills.[46] Following the Assembly election, the Secretary General explained that UNMIK international staff would continue to perform administrative functions after the government was established, but would hand over executive responsibility as soon as possible.[47] Many international Co-Heads remained in place under the title of Principal International Officer and in most ministries policy issues were still controlled by UN international staff. A year after the creation of the PISG, nearly 50 per cent of senior posts remained unfilled and two Permanent Secretary positions in Ministries were still held by UNMIK staff.[48] At the end of 2003, however, UNMIK officially transferred responsibility for all 'non-reserved' competencies to the PISG.[49] International UN officials continued to work closely with the PISG ministries for some time after this, providing advice and ensuring compliance with UNSCR 1244, the Constitutional Framework and applicable law.[50]

As in the PFM institutions, the slow handover of administrative functions to the local government was a contentious issue between the Kosovar politicians and UNMIK, and among international actors. USAID was one of the international donors most critical of UNMIK's policies on the transition to self government: 'Certain authorities have been retained by UNMIK that, in the view of many observers, should legitimately be turned over to the PISG. A prominent view amongst Balkan experts is that UNMIK has proceeded at a slower than optimal pace in turning over authority to the PISG.'[51]

UN officials, for their part, justified the gradual pace of the handover on the need to balance the transfer of responsibility with the requirement for stability and good government, citing concerns about corruption and lack of public accountability. The UN also faced opposition from the Serbian government in Belgrade and Serbs in Kosovo to any transfer of responsibilities to the Kosovo PISG as being outside the terms of UNSCR 1244.[52] One assessment argued that the speed of the hand-over 'needs to be seen in a context in which there has been widespread criticism of bureaucratic ineptitude and inefficiency'.[53] Hans Haekkerup, who was SRSG in early 2002 when the PISG was formed, has argued that the UN 'tried to hand over authority as fast as it could be defended to keep the political momentum. From an administrative point of view it was certainly too fast. Our real difficulty was to build a (multi-ethnic) civil service according to our standards in a place where corruption always has prevailed.'[54]

The gradual pace at which UN officials reduced their involvement in the civil administration did not succeed in insulating government ministries from political interference, or institutionalising high performance standards and bureaucratic values. The UN had neither the resources nor the policy framework needed to achieve this. In fact, in the absence of a clear legal framework for the civil service well after the creation of the PISG, the Kosovarisation process presented further opportunities for patronage-based appointments and the further politicisation of the administration.[55] The slow withdrawal of the UN from the public administration may also have had less to do with the pursuit of good government and more to do with the reluctance of UN staff to relinquish their positions in government departments and municipalities. Unwillingness by UN administrators to hand power to local authorities has been noted in relation to previous UN peacekeeping missions[56] and a former UNMIK official confirmed that this was a problem in Kosovo:

> It was also becoming very difficult for the UN personnel to exit out of Kosovo ... in the PISG, we formed the government, we recruited our counterparts, we trained them, we handed them the power, then what the hell are we doing there? I must go! But I didn't go, that's the problem. So all of us stuck onto our jobs, so that was another challenge.[57]

DFID's Personnel Policies and Procedures Project and Administrative Direction 2003/2

With the formation of the PISG, the JIAS Department of Public Services became the Ministry of Public Services (MPS) and Jakup Krasniqi, a PDK member and former KLA spokesman, was appointed by the coalition government as Minister. Ministers in the new government were provided with well-appointed offices and personal staff, but UN officials remained in many management roles. A Department of Civil Service Administration (DCSA), with forty-three Kosovar staff, nominally assumed responsibility for civil service policies, including finalising DFID's draft Civil Service Administrative Direction and establishing the IOB, but senior UN officials from the former JIAS department continued to control policy development and the passage of legislation through UNMIK's approval processes.

DFID's Personnel Policies and Procedures (PPP) Project, which commenced in 2002, was designed to support the Kosovarised DCSA in approving the Administrative Direction, implementing the Civil Service Law and developing detailed policies and instructions for personnel managers in the PISG administration. The PPP Project was very large, by DFID standards, with £3 million to be spent on consultants and trainers. DFID had high expectations for the project. The planning documents stated that the principal beneficiaries would be 'the people of Kosovo who, perhaps for the first time, will have a civil service in which they can have confidence; and which is dedicated to serving the needs of the whole population'.[58] The project would involve Kosovars in the design of personnel management procedures, provide training to civil service personnel managers and support the IOB and the Senior Public Appointments Committee (SPAC). The contract to implement the project was awarded to the Centre for Management and Policy Studies (CMPS), a British public sector training body (since renamed the National School of Government), in consortium with similar organisations from Germany and Northern Ireland and a local Kosovo NGO.

DFID's planning for the project had noted potential risks to successful implementation, including possible delays in appointing Kosovar staff and in transferring responsibilities from UNMIK. In the event, most of the identified risks were realised. Slowness on the part of UNMIK international officials in implementing their role in the civil service development process emerged as a major issue. The first DFID review of the project noted that these delays had had a direct impact on progress and the ultimate achievement of its goals. Development of the capacities of the Kosovar DCSA staff was hampered by significant personnel changes and delays in the confirmation of appointments which meant that the staff were not able to play a part in policy development as had originally been hoped. The continued involvement of UN officials at senior levels of the MPS was a further obstacle. Unlike normal technical assistance exercises, the ultimate clients, the Kosovar staff of DCSA, were only accessible to the project team through the intermediation of international UNMIK staff and DFID felt that the project team had been kept at a distance from the decision-making process on policies and procedures.[59]

In spite of these obstacles, some aspects of the PPP Project went very well and it was commented on favourably by both international and Kosovar observers. In particular, the cooperative development of detailed personnel procedures through a 'Personnel Managers Forum' and the training of large numbers of personnel management staff seem to have been very successful. A review of the project in early 2003 praised efforts to ensure ownership and a project completion review considered the project 'reasonably successful'.[60] Kosovar staff still working in the DCSA in 2010 spoke glowingly of the assistance they had received from the project's consultants seven years earlier.

However, the lengthy delay in steering the draft Administrative Direction through both the PISG and UNMIK approval processes was a major frustration for DFID and for the PPP consultants. Although the Administrative Direction had been drafted at the same time as the Civil Service Law in early 2001, and did not appear to contain anything particularly contentious, it was not finally approved and issued by UNMIK until January 2003.[61] The Administrative Direction set out detailed provisions on civil service eligibility, selection, contract terms, probation, promotion, work hours, leave entitlements, disciplinary processes, appeals, termination and retirement. By this point, the Kosovo administration had in effect been in existence for almost three and a half years, from late 1999 to early 2003, without any formal regulation of these matters. DFID reviewers generally attributed the delay of the Administrative Direction to failures of UNMIK officials. A senior UNMIK official was himself at a loss to explain the lack of progress on this issue. 'Every country has a civil service set up and the moment we decided which one to have we just needed to adapt it to Kosovo conditions and that's it. So the fact that it took two years to create – recruitment, conditions of service, terms of service – all the things that go with a civil service, took inordinately long.'[62]

Getting to Westminster: The Senior Public Appointments Committee (SPAC)

The SPAC was considered to be an essential component of the proposed system of civil service management and an important measure for preventing the politicisation of the civil service. Its sole purpose was to ensure merit-based and non-political selection of permanent secretaries and chief executive officers. Membership of the Committee would comprise three government ministers, including the Prime Minister and the Minister for Public Services; two appointed non-Albanian ministers; three international members appointed by the SRSG; and three 'eminent inhabitants of Kosovo' representing civil society, who would also be appointed by the SRSG.[63] The elected government would thus be well and truly outnumbered on the Committee. The new government, when it was formed in early 2002, was not at all happy with the idea of the SPAC, or indeed with the concept of a 'permanent secretary', and the appointment process for senior ministry staff was one of the first issues discussed by the new Cabinet when it met.[64]

The drafters of the legislation had chosen a civil service design based on the British system, which envisaged that ministries would have a strong, apolitical permanent secretary who would manage the ministry. It soon became clear, however, that this model was inconsistent with the political system that had been established for Kosovo, which, unlike the Westminster model, separated the elected Assembly from the Executive, with the government to be managed by technocratic, albeit politically appointed, ministers. Kosovo's politicians also much preferred the system found in many jurisdictions where senior officials are appointed by the elected government:

> This model was contested from the outset as most ministers believed (not without reason) that they would encounter difficulties in gaining full control over their ministries. Moreover, Kosovo's political culture is similar to those of its neighbours, where every change in government results in substantial purges in the patronage built civil service. Unfortunately, this culture proved stronger than all well meaning attempts to build sustainable institutions.[65]

The SPAC started work in 2002 but achieving apolitical appointments to senior posts proved difficult. By October 2002 only five of the eleven permanent secretary posts had been recruited. The slow pace was partly due to ministers refusing to accept the candidates selected by the committee:

> Sometimes this did not work very well. You had people bringing in Permanent Secretaries that were sometimes possibly not qualified, who came in for political reasons ... so there was always a problem. Sometimes the minister did not want somebody, or if there was a change of minister he wanted a change, so there was sometimes, you know, without due process sackings and so on.[66]

In 2005 UNDP reported that a fully merit-based selection had proved impossible and that politics continued to interfere in the recruitment of senior executives and permanent secretaries. The report noted, however, that in spite of concerns about politicisation, most senior positions seemed to be staffed by qualified individuals.[67]

A guarantee of fair treatment: the IOB

It was hoped that the evident problem of politicisation of the civil service would, in part, be countered by the proposed establishment of the IOB. The IOB was intended to protect civil servants from unfair treatment. It would hear appeals against employment decisions, review appointments at middle-management level, assess general compliance with the principles set out in the legislation and seek remedies for successful complaints. The Board's seven members were to be selected by the SRSG in consultation with the prime minister, with at least two members to be non-Albanian. An international official was to serve on the Board for the first year.

Establishing the IOB was an exceedingly slow process, however. The appointment of staff for the Board's secretariat was completed in October 2003, almost two years after the regulation that created it had been approved, but the appointment of the seven Board members took even longer. DFID staff attributed the delay in the creation of the IOB to the UN officials who were still the dominant players in the MPS. In 2003, for example, DFID noted that 'although obstacles to its establishment have been addressed, there has been no progress by UNMIK in making appointments to the IOB'.[68] Continued lack of progress the following year was blamed on Pillar II procedures and on delays in the SRSG's office.[69] The failure of UNMIK to establish the IOB was considered by DFID to be a serious obstacle to creating an apolitical, merit-based civil service: 'The number of appeal cases is mounting, covering issues such as sexual harassment, extreme political interference and enforced embezzlement ... the delay in setting up the IOB means that civil servants can see that a major element of the guarantee of their fair treatment is still missing.'[70]

All IOB members were finally recruited in October 2004, but the Board did not start hearing appeals until 2006. In its first year it resolved 129 cases and in 2007 increased this to 386. It had been intended that DFID's PPP Project would train the IOB members, but by this time the consultant team had been disbanded and OSCE took over the role of developing the professional capacities of the Board and its secretariat. It provided the international member for the first year and organised training courses and study tours to the United Kingdom and Canada to observe similar Westminster-based civil service appeals systems in operation.[71]

Even before it started work, however, there were criticisms of the IOB's legal basis and structure. UNDP noted in 2005 that the Board did not have instruments to ensure that its decisions were implemented and that there was an apparent overlap between the functions of the IOB and the DCSA: both bodies had the right to carry out inspections of the implementation of the Civil Service Law, but neither had sufficient staff to actually carry out such inspections.[72] There were also doubts about the legal viability of the IOB concept in Kosovo's civil law system and concerns about its independence. The fact that the IOB was located in the MPS and its staffing and budget were controlled by the Ministry, was taken to imply a lack of independence in decision making.[73] In February 2008 the Civil Service Law was amended to move the IOB from the MPS to report directly to the Assembly.[74]

Civil service salaries and the EU pay and grading project 2004–5

The level of remuneration appropriate for the civil service has been an ongoing source of disagreement between civil servants, the Kosovo government and international actors. When the PISG government took office in 2002 there had been no nominal growth in public sector salaries since the 2000 budget and the newly elected ministers were under pressure to increase wages. Public sector pay at the time ranged from €131 to €191 per month, while average wages in the wider economy, reported by the Kosovo Statistical Office, were around €200 per month. The lowest wages were in health care and education and it was claimed that workers in these sectors needed to seek additional employment to achieve a basic standard of living.[75] The CFA argued, however, that wages in Kosovo were already higher than in most other countries in the region: in Albania, Serbia, Moldova and Ukraine the average monthly wage was below €100 and in Macedonia, Bulgaria and Romania it was around €150.[76] The IMF and the World Bank recommended a policy of wage restraint and the PISG government agreed to comply.[77] Civil service salaries became an increasingly political issue in subsequent years. In July 2003, the government approved a 20 per cent pay increase for staff in health and education but workers in these sectors considered this inadequate and threatened to strike. All respondents to the Early Warning opinion poll rated public sector salaries as a significant problem facing Kosovo.[78] In January 2004, the government implemented a further 5 per cent general wage increase.

International actors were also concerned not only about civil service pay rates but also the ability of the MPS to control salary spending and employment levels effectively.[79] Civil service salaries under the PISG were still based on the simple pay scale first introduced in the 2000 budget as a temporary measure. As the civil service developed, however, the system had been subject to *ad hoc* modifications leading to a far more complex arrangement with widespread manipulation. New categories of staff had been created and intermediate levels introduced to make finer distinctions between the original seven grades. By 2003 there were 69 different salary points and more than 1,200 job designations with no clear rules for deciding the appropriate pay rate for each position. Many of the modifications may have been aimed simply at increasing an individual's salary rather than reflecting a real difference in responsibilities. The salary scale was also very compressed. Based on official pay rates, the salary compression ratio was 4, which is at the lower end of the international range of 3.1 to 20. There was still no possibility of salary increases within a given job based on experience or length of employment, and no consistent policy on allowances or non-monetary benefits such as access to cars and mobile phones.[80]

The DCSA was responsible for the application of pay policy, but a DCSA official reported that the absence of a set of well-defined rules and standard job descriptions, other than the original 1999 memo, made it difficult to ensure consistency across the civil service: 'This gave a chance to every ministry to deal with it as they wanted to in the absence of these documents and regulations. As a consequence they formed hundreds of new positions that were at different salary levels. For the same job people were paid differently, because there was no regulation, no law, no instruction, just that piece of paper.'[81]

A clear distribution of official duties and authorities within a standardised, hierarchical salary structure is regarded as one of the essential characteristics of a traditional public sector bureaucracy. Bringing more order into the civil service grade system and pay rates had therefore long been identified by donors as a priority. In 2003, EAR launched a project intended to address some of the civil service salary issues. Consultants were contracted to develop a uniform grade and salary system for civil servants. The task proved much more difficult than had been envisaged due to the absence of formal job descriptions on which to base the new system, the reluctance of government ministries to provide information, and the inability of DCSA staff to find time to work with the consultants.

A report recommending new pay and grading arrangements was finalised in February 2004. The proposed new system was considerably more complex than the original UNMIK scheme. It grouped jobs into three categories and four salary grades under five work/career streams requiring different qualifications. In addition there were salary steps within each grade allowing salary progression based on performance evaluation. The gap between the highest and lowest salaries was increased to provide better rewards for those in senior positions. The consultants' report described the system as a modern approach consistent with European practice, which would address many of the problems in the current situation, if it was implemented consistently, but the report also noted that a major programme of work would be required to put the new arrangements in place. Each existing civil service position would need to be reviewed against the new job descriptions and reclassified, and incumbent staff would need to demonstrate that they met the qualifications required for their reclassified position. The consultants foresaw risks in this process: poor implementation could result in transferring the problems of the existing system into the new arrangements.[82]

These risks were avoided, however, because this revised pay and grading structure was never implemented. The new system was originally expected to start from 1 January 2005 but EAR funding was not available to support the implementation phase and responsibility fell to the Kosovar DCSA staff. An initial exercise to match existing staff with the appropriate new grade and pay range was undertaken in late 2004 but produced many irregularities and a high degree of grade inflation. Poor fiscal results in 2004 and concern about the first regrading attempts led the government to defer implementation to July 2005,[83] already a considerable time after the consultants had completed their work, but this new target was also not achieved and the exercise was eventually postponed indefinitely. Several Kosovars cited the EAR pay and grading project as a prime example of donor failure and waste of resources. A former government official, for example, described it as 'a complete failure. The project was late and whatever was drafted was impossible to implement. People were trained and instructions were issued and when they were supposed to start implementation they said there was no money in the budget.'[84]

The most common reason cited for the failure of the project was the expected fiscal impact. A senior MFE official complained that the consultants 'never looked at the budget, just worked on some system which at the end of the day we see it is not possible to apply'.[85] The World Bank had argued that the introduction of the new structure should be dependent on more analysis of the fiscal implications.[86] International officials anticipated that, when posts were reclassified, government bodies would push the grades to the highest level they could and the DCSA was not considered powerful enough to counter this. One adviser noted that the fact that the MPA and the MFE were aligned to different political parties further undermined the project. 'The DCSA and the MPA were not really controlling things ... and the link between MPA and MFE was not strong enough and they wouldn't really talk to each other because they were different parties.'[87] Added to this was the potential political reaction to the new salary classifications:

> We know there is going to be quite a lot of problems because those that have been upgraded need now to be graded at their level. If this was implemented people who were upgraded initially would have to be back to their normal grade and for them that would be a downgrading. So we have foreseen a grace period of one year. This was discussed and discussed and discussed and approved by the government and implementation started. Then people started complaining ... there was no commitment from the government to take it to the end. They were afraid of social unrest because salaries were anyway low, if you decrease them it is even worse.[88]

This issue would have been much less problematic if the question of civil service salaries had been addressed more comprehensively earlier in the Mission. By 2004, when the first attempt at reform and standardisation was proposed, the situation had become much more difficult to manage.

Capacity development and public administration reform

From around 2005 UNMIK's executive role was reduced to the point where it was no longer possible simply to blame the UN for any problems in the management of the civil service. The PISG government was now clearly responsible for most public administration functions. International organisations still had significant influence, however. The 'Standards for Kosovo', as a precondition for final status discussions, replaced direct UNMIK oversight as the main mechanism for ensuring compliance with the demands of international actors. Significant improvement in the quality of public administration was among the targets set for future independence and possible EU membership in the first European Commission progress report in 2005.[89] Although Kosovo's public sector institutions had been in existence only a few years and had been established under international supervision, they were a long way from meeting donor expectations in relation to structure or performance.

A succession of reports identified the many improvements needed in public administration capacity. A 'situational analysis and strategy discussion paper' prepared by the UN Department of Economic and Social Affairs (UNDESA) in 2003, at the request of UNMIK, argued that Kosovo 'requires transformational change from the earlier mode of administration'.[90] Its recommendations for improvement included reviewing and strengthening the existing legal framework for the civil service (although at the time one of the main legal instruments, the Administrative Direction on the civil service, had only recently been promulgated), enacting new laws to deter corruption, establishing the proposed IOB, harmonising the 'structural taxonomy' of ministries, rationalising job classifications, stronger minority representation, improved policy coordination, staff performance appraisal, wage decompression and implementing a personnel information system, as well as exploring modern public administration innovations such as citizens' charters, service standards, performance contracts and contracting out the delivery of government services. Several of these tasks were already included in the terms of reference of donor projects then under way or about to commence including the DFID PPP Project, the EAR Pay and Grading Review and a DFID project on policy coordination in the Office of the Prime Minister, which started in 2004. The report praised what the UN had achieved so far but argued that public sector transformation on the scale needed in Kosovo would require clarity of vision, a strong sense of direction, committed and consistent leadership, and a significant amount of resources. Unfortunately, although there have been repeated efforts over the years that followed to formulate a vision and a sense of direction for the public sector, the last two ingredients – leadership and resources – have generally been missing.

The 'Standards for Kosovo Implementation Plan', developed by UNMIK in 2004, included several of the initiatives drawn from the UNDESA report as specific actions to be taken by the PISG as a precondition for negotiations on 'final status'[91] and a draft Public Administration Strategy was thus drafted and issued jointly by UNMIK and the PISG in mid-2004.[92] In 2005, as UNMIK prepared for talks on final status, another assessment of the capacity of the public administration was commissioned by the SRSG. The 'KCAP' report, prepared by UNDP and financed by the European Commission covered similar ground to the previous UNDESA document, identifying similar weaknesses and making similar recommendations.[93]

A year after KCAP, the PISG MPS decided to prepare their own Public Administration Reform Strategy. It established a 'Group of Experts for Reform of Public Administration' (GERAP), with members from the government, civil society and international organisations, and support from DFID, World Bank and EU advisers. In 2007 the GERAP released a Report on Public Administration, a Reform Strategy and an Action Plan.[94] The documents covered much the same topics as previous reports, and the priority actions included familiar issues such as drafting new civil service legislation, changes to the system of salary grades, a strategy for training civil servants, reviews of the structure of all institutions, improved policy coordination and harmonisation with EU standards. Between the UNDESA report, the Standards for Kosovo Implementation Plan, the KCAP assessment and the GERAP reports, therefore, the weaknesses in Kosovo's public administration and the actions required to address them have been very well documented. Achieving the necessary changes, however, has been much harder.

The civil service since independence

In the years since the declaration of independence in early 2008 there has been some progress in reforming the framework for managing the Kosovo civil service. In 2010 several major pieces of legislation relating to the civil service were approved, including a new Civil Service Law and a Law on Salaries of Civil Servants. However, in general, public administration reform has moved slowly due to both a lack of capacity and resources in the responsible government agencies and a lack of political interest in achieving change.

Functional reviews and DFID's FRIDOM project 2008–10

One of the recommendations of the Public Administration Reform Strategy that has been successfully implemented was, in effect, another major review. Although the PISG ministries and other agencies had been created by UNMIK, it was argued that their subsequent development had been uncoordinated. The lack of legislation to regulate staffing structures and the inability of the DCSA to enforce civil service regulations, as well as the different approaches to civil service management taken by the many international advisers and donors in different ministries, were all considered to have contributed to an excessively complex, opaque and inefficient institutional structure. All previous reports on public administration had therefore recommended conducting functional reviews of all government bodies. The reviews were expected to produce agreement on the structure, personnel numbers, grades, skills and job descriptions for all government agencies and to address duplication of duties and ambiguities in terminology which made it 'very difficult to understand who is who, who is responsible for what and who is doing what in an institution.'[95]

DFID funded the reviews through the 'Functional Review of Institutional Design of Ministries' project, referred to as FRIDOM, which started in early 2008 with a total budget of £2.8 million. The project was one of the largest functional review programmes ever designed in Europe and made the reviews the centrepiece of Kosovo's public administration reform strategy. As with many DFID projects it was a 'design and implement' exercise. The successful consortium of British, Latvian, Slovak and Spanish consultants proposed an ambitious programme of sixteen vertical reviews of ministries and fourteen horizontal reviews of administration functions, as well as a Whole of Government Review. The reviews compared Kosovo's 'organisational solutions' with those of small EU states of comparable size and with similar coalition political systems and made recommendations on rationalising and restructuring the government.[96] Implementation of the recommendations was added to the list of public administration reform tasks facing the government and by 2014 new regulations on the internal organisation of ministries had been adopted. In spite of this, however, the structure of the state administration is still considered by external assessments to be fragmented and inefficient.[97]

The Civil Service Law 2010

It had been a struggle to get the original 2001 UNMIK Civil Service Regulation and the associated 2003 Administrative Direction enacted, but the arrangements they put in place were not considered optimal. One of the problems cited was the use of a Westminster-style civil service and a British common law approach, rather than a European civil law model. DFID downplayed this criticism, arguing that it should not be allowed to undermine the basic concepts embodied in the law.[98] However, a British consultant to the MPA agreed that the use of a common law model was an obstacle to gaining acceptance: 'it wasn't done in the Yugoslav legal tradition. It was kind of "regulation Britain" ... from an HR point of view it was a perfectly good system, but it wasn't written in the legal framework that is an absolute necessity in this part of the world. It was more Anglo Saxon.'[99]

The fact that government staff were employed on short-term contracts rather than being permanent career civil servants was perhaps a more significant issue. The 2001 UNMIK Civil Service Regulation had provided for staff to be appointed on three-year, renewable contracts. This was a consequence of the reluctance of international officials to commit any future regime to open-ended employment contracts and the expectation that there would be a need to dismiss people for corruption and incompetence. However, limited-term contracts continued under the PISG and after independence, facilitating political intervention in civil service staffing. It was reported that many contracts were in fact much shorter than three years, with one-year contracts being common.[100] There are arguments both for and against a permanent civil service, but some degree of job security is usually seen as necessary to protect civil servants from political pressures and to compensate for public sector pay that is below private sector levels. Contracts of limited duration, extended by superiors, potentially allow politicisation and discrimination, as well as limiting opportunities for career development. As one Kosovar put it, 'if you don't like the person, you can just get them out and then you get someone that you like'.[101]

The Kosovo government decided to create a traditional permanent civil service, but there were considerable delays in implementing the policy. The MPS started drawing up a new civil service law in 2005 and prepared several drafts before it was eventually finalised and passed by the Assembly in 2010.[102] Assistance in drafting the legislation had been provided by the OECD's SIGMA programme and by the FRIDOM project but, according to one observer, local officials played a much larger role in this drafting exercise than they had in the preparation of previous versions.[103] The new law replaced the contract system with permanent employment, career progression within functional categories, and internal mobility. Senior positions must be filled from the pool of existing civil servants wherever possible rather than through open advertisement. The rights and duties of civil servants are extensively described, with clear prohibitions on illegal or corrupt acts. The legislation also envisages stricter controls on recruitment and a stronger role for the MPA in approving staffing plans. Recruitment procedures include a written test but, according to a senior civil servant, this will only apply to new recruitment because 'if all the existing staff were to undertake these new procedures, it's certain many of them would fail most likely'.[104]

The new Civil Service Law only applies to staff in purely administrative roles. Teachers, health workers and 'uniformed services' such as the police are to be covered by separate arrangements. A comprehensive teacher licensing and professional development process implemented in the education sector in 2008, for example, included new salary scales based on qualifications and experience.[105] Under the new law the centralised SPAC for senior appointments no longer exists. In its place individual assessment commissions are established for each senior level vacancy to interview applicants and refer the three best candidates to the 'head of the institution' for a final decision. The IOB is also now under separate legislation which makes it a body appointed by and reporting to the Assembly of Kosovo.[106] The Kosovo government has thus formulated a civil service management arrangement that adapts the blueprint proposed by DFID advisers to meet the needs of the post-conflict political system, while still incorporating the underlying principles of good civil service management. How well this new law will address the problems of politicisation and administrative effectiveness is still to be seen.

The Law on Salaries of Civil Servants 2010

A new Law on Salaries of Civil Servants was also approved by the Assembly in 2010, finally replacing the two-page memorandum that had been the basis for civil service pay arrangements since early 2000.[107] The law was drafted with assistance from DFID-funded consultants, including some who had been involved in the previous EAR pay and grading project in 2003, and revived some of the work done at that time. It sets out the criteria for classifying jobs to grades based on responsibility, complexity and qualifications required, provides for progress through salary steps within each grade based on performance appraisal and specifies policies on allowances and other conditions of service. The DCSA is responsible for issuing standards and procedures for job classification, approving the grades proposed for each position in the civil service, approving annual salary progression and setting rules for allowances, leave and expenses.

In late 2010 there was considerable scepticism, including among Kosovar officials in DCSA, about the ability of the MPA to complete the work required to implement the law. Evaluations of public administration in Kosovo since the passage of the law note that overall implementation has been slow. Most staff are now on open-ended appointment letters rather than short-term contracts, senior officials have been confirmed in their positions using the new procedures and much of the secondary legislation is in place, but the legislative framework is not complete and the classification of positions to new grades and salaries has been delayed. Recruitment processes remain highly decentralised with limited involvement of DCSA, despite the provisions of the new legislation.[108] The slow progress has been attributed to lack of capacity and staff resources in the relevant areas of the MPA as well as inadequate political support for reform.

Public administration outcomes

It is difficult to find positive assessments of the current state of the civil service in Kosovo. The opinions of both international observers and Kosovars echo the negative assessments in official reports. One donor representative described the civil service as a 'disaster' and a 'black hole in Kosovo's public administration'. Low productivity, a lack of responsibility or accountability and an attitude that public sector employment is a form of social welfare were mentioned by several people. Continuing inequities and lack of transparency in rates of pay and job classifications and the absence of effective control over civil service recruitment were also identified as problems. The most serious criticisms concerned political interference, nepotism, corruption and attempts by politicians to intervene in senior civil service appointments. The various assessments of public sector performance in Kosovo all add up to a convincingly dismal picture of the current state of the administration.

Civil service size and cost

The size and cost of the civil service is sometimes taken as an indicator of the state of public administration in developing countries: a poor performing government is indicated by a bloated but low-paid civil service whose salaries are a drain on public finances. In Kosovo the available data on these measures is inconsistent and open to interpretation. In 2002, for example, the administration employed slightly fewer people per capita compared with other economies in the region, but because of Kosovo's high unemployment rate, low labour participation and high levels of informal economic activity, public sector employment was several times higher as a share of total employment.[109] Donors, advisers and the government have thus found it difficult to agree on the number of civil servants that would be appropriate for Kosovo and the salary levels that would be acceptable. Many people are convinced that the current size of the civil service is excessive. An international donor representative, for example, argued that 'it's a huge bubble in Kosovo. They employ I don't know how many people, thousands and thousands, so it's really big for a place which has less than two million people.'[110] A Kosovar working for an international organisation had much the same opinion:

> We have seen extension of civil service in size booming from year to year ... First, every politician that came there as Minister hired his own relative or his own friends, he provided a job for them. Secondly, UNMIK didn't care as long as there was peace. And employing more people means less people unemployed, less poverty, more quiet, nice, that's it. ... and we ended up with an enormous civil service.[111]

Based on information in official budget documents, however, the size of the administration has been relatively stable over an extended period. The number of civil service staff increased rapidly in 2003 and 2004, when the PISG ministries were created and UNMIK rushed to Kosovarise the functions it had previously been performing on the UN budget, but has remained remarkably steady since then. The 2015 budget provided salaries for around 82,000 staff, only 4,500 more than in 2004, despite the assumption of additional functions following independence and the creation of more municipalities as a result of decentralisation.[112]

The cost of the civil service is a different matter. Before the PISG was established the Pillar IV-led CFA, in keeping with IMF and World Bank advice, sought to keep civil service wage levels down and in 2003 an EAR review concluded that civil service salaries were low in relation to the cost of living.[113] Nevertheless, the IMF argued that, as a percentage of GDP, public sector wages in Kosovo were high compared to those in other transition economies and in the rest of the former Yugoslavia. Only Bosnia and Herzegovina, also a post-conflict territory under international supervision, had higher average public sector salaries.[114] Since then the IMF, the World Bank and other donors have consistently exhorted the government to restrain growth in the salary budget.

Other observers, however, were concerned that low public sector salaries contributed to the loss of trained civil servants and undermined government performance. Paradoxically, the steady development of the private sector, a primary goal of donors, has attracted well-qualified civil servants to better opportunities and higher salaries, particularly in the banking sector.[115] The presence of the international Mission itself and the discrepancy between the high salaries paid by international bodies and the level of government pay have also complicated public sector wage setting and been identified as a detriment to the performance of the government sector. One report described the situation as 'capacity asset stripping' by the international aid system, which denuded not only the public administration but also civil society organisations of leadership and technical and professional skills.[116] Another report concluded that UNMIK 'has apparently siphoned off the available supply of highly educated workers from the rest of the economy'.[117]

In 2010, senior Kosovo government officials saw low civil service salaries as a major problem in retaining staff, and an international adviser expressed concern about the impact on work effort: 'Morale has declined a lot. People are grateful to have a job ... but given the responsibilities and the pressures and the long hours some people work, it's not enough.'[118] Another agreed with this perception: 'I guess what I'm saying is that my guts tell me that there's a certain critical mass of money that you have to make before you just show up and sleep at your desk and go home.'[119] A Kosovar World Bank representative suggested that Kosovo's position relative to the region had changed over the years as a result of increases in public sector salaries in neighbouring countries[120] and this appears to be confirmed by IMF data showing that Kosovo's nominal public sector wages are now the lowest in the region.[121] The evidence on public sector size and cost is thus unclear. The Kosovo civil service is not necessarily too large in relation to the functions it is expected to perform, or too well paid by regional standards, although it may be too expensive for current economic conditions.

Politicisation

The high degree of politicisation of the Kosovo administration has long been a concern. Even when efforts were made to ensure merit-based recruitment, the perception by civil servants that their career depended on political allegiance more than on professional skills meant they only applied for positions in those ministries controlled by their preferred political faction. This led to an alignment of civil servants according to party politics, undermining attempts to ensure political neutrality and putting employees under pressure to act on the basis of political directives rather than following proper procedures.[122] Kai Eide, in 2005, noted a tendency among politicians to see government institutions as their personal domains and to make appointments on the basis of political or clan affiliations rather than competence.[123] This outcome is not surprising given that administrative responsibilities were consistently allocated by the UN on the basis of political affiliation, beginning with the creation of the JIAS departments in early 2000, and the system of coalition government that followed.

'Public Pulse' surveys indicate that recruitment on merit is still rare. In 2014, only 13 per cent of respondents considered education, professional experience and vocational training to be important for gaining employment in the public sector with 79 per cent believing that family connections, bribes and party alliance were most important.[124] Although the new Civil Service Law in 2010 removed the insecurity of short-term contract employment, weak enforcement of civil service management procedures means that ordinary civil servants remain vulnerable to political influence.[125] The annual reports of Kosovo's Auditor General, for example, continue to note evidence of the recruitment of staff without advertisement, additional salary and allowances paid without the necessary evidence, and promotions and appointments made without sufficient justification.[126]

Corruption

Opinions vary about the seriousness of corruption in Kosovo's public administration. In opinion surveys, corruption is identified as the third most serious problem facing Kosovo, although it comes well behind unemployment and poverty. In 2014, only 5 per cent of respondents said corruption was the most serious issue facing the country while 55 per cent nominated unemployment and 24 per cent said it was poverty.[127] Perceptions of the level of corruption in public institutions tend to move in step with changes in attitudes on other issues. According to Public Pulse data, concern about corruption declined significantly in early 2014, as satisfaction with the government improved. By late 2014, however, following a long stalemate over the election outcome, perceptions of corruption increased again, along with a rise in dissatisfaction with the government. This data illustrates the gap that often exists between perceptions of corruption and actual experience of it. Only 8 per cent of respondents reported that they had personally been asked for money, gifts or other favours in exchange for a service. Most people heard about the extent of corruption from the media, or from friends and relatives.[128] Well-publicised anti-corruption activity by EULEX, including the arrest of the head of the government's Anti-Corruption Task Force for alleged corruption, may have the effect of increasing public concern about the problem.[129] A Kosovar donor representative also felt that perceptions did not necessarily reflect reality: 'I think it's mainly perception of corruption ... I think for example if you look at Albania and you look at Kosovo, Albania is suffering much more from petty corruption which gives people alarming sense of corruption ... you don't have that here.'[130] Nevertheless, the number of firms reporting that corruption is a problem in doing business is above the average for South Eastern Europe[131] and Kosovo is currently ranked below all other former Yugoslav entities on Transparency International's 'Corruption Perception Index'.[132]

Productivity, efficiency and government performance

The civil administration in Kosovo clearly does not conform to the Weberian ideal of rule-based operations, employment on merit, political independence and freedom from corruption that is promoted by donors. This may not be important, however, if the government is able to deliver effective services to the public and to pursue economic development goals. Unfortunately Kosovo is also failing on this measure. Many staff do not have the necessary skills for their jobs and are not productively and efficiently employed, largely as a consequence of politicised or nepotistic recruitment and the predominant loyalty-based system of career progression.[133] As a senior MPA official described it, 'They will hire people with no experience at all. All day long they stay in their offices, drink coffee, surf the internet, because they don't have any relevant experience, and this is impacting on the processes of all other institutions and because of this we have stagnation of these processes for other institutions as well.'[134] Numerous international reports confirm poor professionalism, weak capacity and lack of motivation as characteristics of the civil service.[135] The alignment of government ministries to different political parties in an unstable coalition government has also had negative impacts on inter-ministerial cooperation and policy implementation.

Weak capacity and motivation has an adverse effect on service delivery. The Eide Report, in 2005, noted shortcomings in the quality of public services, particularly in health and education, where standards were low and services highly politicised.[136] Subsequent World Bank public expenditure reviews indicate that low standards in service delivery continue. The level of government spending on health is the lowest in the region, even measured as a percentage of Kosovo's low GDP, but hospital facilities are under-used and overstaffed and spending on pharmaceuticals and sophisticated medical equipment is excessive. Public spending on education is also low by regional standards, and maintenance of existing roads, schools and health facilities is under-funded.[137]

Kosovo also rates poorly on World Bank governance indicators, including on measures of government effectiveness and regulatory quality.[138] Deficiencies in bureaucratic and technical capacities at the local and central government levels have been identified as obstacles to economic development.[139] Although Kosovo's GDP has grown faster than other Western Balkan economies over recent years, economic competitiveness is undermined by structural impediments such as deficient public infrastructure, weak governance and a difficult business environment.[140]

Public opinion

The most important indicators of government effectiveness, however, are the opinions of citizens themselves and there is ample evidence from opinion surveys that there is considerable public dissatisfaction with Kosovo's administration. The level of satisfaction with the performance of the government has been declining steadily, from 53 per cent in 2009, a year after independence, to just 19 per cent in late 2014. Only 18.2 per cent of respondents believe that the Kosovo government is working according to the priorities of Kosovo citizens.[141] A much larger proportion, however, around 56 per cent, appear to be satisfied with the performance of their local municipal government.[142] Kosovars have also been 'voting with their feet' in recent times with record numbers of young Kosovars seeking, mostly unsuccessfully, to emigrate to EU countries in search of better opportunities.[143] Twenty-two percent of people surveyed in 2014 said they had plans to leave the country, with the overwhelming majority giving the unfavourable economic situation or seeking a better future as the reason.[144]

A missed opportunity

It is easy to attribute poor outcomes in this sector to inadequate performance by the lead actor in the field, the UN's Civil Administration component. However, the recruitment of a new civil service and the transfer of capacity to a self-governing administration 'presented a challenge of quite staggering proportions'[145] and it is likely that even a well-resourced and clearly targeted effort would have struggled in the conditions that existed in Kosovo immediately following the conflict. The UN Civil Administration, with confused objectives and inappropriate staff, was poorly equipped to prevent the rapid re-establishment of the worst aspects of former administrative practices and left the new Kosovo government with a mountain of public administration reform tasks to deal with.

Unclear objectives

UNMIK's civil administration component was very slow to do what it was mandated to do, that is, to 'establish the multi-ethnic governmental structures essential for the sustainable delivery of public services'.[146] This was primarily due to the absence of an agreed plan on what needed to be done. In contrast to the sense of purpose of PFM development, UNMIK's goals in the area of civil administration were unclear and sometimes disputed. UNSCR 1244 did not provide the Mission with clear objectives in relation to civil administration activities. In particular, to many in the UN, it did not imply engaging in either reform or capacity development. Planning for the Mission had assumed that an orderly transfer of a functioning administration would be possible, and when it was realised that much more would be required there was no effective alternative plan. Moreover, civil service development was just one of the many things on UNMIK's 'to do' list and it was easily crowded out by issues that were apparently more urgent. Progress in developing a local public administration was also hampered by the UN's relatively conservative approach to its administrative responsibilities, reinforced by protests from Belgrade and criticism in the General Assembly, and its reluctance to make decisions or implement reforms that might in any way be construed as prejudging Kosovo's eventual separation from Serbia. Its primary focus on maintaining peace and avoiding civil unrest predisposed it to short-term expediency and appeasement in lieu of assertive action to ensure future good governance.

In the conditions immediately after the end of the conflict, the mass return to work of former public employees may have been difficult to prevent and the proactive creation of a completely new cadre of public sector employees, as was done in most public finance institutions, may not have been feasible. The UN in Pillar II missed a significant opportunity, however, to exert control of the civil service in 1999 and 2000, and did not do enough later to make up for this by developing, implementing and enforcing good management practices in the new administration. More could have been done, perhaps, to ensure that the emergency employment phase, under the 'stipend' arrangement, was temporary and to insist that permanent employment would be based on impartial merit selection and the needs of each organisation, following the model established by Pillar IV. This would have helped to ensure that staff had the ability to do their jobs, and had jobs to do. It may also have opened up more opportunities for younger people and women, rather than preserving the aging, male-dominated workforce of the past.

Instead, the uncontrolled return to previous workplaces and the reactivation of the parallel education and health services, aimed at resolving the immediate issue of restoring economic activity and normality, lent support to pre-existing ideas about public sector employment as an entitlement, a form of social welfare or an instrument of political influence. The civil service in Kosovo soon acquired the features of public sector behaviour found in so many developing countries, characterised by reliance on personal and political connections, vague boundaries between public and private interests, and the diversion of public resources for political objectives.

Inadequate and inappropriate resources

Confusion over exactly what the UN was supposed to do in relation to civil administration was compounded by delays in mobilising the Mission, partly due to the short preparation time allowed by the UNSC, but also because of the UN's administrative practices, procurement bottlenecks and budget inflexibilities. UNMIK had difficulty recruiting enough people to fill all the available positions in the civilian administration, let alone finding staff with appropriate knowledge and experience. Although there were many in the UN Pillar who were competent and motivated, others were inappropriately qualified and sometimes of questionable quality. Their predominantly diplomatic or military experience was not necessarily a relevant background for civil administration tasks:

> The people definitely had political experience. They'd seen a lot of conflict situations, but for administration, I don't think UNMIK could really boast many good people you know ... there was no specific recruitment by the UN. It was the same sort of people who continued to work for the government ... many of them had military background and not really had much experience, but they were eminently suited for the crisis period. But for the administration you needed a lot of people with administrative experience.[147]

Regardless of the quality of the UN personnel, UNMIK's Civil Administration Pillar never had the number of staff that would have been needed to effectively recruit, manage and develop the thousands of Kosovars who made up the civil service. One year after the start of the Mission, when UN employment was at its peak, 906 international staff were meant to oversee the work of around 50,000 public sector workers.[148] In the JIAS Departments of Education and Health, a handful of international officials were nominally responsible for around 38,000 public employees. Not surprisingly, there was little the UNMIK civil administration could do other than cede day-to-day control of these staff to political interests and power brokers.

The support provided by other international actors in this field was also inadequate. The funding made available by EAR for the review of civil service pay grades in 2003, for example, was small relative to the significance of the problems it was intended to address, and did not include the resources to ensure the proposed reforms were implemented. DFID's main contribution during this period had an adequate budget and achieved success in some of its activities but neglected the political dimensions of civil service development and was undermined by the poor performance of its UN partners.

The multinational make-up of UNMIK, with officials drawn from each of the various UN member countries, contributed further confusion and uneven development in civil administration functions. Lacking effective policy coordination within UNMIK, many officials simply replicated practices that were familiar to them. As one UN observer described it, 'in the civil ministries which were under UNMIK, the administration is evolving along the lines of the country from where the senior international officer is coming from, because there is no definitive blueprint. So it is evolving as if it was a mirror of the boss of that department. It was a classic *pot pourri* you know'.[149] This problem was also very apparent to some Kosovars: 'You had an administrator coming from one country in UNMIK for three months and he would have his set of ideas, and then you would have another administrator that would come from somewhere else, somewhere maybe even worse than Kosovo, with his other set of ideas.'[150] Although technical advisers working for USAID and EU projects also sometimes brought divergent ideas from their own past, the organised structure of donor-funded assistance meant they were generally subject to firmer specification of the policies and systems expected to be implemented. UN staff, in contrast, were largely left to run their departments as fiefdoms according to their own preferences.

Reluctant Kosovarisation

The UN civil administration departments were relatively slow to recruit and train local staff to take over administrative responsibilities. While Pillar IV began training Kosovars for management roles in public finance institutions a few months after the start of the Mission, some Pillar II departments, in particular the DPS, were largely staffed by international officials rather than civil servants for a considerable period. A concerted effort by UNMIK to recruit local staff to management positions was still under way in 2003, at a time when PFM institutions such as the MFE and the Tax Administration had already been transferred to Kosovar operational control. This late 'Kosovarisation' of the PISG ministries had the effect of presenting more opportunities for politicisation of the civil service. Although UN officials were involved in the appointment of senior positions, a Kosovar government official noted that at lower levels there was scope for manipulation of the process: 'The idea was to give most of the competencies to locals in order for them to decide … but certainly it was misused because after that they started to hire people, their friends, relatives, political affiliates as well.'[151]

Political challenges

While the performance of UNMIK's civil administration could certainly have been better with clearer objectives, appropriate staff and more resources, it must be acknowledged that the situation in which the administration was working was extremely difficult. The size, diversity and geographical spread of the civil service made effective external control difficult. The UN had enough difficulty managing within its own organisation and between its central and regional offices. Its ability to influence the actions of local civil servants throughout the territory and to prevent the re-activation of earlier traditions of administration, work practices and power relationships was consequently very limited.

Some of the patterns of behaviour established by UNMIK did little to challenge the politicisation of the public sector. When the JIAS administrative departments were established in early 2000, the right to nominate national Co-Heads to manage them was handed to the leading political factions. It is perhaps not surprising, therefore, that there was an expectation that other positions in the bureaucracy could be filled in a similar way. An international Co-Head in Pillar IV reported conflict with his Kosovar counterpart on this question: 'The biggest issue was recruitment because we were trying to run an open, transparent, merit-based recruitment process and he would keep coming to me with "look here's a person I think you should give a job to", so we had some differences on that.'[152] It is not known whether other international Co-Heads were as firm on this issue. The electoral system adopted under international administration to share power between political factions and the consequent allocation of PISG ministries among political parties further contributed to making government ministries into political territories, hampering policy development and implementation and further undermining the idea of merit-based employment. These precedents continue to challenge efforts to establish the concept of apolitical administration and appointment on merit.

Peace versus development

This account of the creation of the civil service in Kosovo reveals a significant difference in approach between the UN, on the one hand, and most development actors on the other. Based on the wording of the Security Council resolution, the UN quite understandably saw its role primarily as ensuring peace and stability in the territory and this, at least in part, motivated its policies of economic stimulation through public sector employment and political appeasement through the allocation of positions of power in the administration.

Most other participants in the post-conflict reconstruction exercise, however, had a completely different set of priorities, determined largely by the economic policies they considered necessary for long-term economic stability and good administrative performance. They pursued the idea of a 'lean and productive' civil service through restraint on public sector numbers and wage levels. Their control of the Kosovo budget and the influence of the IMF on fiscal policy ensured that the size and cost of the administration was controlled. These economic policies could not, however, influence the quality, diligence and political independence of the civil service, leaving Kosovo with an administration that may be sufficiently lean, but is also relatively unproductive.

It is difficult to say which of these two very different approaches to the post-conflict situation was in fact the correct one. A tighter, less politically flexible and more economically rationalist approach by the UN to civil administration may have produced better government performance today, or it may have generated political unrest and stronger resistance to external intervention. Placing control of economic and fiscal policy in the hands of the UN civil administration, as initially proposed, may or may not have resulted in unsustainable levels of public expenditure, lower revenue collections, looser controls on public funds and an extended period of dependence on donors.

The experience of the development of the legal framework for civil service management also shows the limits of imposing existing models and blueprints without adaptation to the environment. While DFID is quite right in arguing that it is the principles underlying the legislation that are important, and complaints by Kosovo's politicians about DFID's 'imposition' of the civil service laws may in fact have stemmed from their reluctance to be constrained by the rules they put in place, a lack of awareness and understanding of the legal and political environment to some extent undermined implementation of the civil service regime. But this was not the main obstacle to DFID's efforts to establish sound management of the civil service. Its work was also undermined by the almost inexplicable tardiness of the UN civil administration in implementing the laws.

Other problems in the establishment of the civil service were perhaps an unavoidable consequence of the post-conflict context and the underdeveloped economic environment. The presence of large numbers of international actors and the lack of other employment opportunities pushed salaries up, drained talent from the civil service and made jobs in the administration valuable political resources. The challenges facing public administration in Kosovo today might not be as serious, however, if more had been done initially to put in place the basics of sound public sector management. Instead the UN used highly paid UN staff to perform tasks that could have been done by Kosovar civil servants, and then faced the problem of transferring these functions to local personnel on much lower salaries. Other donors, however, also showed little apparent interest in this aspect of reconstruction in the early years and most of their subsequent interventions have been under-resourced and intermittent. Donors such as DFID and EAR began to address these issues only as the prospect of an elected Kosovo government became a reality and the absence of the necessary laws, procedures and staff became obvious. By that stage, however, the post-conflict advantage of the (relatively) clean slate had been lost. The absence of decisive steps to establish alternative rules, incentives and norms allowed an ineffective and politicised public administration to become entrenched and subsequent efforts at public administration reform have thus had to confront ingrained traditions and assumptions, as well as the vested interests of political leaders.

Notes

1 H.-J. Chang, *Kicking Away the Ladder: Development Strategy in Historical Perspective* (London: Anthem, 2002) 76–80; E. Kamenka and M. Krygier, *Bureaucracy: The Career of a Concept* (New York: St. Martin's Press, 1979).
2 M. Weber, 'Bureaucracy' in H. H. Gerth and C. Mills (eds), *From Max Weber: Essays in Sociology* (London: Routledge & Kegan Paul, 1970) 196–244.
3 Quoted in Kamenka and Krygier, *Bureaucracy: The Career of a Concept* 24.
4 Weber, 'Bureaucracy'.

5 Johnson, *Japan, who Governs?: The Rise of the Developmental State*; Leftwich, *States of Development: On the Primacy of Politics in Development*; World Bank, *The East Asian Miracle: Economic Growth and Public Policy* (New York: Oxford University Press, 1993).
6 Dimitrova, 'Enlargement, institution-building and the EU's administrative capacity requirement' 177–8.
7 SIGMA, *The Principles of Public Administration* (Paris: OECD, 2014); World Bank, *Country Policy and Institutional Assessments: 2010 Assessment Questionnaire* (Washington, DC: World Bank, 2010).
8 E. Ferlie, L. Ashburner, L. Fitzgerald and A. Pettigrew, *The New Public Management in Action* (Oxford: Oxford Scholarship Online, 1996); D. Osborne and T. Gaebler, *Reinventing Government: How the Entrepreneurial Spirit is Transforming the Public Sector* (New York: Plume, 1992).
9 Goetz, 'Making sense of post communist central administration' 1033.
10 World Bank/European Commission, *Towards Stability and Prosperity* 14.
11 UNSC, *Report of the Secretary General on the United Nations Interim Administration Mission in Kosovo, 12 July 1999* para 56.
12 UNMIK, *UNMIK News Archive 1999*.
13 Power, 'Kosovo dispatch: breathing room' 19.
14 International UNMIK official (IU3).
15 International UNMIK official (IU1).
16 International donor representative (ID1).
17 ICG, *Waiting for UNMIK: Local Administration in Kosovo*, ICG Balkans Report N° 79 (Pristina: International Crisis Group, 1999); World Bank, *Kosovo: Building Peace through Sustained Growth*; World Bank, *Conflict and Change in Kosovo: Impact on Institutions and Society* (Washington, DC: World Bank, 2000).
18 World Bank/European Commission, *Towards Stability and Prosperity* 24.
19 International Civil Service Commission, *Review of the Methodology for Surveys of Best Prevailing Conditions of Employment at Non-Headquarters Duty Stations* (New York: United Nations, 2003).
20 UNMIK, *The New Kosovo Government 2002 Budget*.
21 King and Mason, *Peace at any Price*.
22 European Commission, *Commission Decision on establishing a programme for exceptional targeted support for public services under the 1999 Kosovo budget* (Brussels: European Commission, 1999) 5.
23 del Castillo, *Rebuilding War-Torn States* 150.
24 International UNMIK official (IU3).
25 UNMIK/REG/1999/27, 22 December 1999; UNMIK/European Union, *Kosovo Consolidated Budget 1 January–31 December 2000* (Pristina: Central Fiscal Authority, Pillar IV, 1999) 1.
26 Dixon, *Speech at First Donor's Conference for Kosovo, Brussels, July 28*.
27 World Bank, *Kosovo: Building Peace through Sustained Growth* 17.
28 Dixon, *Speech at First Donor's Conference for Kosovo, Brussels, July 28*; Seale, 'Establishing financial management in the Kosovo interim administration'.
29 UNMIK/REG/ 1999/1, 1 July 1999, Section 1, Clause 2.
30 UN General Assembly, *Financing of the United Nations Interim Administration Mission in Kosovo: Report of the Secretary General, 22 October 1999*, 18–19.
31 Barents Group, Government infrastructure support, United Nations Mission in Kosovo, Pillar IV – Weekly reports 1999, November.
32 International UNMIK official (IU1).

33 UNMIK/REG/1999/16, 6 November 1999, Section 6.
34 World Bank, *Conflict and Change in Kosovo* 19.
35 UNMIK, *UNMIK News Archive 2000*, February.
36 Congressional Research Service, *Kosovo: Reconstruction and Development Assistance* 7; ICG, *Kosovo Report Card* 29.
37 ICG, *Kosovo Report Card* 3.
38 UNMIK/REG/2000/12, 14 March 2000 para 2.1 (b).
39 UNMIK/REG/2001/19, 13 September 2001.
40 DFID, 'Terms of reference: Support to drafting of Kosovo Basic Public Service Law as an UNMIK Regulation' (unpublished document held by DFID Office, Pristina, 2001) para 11.
41 UNMIK/REG/2001/36, 22 December 2001.
42 DFID, 'Kosovo civil service personnel policies and procedures: Implementation programme, project memorandum' (unpublished document held by DFID Office, Pristina, 2001) 18–19.
43 DFID, 'Output to purpose review of Kosovo civil service personnel management project' (unpublished document held by DFID Office, Pristina, 2003) 16.
44 DFID, 'Terms of reference: Support to drafting of Kosovo Basic Public Service Law as an UNMIK Regulation', para 7.
45 Personal communication, PDK member Jakup Krasniqi, 2002.
46 UNMIK, *Kosovo: UNMIK-Government Report for the Donor Coordination Meeting for Kosovo, Brussels, 5 November 2002*, 20.
47 UNSC, *Report of the Secretary General on the United Nations Interim Administration Mission in Kosovo, 15 January 2002* para 12.
48 UNSC, *Report of the Secretary General on the United Nations Interim Administration Mission in Kosovo, 29 January 2003* (New York: United Nations Security Council, 2003) para 3.
49 UN General Assembly, *Performance Report on the Budget of the United Nations Interim Administration Mission in Kosovo for the Period from 1 July 2003 to 30 June 2004, Report of the Secretary General* (New York: United Nations General Assembly, 2004); UNSC, *Report of the Secretary General on the United Nations Interim Administration Mission in Kosovo, 14 April 2003* (New York: United Nations Security Council, 2003).
50 UN General Assembly, *Performance Report on the Budget of the United Nations Interim Administration Mission in Kosovo for the Period from 1 July 2004 to 30 June 2005, Report of the Secretary-General* (New York: United Nations General Assembly, 2005).
51 USAID, *USAID Mission in Kosovo Strategic Plan 2004–2008* (Pristina: United States Agency for International Development, 2003) 2.
52 UNSC, *Report of the Secretary-General on the United Nations Interim Administration Mission in Kosovo, 26 January 2004* (New York: United Nations Security Council, 2004) para 5.
53 DANIDA, *Evaluation: Humanitarian and Rehabilitation Assistance to Kosovo, 1999–2003*, 72.
54 Quoted in ibid. 72. Parentheses in original.
55 Skendaj, *Creating Kosovo: Intenational Oversight and the Making of Ethical Institutions* 79–80.
56 Dobbins, 'The UN's role in nation-building' 87.
57 International UNMIK official (IU4).
58 DFID, 'Kosovo civil service personnel policies and procedures: Implementation Programme, project memorandum' 8.
59 DFID, 'Output to purpose review of Kosovo civil service personnel management project'.
60 Ibid.; DFID, 'Project completion review narrative report: Kosovo civil service personnel management project' (unpublished document held by DFID Office, Pristina, 2004).
61 UNMIK/REG//2003/2, 25 January 2003.
62 International UNMIK official (IU1).

63 UNMIK/REG/19/2001, 13 September 2001, Annex I, Part E.
64 I was an observer at one Cabinet meeting at which ministers from all the coalition partners were essentially of the same view. They complained bitterly about the appointment of permanent secretaries and blamed the international officials for imposing this process on them.
65 Wittkowsky, 'Squaring the circle' 32.
66 International UNMIK official (IU1).
67 UNDP, *Assessment of Administrative Capacity in Kosovo.*
68 DFID, 'Output to purpose review of Kosovo civil service personnel management project' 6.
69 DFID, 'Project completion review narrative report: Kosovo civil service personnel management project' 7.
70 DFID, 'Output to purpose review of Kosovo civil service personnel management project' 6.
71 OSCE, 'Helping Kosovo's institutions improve public service' web page (Pristina: Organisation for Security Cooperation in Europe, 2008).
72 UNDP, *Assessment of Administrative Capacity in Kosovo.*
73 DFID, 'Project completion review narrative report: Kosovo civil service personnel management project', 7; OSCE, Helping Kosovo's institutions improve public service.
74 UNMIK/REG/2008/12, 27 February 2008.
75 Early Warning Report, *Kosovo Early Warning Report No. 1*, 7–8.
76 UNMIK, *The New Kosovo Government 2002 Budget* 33.
77 UNMIK, *Kosovo: UNMIK-Government Report for the Donor Coordination Meeting for Kosovo, Brussels, 5 November 2002*, 25.
78 Early Warning Report, *Kosovo Early Warning Report No. 4*, 28–9.
79 World Bank, *Kosovo: Medium Term Public Expenditure Priorities* (Washington, DC: World Bank, 2002) 38–9.
80 HELM and PAI, 'Kosovo civil service proposed new pay and grading system: Final report' (unpublished work in possession of author, 2004) 12–14; World Bank, *Kosovo: Medium Term Public Expenditure Priorities* 35.
81 Kosovar government official (KG4).
82 HELM and PAI, 'Kosovo civil service proposed new pay and grading system: Final report'.
83 European Agency for Reconstruction, *EAR Annual Report 2004* (Thessaloniki: European Agency for Reconstruction, 2005) 22.
84 Kosovar government official (KG3).
85 Kosovar government official (KG1).
86 World Bank, *Implementation Completion Report: Economic Assistance Grant IV Kosovo* 12.
87 International civil service adviser (IA9).
88 Kosovar technical adviser (KA3).
89 European Commission, *Kosovo 2005 Progress Report.*
90 UNDESA, *Public Administration in Kosovo: Situational Analysis and Strategy, Draft Discussion Paper* (New York: UN Department of Economic and Social Affairs, 2003) viii.
91 UNMIK, *Kosovo Standards Implementation Plan (KSIP)* (Pristina: United Nations Mission in Kosovo, 2004).
92 UNMIK/PISG, *Kosovo: Public Administration Strategy 2004–2006, Towards a Professional, Responsive and Impartial Public Service (Draft)* (Pristina: United Nations Mission in Kosovo; Provisional Institutions of Self Government, 2004).
93 UNDP, *Assessment of Administrative Capacity in Kosovo* 7.
94 Government of Kosovo, *Report on the Status of Public Administration in Kosovo* (Pristina: Ministry of Public Services, Group of Experts for Public Administration Reform, 2007);

Government of Kosovo, *Strategy for Public Administration Reform* (Pristina: Ministry of Public Services, Group of Experts for Public Administration Reform, 2007); Government of Kosovo, *Action Plan for Public Administration Reform in Kosovo (2009 Revision)* (Pristina: Ministry of Public Services, 2009).

95 Government of Kosovo, *Report on the Status of Public Administration in Kosovo* 23.

96 FRIDOM, *Whole of Government Review, Functional Review and Institutional Design of Ministries* (Pristina: Ministry of Public Administration, 2008).

97 SIGMA, *Public Administration Reform Assessment of Kosovo 2014* (Paris: OECD, Support for Improvement in Governance and Management, 2014).

98 DFID, 'Output to purpose review of Kosovo civil service personnel management project' 14.

99 International civil service adviser (IA9).

100 Kosovar technical adviser (KA3).

101 Ibid.

102 Republic of Kosovo Law No 03/L-149, 13 May 2010.

103 International civil service adviser (IA9).

104 Kosovar government official (KG4).

105 World Bank, *Kosovo Public Expenditure Review* (Washington, DC: World Bank, 2010).

106 Republic of Kosovo Law No. 03/L-192, 15 July 2010.

107 Republic of Kosovo Law No 03/L-147, 13 May 2010.

108 European Commission, *Kosovo 2014 Progress Report*; OSCE, *The Implementation of Civil Service Legislation in Kosovo* (Pristina: Organisation for Security and Cooperation in Europe: Mission in Kosovo, 2013); SIGMA, *Assessment: Kosovo 2012*; SIGMA, *Public Administration Reform Assessment of Kosovo 2014*.

109 World Bank, *Kosovo: Medium Term Public Expenditure Priorities* 34.

110 International donor representative (ID1).

111 Kosovar donor representative (KD2).

112 Data from UNMIK Budget Regulations 1999–2008 (www.unmikonline.org) and Kosovo Government Budget Laws 2008–2014 (www.gazetazyrtare.com).

113 HELM and PAI, 'Kosovo civil service proposed new pay and grading system: Final report'.

114 IMF, *Kosovo: Macroeconomic Issues and Fiscal Sustainability* 11.

115 Early Warning Report, *Kosovo Early Warning Report No. 15, October–December 2006* (Pristina: UNDP, 2006) 19.

116 DANIDA, *Evaluation: Humanitarian and Rehabilitation Assistance to Kosovo 1999–2003*.

117 UNMIK, *UNMIK's Impact on the Kosovo Economy: Spending Effects 1999–2006 and Potential Consequences of Downsizing* (Pristina: EU Pillar Economic Policy Office, 2006) 21.

118 International EU customs adviser (IA10).

119 International EU public finance adviser (IA4).

120 Kosovar donor representative (KD2).

121 IMF, *Republic of Kosovo: Staff Report for the 2013 Article IV Consultation*, IMF Country Report No. 222 (Washington, DC: International Monetary Fund, 2013) 32.

122 UNSC, *Report of the Secretary General on the United Nations Interim Administration Mission in Kosovo, 14 April 2003*, 2–3; UNSC, *Report of the Secretary-General on the United Nations Interim Administration Mission in Kosovo, 26 January 2004*, 2.

123 UNSC, *A Comprehensive Review of the Situation in Kosovo (Eide Report)* 9.

124 Public Pulse, *Public Pulse Report No. 8 – November 2014* (Pristina: UNDP, 2014).

125 D. Doli, F. Korenica and A. Rogova, 'The post-independence civil service in Kosovo: A message of politicization', *International Review of Administrative Sciences* 78: 4 (2012) 665–91.

126 Office of the Auditor General, *Annual Audit Report 2013*.

127 Public Pulse, *Public Pulse Report No. 8*.
128 Public Pulse, *Public Pulse Report No. 6, August 2013* (Pristina: UNDP, 2013).
129 Balkan Insight, 'Kosovo anti-corruption chief held for corruption', Balkan Investigative Reporting Network (3 April 2012).
130 Kosovar donor representative (KD4).
131 EBRD, *Business Environment and Enterprise Performance Survey (BEEPS) V: Country Profile Kosovo* (London: European Bank for Reconstruction and Development, 2015); World Bank, *Interim Strategy Note for Kosovo for the period FY08* (Washington, DC: World Bank, 2007) 5.
132 www.transparency.org/cpi2014/results#myAnchor1, accessed 6 May 2015.
133 USAID, *Human and Institutional Capacity Development (HICD) Assessment: Kosovo* (Washington, DC: United States Agency for International Development, 2012); USAID, *Human and Institutional Capacity Development Assessment: Kosovo. Final Report, Part II* (Washington, DC: United States Agency for International Development, 2012); World Bank, *Public Expenditure Management Technical Assistance Project (PEMTAG), Project Appraisal Document* 21.
134 Kosovar government official (KG4).
135 European Commission, *Kosovo 2013 Progress Report*; European Commission, *Kosovo 2014 Progress Report*; SIGMA, *Assessment Kosovo 2013*; SIGMA, *Public Administration Reform Assessment of Kosovo 2014*.
136 UNSC, *A Comprehensive Review of the Situation in Kosovo (Eide Report)* 9.
137 World Bank, *Kosovo Public Expenditure Review*; World Bank, *Kosovo Public Finance Review: Fiscal Policies for a Young Nation* (Washington, DC: World Bank, 2014).
138 World Bank, *Kosovo Public Finance Review*.
139 US Department of State, *Doing Business in Kosovo: 2012 Country Commercial Guide for U.S. Companies* (Washington, DC: U.S. and Foreign Commercial Service and US Department of State, 2012) 2.
140 IMF, *Republic of Kosovo: Staff Report for the 2013 Article IV Consultation*.
141 Public Pulse, *Public Pulse Report No. 8*.
142 Public Pulse, *Public Pulse Report No. 7 – June 2014* (Pristina: UNDP, 2014).
143 Balkan Insight, *Thousands leave Kosovo Seeking Asylum in EU*, Balkan Investigative Reporting Network (9 February 2015).
144 Public Pulse, *Public Pulse Report No. 7*.
145 DANIDA, *Evaluation: Humanitarian and Rehabilitation Assistance to Kosovo, 1999–2003*, 26.
146 UNSC, *Report of the Secretary General on the United Nations Interim Administration Mission in Kosovo, 12 July 1999*, 11.
147 International UNMIK official (IU4).
148 UNMIK Regulation 1999/27 (On the Approval of the 2000 Kosovo Consolidated Budget); UN General Assembly budget for UNMIK 2000–2001.
149 International UNMIK official (IU4).
150 Kosovar technical adviser (KA1).
151 Kosovar government official (KG4).
152 International USAID public finance adviser (IA1).

Conclusion

The events in Kosovo in the early years of the post-conflict period may seem like ancient history to people working there today. The mistakes and inadequacies of previous international efforts cannot be undone and those who are involved in current attempts to make the country conform to ideas about best practice must deal with the situation as they now find it. But the international community continues to find new green fields of post-conflict territory on which to build the type of institutions they consider necessary for future security and prosperity. Since Kosovo, reconstruction exercises of various scales have been launched in East Timor, Afghanistan, Iraq, the Solomon Islands, Liberia and South Sudan, and they have generally adopted a similar programme of building new institutions, or re-engineering old ones, to achieve long-term social, political and economic transformation. Given that international organisations and developed country governments can be expected to continue to launch efforts to transform post-conflict territories, or indeed any country classified as 'underdeveloped', what does the experience in Kosovo tell us about the enterprise? This account of the development of public administration in the post-conflict era in Kosovo provides insights into both the big picture issues of what international actors attempted to achieve and whether they achieved it, and more detailed questions about the effectiveness of the methods they used in pursuit of their objectives.

The goal of transformation

It is clear that the goal of most international actors in Kosovo was, and still is, to transform it into a society with 'Western' or more specifically 'European' institutions, values and behaviours. As King and Mason observe, this 'would require Kosovo to become a kind of society it had never been before'.[1] For most this meant a multi-ethnic, law-abiding, democratic society with a free market economy. The international enterprise in Kosovo therefore followed, more or less, the patterns that had been applied in previous decades by the same actors in the transition countries of Eastern and Central Europe, in previous post-conflict missions, and indeed in most less developed economies. Only the UN itself was not fully committed to the vision of transformation and this had a significant impact on what it did in the field of public administration development. The Security Council resolution said nothing that could be construed as authorising radical change and the policies of the UN Mission in this respect were thus unclear and inconsistent. UNMIK officials were often 'making it up as they went along'.[2] In carrying out its civil administration role, therefore, the UN often simply reacted, sometimes reluctantly, to the development initiatives of its partners in the Mission, rather than leading or coordinating this process.

The transformation strategy

The transformational objective of the majority of international actors was pursued in several ways. One of these was by adopting a 'blank slate' approach to the administration of Kosovo and assuming a complete break with the institutions and practices of the FRY. While the exact details of the Western, modern or 'rational' institutions and behaviours considered necessary for Kosovo were not always fully agreed by the international actors themselves, whatever the best model was, it was not what Kosovo already had. The legitimacy of this approach under the terms of UNSCR 1244 hinged on how the Mission could reconcile the idea of 'substantial autonomy and meaningful self-administration for Kosovo' with the commitment of UN member states to 'the sovereignty and territorial integrity of the Federal Republic of Yugoslavia'.[3] Most actors took the view that rationality and modernisation should take precedence over any attempt to retain institutional links with the government in Belgrade, and the political regime in Belgrade at the time in any case made this the simplest option. Kosovo thus soon had a different currency, its own customs rates and tax laws, and new budget institutions, payment systems and accounting processes.

In most cases the new institutions and procedures were based on established pre-existing models. These practices provide ample support to critics who see development assistance and post-conflict reconstruction in terms of the imposition of the norms of the dominant power. USAID applied the template it had used in transition economies, based on its own ideological assumptions about what was necessary. The EU explicitly used the 'blueprints' it had developed for its own members and other prospective accession candidates. Sometimes this approach was successful. In fields that are largely technical and where there is limited scope for variation, introducing procedures or systems that have been tested elsewhere is as good a place to start as any. However, one of the main problems with the use of existing models, imported from different national governments or other development assistance projects, in this context was the lack of effective policy coordination between international actors. DFID's attempt to insert an ideal type Westminster civil service into an electoral system based on proportional representation and a political distribution of ministry responsibilities, for example, was bound to run into trouble. The UN had already established the precedent of administrative ministries as political property and the idea of an apolitical 'permanent secretary' did not fit this model. This example illustrates several common potential problems in international intervention including failure to appreciate the political implications of an apparently technical reform, and the need for effective coordination between international actors that may have avoided this problem. The DFID project was also one of the many examples of the use of divergent and incompatible legal drafting conventions and terminologies which has left Kosovo with a mishmash of sometimes conflicting and inconsistently drafted laws and systems.[4]

Conditionality has been another important strategy of the international actors in Kosovo. The international organisations had a significant carrot to offer: the possibility of independence. For Albanian Kosovars, independence was the primary and indeed only objective and Kosovo's leaders would quite probably have been prepared to comply with almost any externally imposed policy agenda that appeared likely to deliver a future outside Serbia. The Kosovars were therefore generally willing to cooperate with the wishes of the international actors and this provided the opportunity to introduce new ideas and practices. Some organisations grabbed this opportunity with enthusiasm. Others were more reluctant.

Now that the independence goal has been largely achieved it has been replaced by a new carrot, the possibility of membership of the EU and the financial and social benefits it might bring. EU conditionality associated with Kosovo's potential membership aspirations has had a significant impact in stimulating institutional reform action on the part of the Kosovo authorities, although it is not clear to what extent the demanding agenda of EU-imposed reforms is in fact benefiting Kosovo. Questions remain about the appropriateness of some EU institutional models in this context and there is concern that the government may simply be going through the motions of reform without real commitment. The assumed benefits of EU integration seem as far away as ever for Kosovo, and the discipline applied by the EU enlargement process may simply be creating resistance to external interference, as evidenced by the growth in support for the nationalist Vetëvendosje party.

Conditionality has also been used by other actors. The World Bank offered budget grants to support its recommended fiscal policies and financial procedures, and the IMF is also now, since Kosovo became a member, in a position to use its financial influence to gain compliance with its policies. The demands of these programmes are more narrowly targeted at achieving specific fiscal policy outcomes than the EU's reform menu. EU, IMF and World Bank conditionality has arguably had a much greater impact on the actions of the government than any of the aid projects that have been implemented by international organisations.

Kosovo has been subjected to a very lengthy period of international tutelage. The international administration under UNMIK lasted longer than perhaps most people anticipated and technically it still continues, as the resolution that established it has not been rescinded. Even after local and national elections the UN maintained a high level of control over the activities of the government and the deliberations of the Assembly. Since independence EULEX has continued to be closely involved in some aspects of the administration, and the OCR's 'supervised independence' role continued until 2012. The UN Mission in Kosovo was, therefore, somewhat closer to Roland Paris's proposed 'institution building first' strategy of extended and intrusive international intervention while the basics of stable institutions are built.[5] It is clear from the different development paths of Kosovo's institutions, however, that an intrusive international presence on its own is not sufficient. What the international presence does and how it is done is also important. The UN Mission did not appear to have an agreed script on this issue. On the one hand, UNMIK's tendency to unilaterally overrule the elected Kosovo Assembly, rewrite legislation and revise the budget generated hostility and resistance in the local population, potentially undermining the achievements of the Mission. On the other hand, in many areas of administration a tentative, minimalist UN approach has left Kosovo with ineffective institutions. Largely as a result of resource constraints and a policy vacuum, the UN often simply abrogated responsibility, failing to intervene, for example, in the spontaneous formation of the civil service, or to effectively manage it subsequently. The balance between these extremes of international supervision is difficult to find and was not found by the UN in Kosovo. The approach taken in some PFM institutions may be closer to what Paris had in mind. International actors retained a degree of high-level control while nevertheless enabling local personnel to manage day-to-day operations. Close attention to issues of merit, ethics and performance resulted in several well-functioning state institutions.

Outcomes

Many believed that the transformation of Kosovo should have been possible given the massive investment of resources and the number of well-intentioned foreigners involved. International intervention has not, however, been able to turn Kosovo into a multi-ethnic, law-abiding, democratic society. Numerous assessments describe the ways in which Kosovo today is considered to fall short of these ambitious ideals. In the sphere of public administration, reports of corruption, politicisation and mismanagement, and the negative opinions of Kosovo's own citizens suggest that this goal is still some distance away.

International intervention has also failed to transform the economy. Despite success in developing economic institutions, international actors have not achieved the economic growth and prosperity initially proposed as the path to political stability. While living conditions have certainly improved for many people since the end of the conflict, performance on most economic and human development indicators is disappointing. Kosovo is still a relatively poor country with high unemployment, high levels of poverty, dependence on diaspora remittances, and slow and uneven economic growth.[6] The continuing problems of unemployment, low exports and limited foreign investment are all the more disappointing given that, under the policies promoted by international organisations, Kosovo's business environment has been made particularly attractive to investors. It has a relatively flexible labour market, few constraints on hiring and firing, an open trade regime, and a strong, competitive banking sector.[7]

Kosovo has not been transformed by international actors, but many other objectives of the international involvement have been achieved. For the majority of the population, life is now more secure and rewarding. Thousands of Kosovars have had access to training and new experiences that would never have been possible otherwise. The country has a relatively stable government and has been provided with a set of public institutions that are, on the whole, no worse and sometimes much better than those of other places with similar economic circumstances. Thus, measured against a relatively modest set of benchmarks, much of what the international community has done over the past decade and a half can be considered a success. There is undoubtedly scope for further improvement, but the Kosovo authorities have some of the basic tools for effective public administration, if they choose to use them. None of this would have been achieved if the international community had simply stuck to the holding pattern of keeping the peace, substantial autonomy and a return to Serb sovereignty outlined in UNSCR 1244.

What worked and what didn't?

In donors' plans for development assistance they are constantly striving to 'control the variables, manipulate the incentives, remove the constraints, realign the connections, set the sequence and timing of things and build an orderly process'.[8] The real world of project implementation, however, is much more complex. Development assistance is not a science. Its outcomes are not predictable or controllable. It is a political activity, sometimes motivated by self-interest and often much closer to the 'chaos' described by my friend in Kosovo than the rational, harmonised process illustrated in the flowcharts and logframes in donor reports.

The various international activities in public finance and the civil service suffered from the same obstacles and pitfalls that have affected development projects elsewhere, but some suffered more than others. Success in institution building and capacity development depended, firstly, on the capacities of the international actors themselves and their experience in this kind of activity. Agreement on the goals and a willingness to work together, the level of resources and the intensity of effort were also clearly important. The unprecedented level of international control over the new institutions that was possible in this post-conflict environment and what the international personnel chose to do with it, in particular their ability to ensure merit recruitment and insulation from political interference, were also crucial.

Donor capacities

Each of the international actors involved in Kosovo's public administration development brought different interests, resources and capacities to the task. Their activities were influenced by their ideological and economic objectives and organisational capabilities, and there was often competition between them and between their representatives on the ground including individual consultants and experts. One commentator has suggested that the divided pillar structure of the Kosovo Mission caused poorer outcomes compared to the single UN pillar in East Timor.[9] It is probably more accurate, however, to say that the pillar structure in Kosovo succeeded in rescuing some parts of the reconstruction exercise from the ineffectiveness of the UN-run civil administration. The division of responsibility for public administration between different international organisations, and in particular between the UN-run civil administration and the actors who worked together in Pillar IV, largely explains the different development trajectories of public finance institutions and the wider civil service. The significance of this is not generally apparent in most official accounts, which attempt to present the Mission as a united effort.

International diplomacy determined the role assigned to the UN, and at the same time limited its ability to fulfil that role by setting unclear and contradictory objectives and providing inadequate resources. The UN had a high level of formal authority and performed well within its areas of specialist expertise, in particular political negotiations with Kosovo's politicians. These successes in the political and diplomatic fields arguably made the achievements of other participants possible. However, the UN was not organisationally equipped to deal with all the tasks assigned to it. In the field of civil administration it lacked experience, had no firm agenda, the wrong staff, and was constrained by conflicting political demands. The UN's primary focus on the peace and security agenda also generated a desire to apply short-term solutions and to appease potentially disruptive elements.

USAID, an experienced and well-resourced development actor, appears to have been better able to deal with the situation in Kosovo and in this context, and in this sector, its programme appears to have had significant success in accomplishing what it set out to do. Although not the largest overall donor, USAID had very clear objectives, was able to mobilise quickly and fielded highly experienced staff and advisers who largely replicated what they normally did elsewhere. It also enjoyed a high level of local support. The successive USAID projects in economic governance stand out in terms of their size and scope, rapid mobilisation, continuity over time and clear objectives. The magnitude of the resources deployed by the US on this rather narrow set of institutions was significantly larger than the amounts other donors were able to devote to the sector.

The EU and USAID worked surprisingly well together, for a time, on economic governance issues and they share the credit for outcomes achieved in these areas. However, the EU's development agency, EAR, adopted a highly bureaucratic project approach and appears to have replicated all the deficiencies in aid administration identified in decades of previous literature on the subject. Its activities comprised a multiplicity of small scale, short-term, discontinuous interventions in several unconnected fields. The small size and limited scope of each project, their considerable administrative overheads and implementation delays undermined the effectiveness of EAR's assistance.

The other major bilateral donor in this area, DFID, was a relatively small player in the overall Kosovo context but had the strongest interest in supporting civil service development. This focus on civil service issues reflected British assumptions about the value of its own civil service model and the benefits of transferring it to other contexts. DFID's work was severely hampered, however, by the inadequacies and failings of UNMIK's Pillar II, which was the gatekeeper for its reform efforts. The impact of the small amount of technical assistance funding provided by the World Bank through the PEMTAG project is doubtful and it is not clear why the World Bank needed to engage in this kind of activity given the resources already deployed by other donors.

Clear goals

Having an agreed goal to work towards and a plan to achieve it was clearly more likely to produce good results. In this respect there was a significant gap between the UN and almost everyone else. Within the UN civil administration there was considerable confusion and indecision in relation to the future governance of Kosovo and sometimes passive or active resistance to the policies being pursued by other actors. Even within the group of actors who were agreed on the democratic, free market transformation model, however, there was scope for disagreement. Where these differences were significant and lingered for an extended period, as in the area of procurement policy, they undermined the long-term results for Kosovo.

Consistency, continuity and adequate resources

Long-term assistance and continuity of effort also produced better results. The EU's extended commitment to Pillar IV and the Customs Service, and USAID's commitment to economic governance stand out in this respect compared to the relatively short, small-budget projects implemented by EAR. World Bank activities also tended to have long lead times and delayed implementation resulting in gaps in assistance and the loss of momentum.

Merit recruitment and political insulation

The more successful institutions in Kosovo today are those that the international community was able to insulate from the influence of local politics and thus ensure merit-based recruitment and Weberian bureaucratic management over an extended period. The international actors in these cases were clear from the start that the functions of government should be performed by Kosovar staff and that the new institutions, or at least their operational aspects, should be handed over to them as soon as possible. There was thus considerable investment in recruitment, training and performance management of local personnel at a very early stage and a progressive transfer of tasks and responsibilities. In all the successful examples of post-conflict institution building, the merit-based recruitment of staff and assiduous attention to their training and development were prominent features of donor activities and an important factor in long-term sustainability. In this respect the first few years were crucial. International technical experts motivated performance, penalised corruption and established the patterns of behaviour that enabled an effective bureaucracy. Employees learned that advancement would depend on adopting these behaviours and also saw that bias, corruption and lack of impartiality were likely to be penalised. Over time these behaviours became entrenched and self-sustaining.[10]

In other parts of the interim administration, however, well-paid UN staff, both international and local, directly delivered many public services rather than developing the skills of Kosovars to do so. In other functions, the inability of international actors to control recruitment, the lack of clear rules about civil service employment, unclear salary entitlements and the absence of mechanisms to either discipline employees or protect their rights, meant that civil servants soon learned that their interests were best served by aligning themselves with political powerbrokers, reinforcing tendencies to inefficiency and corruption.[11]

Kosovo's lessons

Most analyses of post-conflict reconstruction exercises end with a list of 'lessons learned'. In many cases these are fairly obvious but difficult to implement in practice. Clearly donors should do their best to coordinate, plan and consult with each other and with the people in whose lives they are intervening. The experience in Kosovo raises many of the contested issues in development policy but in most cases does little to resolve them definitively. Some of the successful donor activities reinforce previous lessons about aid effectiveness while others challenge assumptions about best practice.

The UN and civil administration

Perhaps one of the lessons from Kosovo is that the UN is not an appropriate organisation to be given responsibility for managing and developing a public administration. It seems that this is a lesson that has been learned by the international community: no UN-led civil administration mission has been authorised since Kosovo and East Timor. On the other hand, there have also been no conflict situations quite like these, where the departing authorities left the territory with no effective institutional infrastructure, thus requiring an international administration. While the UN is uniquely qualified as a neutral actor to lead peacekeeping and reconstruction missions, and has a clear advantage in political negotiation and diplomacy, its very neutrality on many issues of economic policy and governance suggests that civil administration and development tasks would be better contracted out to organisations with the relevant experience and capacity to deliver them.

The value of technical assistance

Another lesson would be that technical assistance, in the right circumstances and if done well, can be very beneficial. The experience in Kosovo suggests that worries about the potential adverse effects of using technical advisers are exaggerated and need to be balanced against the potential benefits and the lack of feasible alternatives. Technical assistance in development is, after all, simply an extension of professional consulting in the developed world. It is often, in fact, delivered by the same private sector consulting companies. The academic literature on 'policy transfer' or 'policy learning' discusses the process by which developed countries share and adapt policy ideas and presents it as an almost entirely positive phenomenon.[12] When the policy sharing is between developed and developing countries, however, and there is an aid donor in the relationship, it is often regarded negatively. Although there are certainly risks in this three-party arrangement, in particular the temptation for governments to see donor-funded advisers as a free good to be either overused or ignored,[13] this is not always the case and the value of the knowledge, technical capacities and systems that are created by the activities of technical experts generally outweighs other risks.

Ownership and aid effectiveness

The literature on development insists that programmes implemented by external actors must be 'owned' by the receiving country. Exactly what this means, however, and how donors should achieve the required degree of national ownership has proven perennially difficult. As Boughton and Mourmouras point out, the true extent of ownership is not directly observable but requires judgement about the state of mind and degree of internal commitment of government officials. Moreover, not all government participants and special interest groups will agree on a policy, so there may be many potential 'owners'.[14] In a post-conflict situation, where political authority or social legitimacy to make decisions is unclear, judging the real extent of support for a particular policy is even more difficult. Waiting, however, until a settled government is available to take decisions is not an attractive option for donors who are in a hurry to see their recommended policies implemented.

In Kosovo, international actors all expressed their commitment to consultation with local stakeholders and the pursuit of 'ownership', but they differed in their understanding of what this meant and for most it quickly became a second-order priority behind seizing the 'window of opportunity' to implement reform. For many, ownership was simply a question of marketing their ideas to a relatively receptive group of local leaders. However, the lack of ownership, in the sense of the involvement of Kosovo's people in determining the direction of policy, does not appear to have adversely affected outcomes. The most effective public administration interventions in Kosovo were in fact those that were able to adopt a 'greenfield' approach and where foreign advisers and officials had a high level of control over policy. Donors set the reform agenda well before local political representatives had been democratically identified and technical advisers more or less imposed systems, rules and procedures with relatively little consultation, local input or adaptation to context. On the whole they avoided trying to revive or reform what may have existed previously, largely because the previous systems were at odds with the principles and values they were promoting. It is difficult to argue, therefore, that these public institutions, legal frameworks and administrative systems constructed by international actors under international administration were 'owned' by Kosovars, but the high level of public satisfaction with some of them today suggests this has not undermined their effectiveness.

The UN's approach to this issue was quite different, but no more consistent with the ideal of local ownership. UNMIK made efforts to engage local leaders in decision making to ensure that the policies of the international Mission were responsive to local opinion, but these opinions were regularly overridden by international staff.[15] The IAC and the JIAS co-opted political leaders into the administration but much of the day-to-day authority remained in the hands of UNMIK officials and Kosovars complained that they had little real involvement in decision making. Even the election of a Kosovo government did not ensure local decision-making processes were respected, as illustrated by UNMIK-imposed changes to approved legislation and the SRSG's revisions to the annual budget. The UN's promise of participation and local control without actually delivering it contributed to difficult relations between the Mission and the Kosovo government, while in other areas of governance, relinquishing control over important aspects of the administration in the name of 'ownership', or from a desire to avoid appearing 'colonial', merely perpetuated bad practices.

The need for large investments

The success of PFM development relative to other sectors suggests that large amounts of investment are required to get results. Such exercises cannot be done on the cheap through intermittent advisers and short-term projects. This is problematic for donors on several fronts. Regardless of how much is invested, results are still uncertain and are affected by political circumstances beyond the control of any donor. Even large, well-planned and well-resourced projects are high-risk activities. Gaining domestic political support in donor countries for large volumes of aid is difficult and the scale of the intervention may be determined more by donors' economic circumstances than by the needs of the recipient country. In addition, large inputs of foreign funding can have adverse impacts on the local economy through pressure on prices and labour market distortions. Perversely, the use of technical advisers has an advantage in this respect: the knowledge and expertise imparted by advisers is, in theory, retained, but most of the money they are paid remains outside the economy.[16]

Setting priorities

Aid resources are usually limited so international actors face the question of priorities and sequencing. Where should their efforts be focused? Good results in PFM were achieved largely because several important and well-resourced international actors made it their priority. Indeed in almost all post-conflict countries, establishing effective PFM institutions is the first order of business, partly because these functions make almost everything else possible, but also because of the leadership provided in this area by powerful international organisations, in particular the IMF. Other aspects of governance do not seem to receive quite the same level of attention nor have such powerful sponsors. Justice, the rule of law and effective management of other government functions, for example, are arguably as important as sound public finances but do not enjoy as much donor unity or investment of resources. The benefits of an effective PFM system will not be realised, however, if the government cannot implement the budget it has formulated or spend the revenue it has raised, nor if the economic laws it passes cannot be enforced because of an ineffective legal system.

The future

Many people had very high expectations of the international intervention in Kosovo, and most have been disappointed. Donors have not yet achieved the deep transformation of the economic, political and social environment described in early donor plans. But events in Kosovo continue to evolve. The steadily increasing competence of the Kosovo government and incremental developments on some of the many EU accession criteria are noted in each annual EU progress report, and EU sponsored discussions between Kosovo and Serbia aimed at normalisation of relations have made some progress.[17] The country and its institutions continue to be the subject of close attention from international actors.[18]

A positive future is not guaranteed, however. A decline in EU interest in enlargement, or adverse political and economic developments in the region or elsewhere in the world, may cause the past efforts of international actors to unravel quite rapidly and make the self-congratulatory statements of donors sound premature. On the other hand, exposure of this previously remote and culturally isolated corner of Europe to a much wider world of ideas and aspirations over the past decade and a half, and the inevitable generational change as leaders who emerged during the conflict years are replaced, may mean that Kosovo continues on its path towards the goals that international actors set for it. Ultimately, however, the ability of outsiders to dictate Kosovo's future is limited and the people may be losing patience with their apparently endless interference. It will ultimately be up to the Kosovars themselves to determine their own course. As one Kosovar explained it,

> Kosovar people generally are welcoming but then at one point people get fed up, even though there is still an inferiority complex, especially with people who haven't gone abroad a lot ... But another class of people in Kosovo who have been all over the place and who know that not everybody that comes from abroad has it right. And this is a new movement, a new feeling among Kosovars, not maybe the government but other people are saying, OK there's a lot of things we can do ourselves if we want to do it right, and we don't need to listen to the US Ambassador to tell us how.[19]

Notes

1 King and Mason, *Peace at any Price* 245.
2 Ibid. 48.
3 United Nations Security Council Resolution 1244, 10 June 1999, 2.
4 M. Roccia, 'Reforming property law in Kosovo: A clash of legal orders, *European Review* 23: 4 (2015) 566–82 describes one effect of this.
5 Paris, *At War's End* 213.
6 IMF, *Republic of Kosovo, 5th Review under the Stand-By Arrangement*, IMF Country Report No. 13/379 (Washington, DC: International Monetary Fund, 2013) 5.
7 World Bank, *IDA/IFC Interim Strategy Note for Republic of Kosovo for the Period FY10-FY11*, 10–11.
8 Dichter, *Despite Good Intentions* 290.
9 L. M. Howard, 'Kosovo and Timor-Leste: Neotrusteeship, neighbours, and the United Nations', *The Annals of the American Academy of Political and Social Science* 656 (2014) 116–35.
10 Skendaj, *Creating Kosovo: Intenational Oversight and the Making of Ethical Institutions.*
11 Ibid.
12 D. Benson and A. Jordan, 'what have we learned from policy transfer research? Dolowitz and Marsh revisited', *Political Studies Review* 9 (2011) 366–78; D. Dolowitz and D. Marsh, 'Learning from abroad: The role of policy transfer in contemporary policy making', *Governance* 13: 1 (2000) 5–24; R. Rose, 'What is lesson drawing?' *Journal of Public Policy* 11: 1 (1991) 3–30; D. Stone, 'Learning lessons and transferring policy across time, space and disciplines', *Politics* 19: 1 (1999) 51–9.
13 S. I. Ajayi and J. Afeikhena, 'Opportunity costs and effective markets', *UNDP Development Policy Journal* 2 (December 2002) 23–45.
14 J. M. Boughton and A. Mourmouras, *Is Policy Ownership an Operational Concept?* IMF Working Paper WP/02/72 (Washington, DC: International Monetary Fund, 2002).
15 S. Chesterman, 'Ownership in theory and practice: Transfer of authority in UN statebuilding operations', *Journal of Intervention and Statebuilding* 1: 1 (2007) 18.

16 P. Collier, *The Bottom Billion: Why the Poorest Countries Are Failing and What Can Be Done about it* (Oxford; New York: Oxford University Press, 2007) 122.

17 Ashton, *Statement by EU High Representative Catherine Ashton following Today's Meeting in the Framework of the EU-facilitated Dialogue.*

18 The EU has announced a commitment of €645.5 million for Kosovo in the current phase of the IPA 2014–20 and remains engaged through EULEX (http://ec.europa.eu/enlargement/instruments/funding-by-country/kosovo/index_en.htm, accessed 17 June 2015). USAID's strategy document for 2014–18 sets out plans for ongoing assistance including in public finance and economic policy (USAID, *Kosovo Country Development Cooperation Strategy 2014–2018*).

19 Kosovar technical adviser (KA1).

References

3rd High Level Forum on Aid Effectiveness, *Accra Agenda for Action* (2008) http://siteresources.worldbank.org/ACCRAEXT/Resources/4700790-1217425866038/AAA-4-SEPTEMBER-FINAL-16h00.pdf, accessed 9 September 2011

4th High Level Forum on Aid Effectiveness, *Busan Partnership for Effective Development Cooperation* (2011) www.aideffectiveness.org/busanhlf4/component/content/article/698.html, accessed 28 February 2012

Abdela, L., 'Kosovo: Missed opportunities, lessons for the future', *Development in practice* 13: 2–3 (2003) 208–16

Abrahamsen, R., 'The power of partnerships in global governance', *Third World Quarterly* 25: 8 (2004) 1453–67

Abramovitz, M., 'The elements of social capability' in B. H. Koo and D. H. Perkins (eds), *Social Capability and Long Term Economic Growth* (New York: St Martins Press/Korean Development Institute, 1995) 19–47

Addison, T., A. R. Chowdhury and S. M. Murshed, 'Financing reconstruction' in G. Junne and W. Verkoren (eds), *Postconflict Development: Meeting New Challenges* (Boulder CO; London: Lynne Rienner Publishers, 2005) 211–22

AFP, 'Official pleads for urgent aid for Kosovo', *Agence France-Presse* (21 September 1999) www.afp.com, accessed October 2008

AFP, 'Blood feud cripples lives in Kosovo', *Agence France-Presse* (12 July 2011) http://news.asiaone.com/News/AsiaOne+News/World/Story/A1Story20110712-288754.html, accessed 4 April 2012

Aid/Watch, *Action for Aid Justice: Australian Aid Priorities and Technical Assistance*, Fact Sheet (Erskineville, NSW: Aid Watch, no date) www.aidwatch.org.au, accessed 10 October 2009

Ajayi, S. I. and J. Afeikhena, 'Opportunity costs and effective markets', *UNDP Development Policy Journal* 2 (December 2002) 23–45

Albright, M., *Madam Secretary: A Memoir* (London: Macmillan, 2003)

Alesina, A. and R. Perotti, *Budget Deficits and Budget Institutions*, NBER Working Paper No. 5556 (Cambridge, MA.: National Bureau of Economic Research, 1996)

Anastasakis, O., 'The Europeanization of the Balkans', *Brown Journal of World Affairs* 12: 1 (2005) 77–88

Andrews, M., 'The logical limits of best practice administrative solutions in developing countries', *Public Administration and Development* 32 (2012) 137–53

Appleby, J., *The Relentless Revolution: A History of Capitalism* (New York; London: W W Norton & Company, 2010)

Arandarenko, M. and P. Golicin, 'Serbia' in B. Deacon and P. Stubbs (eds), *Social Policy and International Interventions in South East Europe* (Cheltenham, UK; Northampton, MA: Edward Elgar, 2007)

Ashton, C., *Statement by EU High Representative Catherine Ashton following Today's Meeting in the Framework of the EU-facilitated Dialogue* (Brussels: European Union External Action, 2014) http://eeas.europa.eu/statements/docs/2014/140212_02_en.pdf, accessed 22 February 2015

Autesserre, S., *Peaceland: Conflict Resolution and the Everyday Politics of International Intervention* (New York: Cambridge University Press, 2014)

Bache, I. and A. Taylor, 'The politics of policy resistance: Reconstructing higher education in Kosovo', *Journal of Public Policy* 23: 3 (2003) 279–300

Balkan Insight, 'Kosovo anti-corruption chief held for corruption', Balkan Investigative Reporting Network (3 April 2012) www.balkaninsight.com/en/article/kosovo-s-anti-corruption-chief-arrested-for-corruption, accessed 4 April 2012

Balkan Insight, 'Thousands leave Kosovo seeking asylum in EU', Balkan Investigative Reporting Network (9 February 2015) www.balkaninsight.com/en/article/kosovo-migrants-leave-the-country-in-thousands, accessed 11 February 2015

Balkan Insight, 'European leaders greet EU's green light to Serbia', Balkan Investigative Reporting Network (23 April 2013) www.balkaninsight.com/en/article/eu-officials-welcome-brussels-report-on-serbia, accessed 12 July 2013

Banuri, T., 'Development and the politics of knowledge: A critical interpretation of the social role of modernization theories in the development of the third world' in F. A. Marglin and S. A. Marglin (eds), *Dominating Knowledge: Development, Culture and Resistance* (Oxford: Clarendon Press, 1990) 29–72

Barents Group, Government infrastructure support, United Nations Mission in Kosovo, Pillar IV – Weekly reports 1999 (Pristina: unpublished reports in possession of author, 1999)

Barents Group, Government infrastructure support, United Nations Mission in Kosovo, Pillar IV – Monthly and weekly reports 2000 (Pristina: unpublished reports in possession of author, 2000)

Barents Group, Government infrastructure support, United Nations Mission in Kosovo – Monthly reports 2001 (Pristina: unpublished reports in possession of author, 2001)

Barents Group, Government infrastructure support, United Nations Mission in Kosovo – Monthly reports 2002 (Pristina: unpublished reports in possession of author, 2002)

Bartlett, W., *Europe's Troubled Region: Economic Development, Institutional Reform and Social Welfare in the Western Balkans* (London: Routledge, 2006)

Begu, A., *Statement by Mr. Ajri Begu, Economic Policy Advisory Board, Kosovo, Second Donors' Conference, Brussels, November 17* (Brussels: Joint Office for South Eastern Europe, 1999) http://ec.europa.eu/enlargement/archives/seerecon/calendar/1999/events/k2dc/sd/ab.htm, accessed 24 January

Bellamy, A. J., *Kosovo and International Society* (Basingstoke: Palgrave Macmillan, 2002)

Bello, W., 'The rise of the relief and reconstruction complex', *Journal of International Affairs* 59: 2 (2006) 281–96

Benson, D. and A. Jordan, 'What have we learned from policy transfer research? Dolowitz and Marsh revisited', *Political Studies Review* 9 (2011) 366–78

Berg, E. J., *Rethinking Technical Cooperation: Reforms for Capacity Building in Africa* (New York: United Nations Development Program, 1993)

Birdsall, N., *Seven Deadly Sins: Reflections on Donor Failings*, Working Paper No. 50 (Washington, D.C.: Center for Global Development, 2004)

Blair, S. A., D. Eyre, B. Salome and J. Wasserstrom, 'Forging a viable peace: Developing a legitimate political economy' in J. Covey, M. J. Dziedzic and L. Hawley (eds), *The Quest for Viable Peace: International Intervention and Strategies for Conflict Transformation* (Washington, DC; Arlington, VA: United States Institute of Peace Press; Association of the United States Army, 2005) 205–43

Bohle, D., 'Neoliberal hegemony, transnational capital and the terms of the EU's eastward expansion', *Capital & Class* 30: 1 (2006) 57–86

Boughton, J. M. and A. Mourmouras, *Is Policy Ownership an Operational Concept?*, IMF Working Paper WP/02/72 (Washington, D.C.: International Monetary Fund, 2002)

Brinkerhoff, D. W., 'Rebuilding governance in failed states and post-conflict societies: Core concepts and cross-cutting themes', *Public Administration and Development* 25 (2005) 3–14

Buwa, D. and H. Vuori, 'Rebuilding a health care system: War, reconstruction and health care reforms in Kosovo', *European Journal of Public Health* 17: 2 (2007) 226–30

Campbell, J., V. Percival and A. Zwi, 'Ministerial challenges: Post-conflict, post election issues in Kosovo's health sector', *European Journal of Public Health* 13: 2 (2003) 177–81

Caplan, R., *International Governance of War-Torn Territories: Rule and Reconstruction* (New York: Oxford University Press, 2005)

Capussela, A., 'Road to ruin: An unnecessary highway in Kosovo could bankrupt Europe's poorest state', *Transitions Online* (13 January 2012) www.tol.org/client/article/22939-road-to-ruin.html, accessed 19 January 2016

Carothers, T., *Aiding Democracy Abroad: The Learning Curve* (Washington, D.C.: Carnegie Endowment for International Peace, 1999)

Cassen, R., *Does Aid Work? Report to an Intergovernmental Task Force* (Oxford; New York: Clarendon Press; Oxford University Press, 1986)

Center for Public Integrity, *U.S. Official Says Government Wasted $6–8 billion in Iraq Reconstruction* (Washington, D.C.: Center for Public Integrity, 2012) www.publicintegrity.org/2012/07/17/9701/us-official-says-government-wasted-6-8-billion-iraq-reconstruction, accessed 18 January 2013

Chandler, D., *Empire in Denial: The Politics of Statebuilding* (London; Ann Arbor, MI: Pluto Press, 2006)

Chang, H.-J., *Kicking Away the Ladder: Development Strategy in Historical Perspective* (London: Anthem, 2002)

Chang, H.-J., 'Institutional development in historical perspective' in H.-J. Chang (ed.) *Rethinking Development Economics* (London: Anthem Press, 2003)

Chang, H.-J., 'The market, the state and institutions in economic development' in H.-J. Chang (ed.) *Rethinking Development Economics* (London: Anthem Press, 2003)

Chesterman, S., *You, the People: The United Nations, Transitional Administration and State Building* (Oxford: Oxford University Press, 2004)

Chesterman, S., 'Ownership in theory and practice: Transfer of authority in UN statebuilding operations', *Journal of Intervention and Statebuilding* 1: 1 (2007) 18

Cohen, L. J., 'Kosovo: "Nobody's country"', *Current History* 99: 635 (2000) 117–23

Collier, P., *Social Capital and Poverty*, Social Capital Initiative Working Paper No. 4 (Washington, D.C.: World Bank, 1998)

Collier, P., *The Bottom Billion: Why the Poorest Countries Are Failing and What Can Be Done about it* (Oxford; New York: Oxford University Press, 2007)

Congressional Research Service, *Kosovo: Reconstruction and Development Assistance*, RL30453 (Washington, D.C.: US Library of Congress, 2001)

Conyers, D. and R. Mellors, 'Aid effectiveness in Sub Saharan Africa: The problem of donor capacity', *IDS Bulletin* 36: 3 (2005) 83–9

Corrin, C., 'Developing policy on integration and re/construction in Kosova', *Development in practice* 13: 2–3 (2003) 189–207

Council of the European Union, Council Regulation (EC) No 1085/2006 of 17 July 2006 establishing an Instrument for Pre-Accession Assistance (IPA), (2006) http://ec.europa.eu/enlargement/instruments/overview/index_en.htm, accessed 5 October 2012

Covey, J., 'Making a viable peace: Moderating political conflict' in J. Covey, M. J. Dziedzic and L. Hawley (eds), *The Quest for Viable Peace: International Intervention and Strategies for Conflict Transformation* (Washington, DC; Arlington, VA: United States Institute of Peace Press; Association of the United States Army, 2005) 99–122

DANIDA, *Evaluation: Humanitarian and Rehabilitation Assistance to Kosovo, 1999–2003*, (Copenhagen: Ministry of Foreign Affairs, 2004) www.um.dk, accessed 29 September 2008

del Castillo, G., *Rebuilding War-torn States: The Challenge of Post-Conflict Economic Reconstruction* (Oxford: Oxford University Press, 2008)

DFID, 'Kosovo civil service personnel policies and procedures: Implementation programme, project memorandum' (unpublished document held by DFID Office, Pristina, 2001)

DFID, *Kosovo: Strategy Paper 2001–2004* (London: UK Department for International Development, 2001)

DFID, 'Terms of reference: Support to drafting of Kosovo Basic Public Service Law as an UNMIK Regulation' (unpublished document held by DFID Office, Pristina, 2001)

DFID, 'Output to purpose review of Kosovo civil service personnel management project' (unpublished document held by DFID Office, Pristina, 2003)

DFID, Project completion review narrative report: Kosovo civil service personnel management project (unpublished document held by DFID Office, Pristina, 2004)

DFID, *Regional Program Evaluation: Western Balkans, Evaluation Report EV693* (London: UK Department for International Development, 2008)

Di Lellio, A., 'Empire lite as a swamp', *Transitions* XLV: 1 (2005) 63–80

Dichter, T. W., *Despite Good Intentions: Why Development Assistance to the Third World Has Failed* (Boston, MA: University of Massachusetts Press, 2003)

Dimitrova, A., 'Enlargement, institution-building and the EU's administrative capacity requirement', *West European Politics* 25: 4 (2002) 171–90

Dixon, J., *Pillar IV's Role within UNMIK*, paper prepared for the first donor conference, 28 July (Brussels: Joint Office for South East Europe, 1999) http://ec.europa.eu/enlargement/archives/seerecon/calendar/1999/events/kdc/sd/dixon.pdf, accessed 24 January 2016

Dixon, J., *Speech at First Donor's Conference for Kosovo, Brussels, July 28* (Joint Office for South East Europe, 1999) http://ec.europa.eu/enlargement/archives/seerecon/calendar/1999/events/kdc/sd/unmik.htm, accessed 24 January 2016

Dobbins, J., 'The UN's role in nation-building: From the Belgian Congo to Iraq', *Survival* 46: 4 (2004) 81–102

Doli, D., F. Korenica and A. Rogova, 'The post-independence civil service in Kosovo: A message of politicization', *International Review of Administrative Sciences* 78: 4 (2012) 665–91

Dolowitz, D. and D. Marsh, 'Learning from abroad: The role of policy transfer in contemporary policy making', *Governance* 13: 1 (2000) 5–24

Duffield, M., 'Social reconstruction and the radicalization of development: Aid as a relation of global liberal governance', *Development and Change* 33: 5 (2002) 1049–71

Duli, I. Q., *Public Procurement in Kosovo* (Pristina: UBT publications, 2008)

Early Warning Report, *Kosovo Early Warning Report No. 1, May–August 2002* (Pristina: UNDP/Riinvest, 2002)

Early Warning Report, *Kosovo Early Warning Report No. 2, Sept–Dec 2002* (Pristina: UNDP/Riinvest, 2002)

Early Warning Report, *Kosovo Early Warning Report No. 3, January–April 2003* (Pristina: UNDP/Riinvest, 2003)

Early Warning Report, *Kosovo Early Warning Report No. 4, May–August 2003* (Pristina: UNDP/Riinvest, 2003)

Early Warning Report, *Kosovo Early Warning Report No. 5, September–December 2003* (Pristina: UNDP/Riinvest, 2003)

Early Warning Report, *Kosovo Early Warning Report No. 9, January–March 2005* (Pristina: USAID/UNDP/Riinvest, 2005)

Early Warning Report, *Kosovo Early Warning Report No. 15, October–December 2006* (Pristina: UNDP, 2006)

EBRD, *Business Environment and Enterprise Performance Survey (BEEPS) V: Country Profile Kosovo* (London: European Bank for Reconstruction and Development, 2015) http://ebrd-beeps.com, accessed 14 April 2015

ESI, *De-industrialisation and its Consequences: A Kosovo Story* (Pristina; Berlin: European Stability Initiative, 2002)

Essex, J., 'The neoliberalization of development: Trade capacity building and security at the US Agency for International Development', *Antipode* 40: 2 (2008) 229–51

European Agency for Reconstruction, *Kosovo 1999 Action Programme* 5 (Thessaloniki: European Agency for Reconstruction, 1999) http://ec.europa.eu/enlargement/archives/ear/home/default.htm, accessed 1 March 2010

European Agency for Reconstruction, *Kosovo 2000 Action Programme* (Thessaloniki: European Agency for Reconstruction, 2000) http://ec.europa.eu/enlargement/archives/ear/kosovo/kosovo.htm, accessed 1 March 2010

European Agency for Reconstruction, *EAR Annual Report 2000* (Thessaloniki: European Agency for Reconstruction, 2001) http://ec.europa.eu/enlargement/archives/ear/home/default.htm, accessed 1 March 2010

European Agency for Reconstruction, *Evaluation of the Implementation of Council Regulation 2667/2000 on the European Agency for Reconstruction, Synthesis Report Volume I Part C – Main Evaluation Report* (Development Researchers' Network Consortium, 2004) http://ec.europa.eu/enlargement/archives/ear/publications/main/documents/Evaluation_on_the_work_of_EAR_June2004.pdf, accessed 10 February 2014

European Agency for Reconstruction, *EAR Annual Report 2004* (Thessaloniki: European Agency for Reconstruction, 2005) http://ec.europa.eu/enlargement/archives/ear/home/default.htm, accessed 28 February 2010

European Agency for Reconstruction, *EAR Annual Report 2005* (Thessaloniki: European Agency for Reconstruction, 2006) http://ec.europa.eu/enlargement/archives/ear/home/default.htm, accessed 13 January 2009

European Agency for Reconstruction, *Kosovo Annual Action Programme 2006: Sector Fiche 2.3 Strengthening Public Administration Reform and EU Integration at Central and Municipal Levels* (Thessaloniki: European Agency for Reconstruction, 2006) http://ec.europa.eu/enlargement/archives/ear/kosovo/main/documents/2006PublicAdmin.pdf, accessed 10 February 2014

European Agency for Reconstruction, *Institutional Capacity Building Support (Kosovo) Executive Summary* Evaluation (EU/11/05/07) (Thessaloniki: European Agency for Reconstruction,

2008) http://ec.europa.eu/enlargement/archives/ear/publications/main/documents/Evaluation_ExSum_ICB_Kosovo.pdf, accessed 28 February 2010

European Commission, *Commission Decision of 15 December 1999 Establishing a Programme for the Agency for the Reconstruction of Kosovo* (Brussels: European Commission, 1999) http://ec.europa.eu/enlargement/archives/seerecon/kosovo/documents/ec-dec-agency.pdf, accessed 10 January 2014

European Commission, *Commission Decision on Establishing a Programme for Exceptional Targeted Support for Public Services under the 1999 Kosovo Budget* (Brussels: European Commission, 1999) http://ec.europa.eu/enlargement/archives/seerecon/kosovo/ec/ec_dec_pubserv.htm, accessed 7 October 2015

European Commission, *Commission Proposes a Stabilisation and Association Process for Countries of South-Eastern Europe* (press release) (Brussels: European Commission, 1999) http://europa.eu/rapid/press-release_IP-99-350_en.htm?locale=en, accessed 10 February 2014

European Commission, *Annual Programme 2002 for Kosovo* (Brussels: European Commission, 2002) http://ec.europa.eu/enlargement/pdf/financial_assistance/cards/publications/kosovo_programme_2002_en.pdf, accessed 23 January 2016

European Commission, *Cooperation in the field of Customs and Taxation: The European Union and the Western Balkans* (Brussels: Directorate-General for Enlargement, 2005)

European Commission, *Kosovo 2005 Progress Report* (Brussels: European Commission, 2005)

European Commission, *Welcome to the World of Public Internal Financial Control (PIFC)* (Brussels: Directorate-General for Budget, 2006) http://ec.europa.eu/budget/library/biblio/documents/control/brochure_pifc_en.pdf, accessed 15 June 2011

European Commission, *2007 Project Fiche Kosovo, IPA Centralised Programme, Meeting EU Standards in Public Procurement* (Brussels: European Commission, 2007) http://ec.europa.eu/enlargement/pdf/serbia/kosovo/ipa/10._kosovo_ipa_2007_eu_standards_in_public_procurement.pdf accessed 20 February 2010

European Commission, *2008 Project Fiche Kosovo– IPA Centralised Programmes, Support to Customs and Taxation Administrations* (Brussels: European Commission, 2008) http://ec.europa.eu/enlargement/pdf/kosovo/ipa/2008/ipa_2008_pf_19_customs_and_taxation_090608_en.pdf accessed 20 February 2010

European Commission, *2008 Project Fiche Kosovo IPA Centralised Programme: Public Finance* (Brussels: European Commission, 2008) http://ec.europa.eu/enlargement/potential-candidates/kosovo/financial-assistance/index_en.htm, accessed 6 May 2011

European Commission, *Instrument for Pre-Accession Assistance (IPA) Multi-Annual Indicative Planning Document (MIPD) 2008–2010, Kosovo* (Brussels: European Commission, 2008) www.eulex-kosovo.eu/docs/info/basic/Basic-ENG.jpg, accessed 12 January 2016

European Commission, *Kosovo 2008 Progress Report* (Brussels: European Commission, 2008) http://ec.europa.eu/enlargement/pdf/press_corner/key-documents/reports_nov_2008/kosovo_progress_report_en.pdf, accessed 14 February 2010

European Commission, *Kosovo 2009 Progress Report* (Brussels: European Commission, 2009) http://ec.europa.eu/enlargement/pdf/key_documents/2009/ks_rapport_2009_en.pdf accessed 20 February 2010

European Commission, *Kosovo – Fulfilling its European Perspective* (Brussels: European Commission, 2009) http://ec.europa.eu/enlargement/pdf/key_documents/2009/kosovo_study_en.pdf, accessed 20 May 2011

European Commission, *Retrospective Evaluation of the CARDS Programmes: Kosovo, Final Evaluation Report* (Brussels: Enlargement Directorate-General, 2009) http://ec.europa.eu/enlargement/pdf/financial_assistance/cards/evaluation-reports/05-fr_cards_kosovo_160709.pdf, accessed 10 February 2014

European Commission, *2009 Annual Report on the Implementation of the Instrument for Pre-Accession Assistance (IPA)* (Brussels: European Commission, 2010) http://ec.europa.eu/enlargement/pdf/press_corner/key-documents/financial_assistance/2009/annex_working_document_en.pdf, accessed 23 January 2016

European Commission, *Kosovo 2010 Progress Report* (Brussels: European Commission, 2010) http://eeas.europa.eu/delegations/kosovo/eu_kosovo/key_documents/index_en.htm, accessed 28 April 2012

European Commission, *Kosovo 2011 Progress Report* (Brussels: European Commission, 2011) http://eeas.europa.eu/delegations/kosovo/eu_kosovo/key_documents/index_en.htm, accessed 28 April 2012

European Commission, *Proposal for a Regulation of the European Parliament and of the Council on the Instrument for Pre-accession Assistance (IPA II)* (Brussels: European Commission, 2011) http://ec.europa.eu/enlargement/news_corner/key-documents/index_en.htm, accessed 3 October 2012

European Commission, *Kosovo 2012 Progress Report, Commission Staff Working Document accompanying the document Commission Communication on a Feasibility Study for a Stabilisation and Association Agreement between the European Union and Kosovo* (Brussels: European Commission, 2012) http://ec.europa.eu/enlargement/pdf/key_documents/2012/package/ks_analytical_2012_en.pdf, accessed 13 February 2013

European Commission, 'Conditions for membership' web page (European Commission, 2013) http://ec.europa.eu/enlargement/policy/conditions-membership/index_en.htm, accessed 12 July 2013

European Commission, *IPA: Interim Evaluation and Meta-evaluation of IPA Assistance – Country Report Kosovo*, EuropeAid/131184/C/SER/Multi (Brussels: European Commission, 2013)

European Commission, *Joint Report to the European Parliament and the Council on Serbia's Progress in Achieving the Necessary Degree of Compliance with the Membership Criteria and Notably the Key Priority of Taking Steps towards a Visible and Sustainable Improvement of Relations with Kosovo* (Brussels: High Representative of the European Union for Foreign Affairs and Security Policy, 2013) http://ec.europa.eu/enlargement/pdf/key_documents/2013/sr_spring_report_2013_en.pdf, accessed 16 January 2014

European Commission, *Kosovo 2013 Progress Report, Commission Staff Working Document accompanying the document Enlargement Strategy and Main Challenge 2013–2014* (Brussels: European Commission, 2013) http://ec.europa.eu/enlargement/pdf/key_documents/2013/package/brochures/kosovo_2013.pdf, accessed 28 January 2014

European Commission, *2013 Annual Report on Financial Assistance for Enlargement* (Brussels: European Commission, 2014)

European Commission, *Instrument for Pre-Accession Assistance (IPA: II): Indicative Strategy Paper for Kosovo (2014–2020)* (Brussels: European Commission, 2014)

European Commission, *Kosovo 2014 Progress Report, Enlargement Strategy and Main Challenges 2014–2015* (Brussels: European Commission, 2014)

European Commission/World Bank, *Donor Polling for Kosovo (Under UNSCR 1244)*, (Brussels: Joint Office for South East Europe, 2006) http://web.archive.org/web/20060719071248/http://www.seerecon.org/kdm/Kosovopolling.pdf, accessed 24 January 2016

Evans, P., 'Development as institutional change: The pitfalls of monocropping and the potentials of deliberation', *Studies in Comparative International Development* 38: 4 (2004) 30–52

Ferguson, N., *Civilization: The West and the Rest* (London: Allen Lane, 2011)

Ferlie, E., L. Ashburner, L. Fitzgerald and A. Pettigrew, *The New Public Management in Action* (Oxford: Oxford Scholarship Online, 1996)

Fidler, S., 'Albright irked by Kosovo funds delay', *Financial Times* (28 January 2000)

FRIDOM, *Whole of Government Review, Functional Review and Institutional Design of Ministries* (Pristina: Ministry of Public Administration, 2008). Formerly available online. Text in possession of author

FRIDOM, *Horizontal Review of Internal Audit Function, Functional Review and Institutional Design of Ministries* (Pristina: Ministry of Public Administration, 2009) http://testmap.rks-gov.net/userfiles/file/FRIDOM/Fridom_en/Horizontal_Reviews/Horizontal_Review_of_Internal_Audit_Function_210e.pdf, accessed 21 January 2016

FRIDOM, *Functional Review of Public Expenditure Management Systems, Functional Review and Institutional Design of Ministries* (Pristina: Ministry of Public Administration, 2010) http://testmap.rks-gov.net/userfiles/file/FRIDOM/Fridom_en/Horizontal_Reviews/Functional_Review_of_Public_Expenditure_Management_Systems_205e.pdf, accessed 21 January 2016

FRIDOM, *Functional Review of the Ministry of Finance and Economy, Functional Review and Institutional Design of Ministries* (Pristina: Ministry of Public Administration, 2010) http://map.rks-gov.net/getattachment/b1b822bc-15b8-4abc-a09f-4cc722013178/Ministria-e-Ekonomise-dhe-Financave.aspx, accessed 21 January 2016

Fukuyama, F., *State-building: Governance and World Order in the Twenty-first Century* (London: Profile Books, 2004)

Garton Ash, T., *History of the Present: Essays, Sketches and Despatches from Europe in the 1990s* (London: Penguin, 2000)

GHK/Technopolis, *Evaluation to Support the Preparation of Pre-accession Financial Instruments beyond 2013: Final Report* (Brussels: European Policy Evaluation Consortium (EPEC), 2011) http://ec.europa.eu/enlargement/news_corner/key-documents/index_en.htm, accessed 3 October 2012

Glenny, M., *The Fall of Yugoslavia* (London: Penguin, 1996)

Gligorov, V., 'The economics of Kosovo: Does viability matter?' *The International Spectator* 35: 2 (2000) 87–101

Goetz, K. H., 'Making sense of post communist central administration: Modernization, Europeanization or latinization?' *Journal of European Public Policy* 8: 6 (2001) 1032–51

Government of Kosovo, *Report on the Status of Public Administration in Kosovo* (Pristina: Ministry of Public Services, Group of Experts for Public Administration Reform, 2007)

Government of Kosovo, *Strategy for Public Administration Reform* (Pristina: Ministry of Public Services, Group of Experts for Public Administration Reform, 2007). Formerly available online. Text in possession of the author

Government of Kosovo, *Action Plan for Public Administration Reform in Kosovo (2009 Revision)* (Pristina: Ministry of Public Services, 2009). Formerly available online. Text in possession of the author

Gow, D. D. and E. R. Morss, 'The notorious nine: Critical problems in project implementation', *World Development* 16: 12 (1988) 1399–418

Griffiths, P., *The Economist's Tale: A Consultant Encounters Hunger and the World Bank* (London; New York: Zed Books, 2003)

Grindle, M. S., 'Good enough governance: Poverty reduction and reform in developing countries', *Governance: An International Journal of Policy, Administration, and Institutions* 17: 4 (2004) 525–48

Grootaert, C., *Social Capital: The Missing Link?* Social Capital Initiative Working Paper No. 3 (Washington, D.C.: World Bank, 1998)

Hajrizi, M., *The Donor Community's Assistance: A Strong Foundation for a Prosperous Future for Kosova*, Speech by Mehmet Hajrizi, Co-Head of the Department of Reconstruction,

UNMIK, Kosovo Donors' Meeting 25–26 February (Pristina: Joint Office for South East Europe, 2001) http://ec.europa.eu/enlargement/archives/seerecon/calendar/2001/events/kdcm/statements/hajrizi.htm, accessed 24 January 2016

Hameiri, S., 'Capacity and its fallacies: International state building as state transformation', *Millennium – Journal of International Studies* 38: 1 (2009) 55–81

Harrison, L. E., *Underdevelopment is a State of Mind: The Latin American Case* (Lanham, MD: Centre for International Affairs, Harvard University and University Press of America, 1985)

Harrison, L. E. and J. Kagan (eds), *Developing Cultures: Essays on Cultural Change* (New York; London: Routledge, 2006)

Hehir, A., 'Autonomous province building: Identification theory and the failure of UNMIK', *International Peacekeeping* 13: 2 (2006) 200–13

HELM and PAI, 'Kosovo civil service proposed new pay and grading system: Final report' (unpublished work in possession of author, 2004)

Herrero, J. L., 'Building state institutions' in G. Junne and W. Verkoren (eds), *Postconflict Development: Meeting New Challenges* (Boulder, CO; London: Lynne Rienner Publishers, 2005) 43–58

Hill, C. R., *Outpost: Life on the Frontlines of American Diplomacy: A Memoir* (New York: Simon and Schuster, 2014)

Hirsh, M., 'The fall guy: Washington's self-defeating assault on the UN', *Foreign Affairs* 78: 6 (1999) 2–8

Hirsh, M. and J. Terzieff, 'Holbrooke's ultimatum: Perform or perish', *Newsweek* (30 August 1999) 27

Holohan, A., *Networks of Democracy: Lessons from Kosovo for Afghanistan, Iraq and Beyond* (Stanford, CA: Stanford University Press, 2005)

Honadle, G. H. and J. K. Rosengard, 'Putting 'projectized' development in perspective', *Public Administration and Development* 3: 4 (1983) 299–306

Howard, L. M., 'Kosovo and Timor-Leste: Neotrusteeship, neighbours, and the United Nations', *The Annals of the American Academy of Political and Social Science* 656 (2014) 116–35

Huddleston, M. W., 'Innocents abroad: Reflections of a public administration consultant in Bosnia', *Public Administration Review* 59: 2 (1999) 147–60

Hysa, Y., 'Kosovo: A permanent international protectorate?' in E. Newman and R. Rich (eds), *The UN Role in Promoting Democracy: Between Ideals and Reality* (Tokyo; New York: UN University Press, 2004) 282–301

ICG, *Kosovo Spring*, (Pristina; Sarajevo: International Crisis Group, 1998)

ICG, *Kosovo: Let's Learn from Bosnia. Models and Methods of International Administration*, Balkans Report No. 66 (Sarajevo: International Crisis Group, 1999)

ICG, *The New Kosovo Protectorate*, Balkans Report No. 69 (Sarajevo: International Crisis Group, 1999)

ICG, *Waiting for UNMIK: Local Administration in Kosovo*, Balkans Report No. 79 (Pristina: International Crisis Group, 1999)

ICG, *Who's Who in Kosovo*, Balkan's Report No. 76 (Pristina: International Crisis Group, 1999)

ICG, *Kosovo Report Card*, Balkans Report No. 100 (Pristina: International Crisis Group, 2000)

ICG, *Kosovo: A Strategy for Economic Development*, Balkans Report No. 123 (Pristina; Brussels: International Crisis Group, 2001)

ICG, *Kosovo's First Month*, Europe Briefing No. 47 (Pristina; Belgrade; Brussels: International Crisis Group, 2008)

ICG, *Kosovo's Fragile Transition*, Europe Report No. 196 (Pristina; Brussels: International Crisis Group, 2008)

ICO, *State Building and Exit. The International Civilian Office and Kosovo's Supervised Independence 2008–2012* (Pristina: Kosovo International Civilian Office, 2012)

Ilcan, S. and L. Phillips, 'Global developmentalities: Keynote address', Technocracy@Development Conference, The University of Wageningen, The Netherlands, 26–28 June 2006

Iles, C., *Implementing Financial Management and Governance in Transitional States: Reflections on Introducing Western Normative Models of Public Internal Financial Control in the New Republic of Kosovo*, (London: Middlesex University, 2012) http://eprints.mdx.ac.uk/9352/ accessed 1 February 2013

IMF, *Kosovo: Macroeconomic Issues and Fiscal Sustainability* (Washington, DC: International Monetary Fund, 2001)

IMF, *Kosovo: Progress in Institution-Building and the Economic Policy Challenges Ahead* (Washington, DC: International Monetary Fund, 2001)

IMF, *Rebuilding Fiscal Institutions in Post Conflict Countries* (Washington, DC: Fiscal Affairs Department, International Monetary Fund, 2004)

IMF, *Kosovo: Gearing Policies Toward Growth and Development* (Washington, DC: International Monetary Fund, 2005)

IMF, *Technical Assistance Evaluation Program: Findings of Evaluations and Updated Program* (Washington, DC: International Monetary Fund, 2006)

IMF, *Manual on Fiscal Transparency* (Washington, DC: International Monetary Fund, 2007)

IMF, *Republic of Kosovo: First Assessment under the Staff-Monitored Program*, IMF Country Report No. 11/374 (Washington, DC: International Monetary Fund, 2011)

IMF, *IMF Mission to Kosovo Assesses Performance under the Staff-Monitored Program and Reaches Staff-Level Agreement on a Stand-By Arrangement*, press release no. 12/65 (Washington, DC: International Monetary Fund, 2012)

IMF, *IMF Executive Board Completes Fifth Review Under the SBA with Kosovo; Approves €4.8 Million Disbursement*, press release no. 13/537 (Washington, DC: International Monetary Fund, 2013)

IMF, *Republic of Kosovo, 5th Review under the Stand-By Arrangement*, IMF Country Report No. 13/379 (Washington, DC: International Monetary Fund, 2013)

IMF, *Republic of Kosovo: Staff Report for the 2013 Article IV Consultation*, IMF Country Report No. 222 (Washington, DC: International Monetary Fund, 2013)

IMF/World Bank, *The Economic Consequences of the Kosovo Crisis: A Preliminary Assessment of External Financing Needs and the Role of the Fund and the World Bank in the International Response* (Washington, DC: International Monetary Fund, 16 April 1999) www.imf.org/external/pubs/ft/kosovo/041699.htm, accessed 20 October 2012

IMF/World Bank, *International Community Responds to the Kosovo Crisis*, press release, 27 April (Washington, DC: International Monetary Fund, 1999) www.imf.org/external/pubs/ft/kosovo/stm.htm, accessed 29 September 2013

IMF/World Bank, *Update on Economic Policy Issues and Institutional Development, First Donors' Conference*, Statement of the IMF and World Bank staff at the Informal Donor Meeting for Kosovo, Brussels, July 28, 1999 (Brussels: Joint Office for South East Europe, 1999) http://ec.europa.eu/enlargement/archives/seerecon/calendar/1999/events/kdc/sd/imf.htm, accessed 24 January 2016

International Civil Service Commission, *Review of the Methodology for Surveys of Best Prevailing Conditions of Employment at Non-headquarters Duty Stations* (New York: United Nations, 2003)

IWPR, 'Blood feuds revive in unstable Kosovo', *Institute for War and Peace Reporting* (21 February 2005) http://iwpr.net/report-news/blood-feuds-revive-unstable-kosovo, accessed 4 April 2012

Jennings, C., 'New honour code aims to cut killings', *Scotsman* (23 April 2005) www.scotsman.com/news/world/new-honour-code-aims-to-cut-killings-1-708898, accessed 4 April 2012

Johnson, C., *Japan, Who Governs?: The Rise of the Developmental State* (New York: Norton, 1995)

Jones, B. D., 'The challenges of strategic coordination' in S. J. Stedman, D. Rothchild and E. M. Cousens (eds), *Ending Civil Wars: The Implementation of Peace Agreements* (Boulder, CO; London: Lynne Reiner, 2002) 89–115

Judah, T., *Kosovo: War and Revenge* (New York; London: Yale University Press, 2000)

Kamenka, E. and M. Krygier, *Bureaucracy: The Career of a Concept* (New York: St. Martin's Press, 1979)

Kamphuis, B., 'Economic policy for building peace' in G. Junne and W. Verkoren (eds), *Postconflict Development: Meeting New Challenges* (Boulder, CO; London: Lynne Rienner Publishers, 2005) 185–210

Kanin, D. B., 'Big men, corruption, and crime', *International Politics* 40 (2003) 491–526

Keukeleire, S., A. Kalaja and A. Çollaku, *The EU and Kosovo: Structural Diplomacy in Action – But on the Basis of One-sided Paradigms?* Policy Paper 4, The Diplomatic System of the European Union (Loughborough: Loughborough University, 2011) http://dseu.lboro.ac.uk/Documents/Policy_Papers/DSEU_Policy_Paper04.pdf, accessed 20 April 2012

Khan, M. H., 'Corruption and governance in early capitalism: World Bank strategies and their limitations' in J. Pincus and J. Winters (eds), *Reinventing the World Bank* (Ithaca, NY: Cornell University Press, 2002) 164–84

King, I. and W. Mason, *Peace at any Price: How the World Failed Kosovo* (London: Hurst & Company, 2006)

Kitching, G. N., *Development and Underdevelopment in Historical Perspective: Populism, Nationalism and Industrialization* (London; New York: Routledge, 1989)

Klasnja, M., 'The EU and Kosovo: Time to rethink the enlargement and integration policy?' *Problems of Post Communism* 54: 4 (2007) 15–32

Klein, J.-P., 'The United Nations and administration of territory: Lessons from the front line: The United Nations transitional administration in Eastern Slavonia (UNTAES)', *ASIL Proceedings* (2003) 205–9

Klein, N., 'Baghdad Year Zero: Pillaging Iraq in pursuit of a neocon utopia', *Harpers Magazine* (September, 2004) 43–53

Knaus, G. and M. Cox, 'The "Helsinki Moment" in Southeastern Europe', *Journal of Democracy* 16: 1 (2005) 39–53

Knudsen, R. A., *Privatization in Kosovo: The International Project 1999–2008* (Oslo: Norwegian Institute of International Affairs, 2010)

Koeth, W., 'State building without a state: The EU's dilemma in defining its relations with Kosovo', *European Foreign Affairs Revie*, 15: 2 (2010) 227–47

KPMG Consulting Group, 'Kosovo Project, Central Fiscal Authority exit report, 4 March 2000 to 28 February 2002' (unpublished document, copy held by author, 2002)

Land, T., *Joint Evaluation Study of the Provision of Technical Assistance Personnel: What Can We Learn from Promising Experiences? Synthesis Report*, ECDPM Discussion Paper No. 78 (Maastricht: European Centre for Development Policy Management, 2007) www.ecdpm.org/dp78, accessed 7 November 2007

Landes, D. S., *The Wealth and Poverty of Nations: Why Some Are so Rich and Some so Poor* (New York: W W Norton, 1998)

Leftwich, A., *States of Development: On the Primacy of Politics in Development* (Cambridge, U.K.; Malden, MA.: Polity; Blackwell, 2000)

Lewarne, S. and D. Snelbecker, *Economic Governance in War Torn Economies: Lessons Learned from the Marshall Plan to the Reconstruction of Iraq* (Washington, DC: United States Agency for International Development, 2004)

Linn, J., *Statement by Vice President of the World Bank*, First Donors' Conference for Kosovo, 28 July (Brussels: Joint Office for South East Europe, 1999) http://ec.europa.eu/enlargement/archives/seerecon/calendar/1999/events/kdc/sd/worldbank.htm, accessed 24 January 2016

MacGinty, R. and O. P. Richmond, 'Myth or reality: Opposing views on the liberal peace and post-war reconstruction', *Global Society* 21: 4 (2007) 491–7

Maddison, A., *Foreign Skills and Technical Assistance in Economic Development* (Paris: Development Centre of the Organisation for Economic Co-operation and Development, 1965)

Magalachvili, D., 'Kosovo: A critique of a failed mission', *Mediterranean Quarterly* Summer (2005) 118–41

Malcolm, N., *Kosovo: A Short History* (New York: Harper Perennial, 1999)

Marglin, S. A., 'Towards a decolonisation of the mind' in F. A. Marglin and S. A. Marglin (eds), *Dominating Knowledge: Development, Culture and Resistance* (Oxford: Clarendon Press, 1990) 1–28

Mehmet, O., *Westernizing the Third World: The Eurocentricity of Economic Development Theories* (London; New York: Routledge, 1999)

MFE, *Public Expenditure and Financial Accountability (PEFA) Assessment* (Pristina: Government of Kosovo, 2007)

MFE, *Public Expenditure and Financial Accountability (PEFA) Public Financial Management Assessment* (Pristina: Republic of Kosovo, 2009)

MFE, *Public Expenditure and Financial Accountability (PEFA) Public Financial Management Assessment* (Pristina: Republic of Kosovo, 2013) http://mf.rks-gov.net/en-us/Reports/Reports-and-Publications/Public-Expenditure-and-Financial-Accountability, accessed 2 January 2015

Mikesell, R. F., 'The emergence of the World Bank as a development institution' in K. Acheson, J. F. Chant and M. Prachowny (eds), *Bretton Woods Revisited: Evaluations of the IMF and the IBRD* (Toronto: University of Toronto Press, 1972) 70–84

Miller, A. J., 'UNMIK: Lessons from the early institution building phase', *New England Law Review* 39: 9 (2004) 9–24

Montgomery, J. D., *The Politics of Foreign Aid: American Experience in Southeast Asia* (New York: Published for the Council on Foreign Relations by Praeger, 1962)

Moore, D., 'Levelling the playing fields and embedding illusions: 'Post-conflict' discourse and neo-liberal 'development' in war-torn Africa', *Review of African Political Economy* 27: 83 (2000) 11–28

Morgan, P., 'Technical assistance: Correcting the precedents', *UNDP Development Policy Journal* 2 (2002) 1–22

Moyo, D., *Dead Aid: Why Aid is not Working and How There Is Another Way for Africa* (London: Allen Lane, 2009)

Murphy, C., *The United Nations Development Programme: A Better Way?* (Cambridge: Cambridge University Press, 2006)

Muscat, R. J., *Selected Lessons from Evaluations of Responses to Complex Humanitarian Emergencies: Implications for the Kosovo Crisis* (Washington, DC: USAID Bureau for Europe and the New Independent States/USAID Mission to Yugoslavia, 1999) https://dec.usaid.gov/dec/home/Default.aspx, accessed 14 October 2008

Narten, J., 'Dilemmas of promoting "local ownership": The case of postwar Kosovo' in R. Paris and T. Sisk (eds), *The Dilemmas of Statebuilding: Confronting the Contradictions of Postwar Peace Operations* (London; New York: Routledge, 2008) 252–83

North, D., *An Introduction to Institutions and Institutional Change* (Cambridge; New York: Cambridge University Press, 1990)

Nove, A., *The Economics of Feasible Socialism* (London; New York: Routledge, 2003)

OECD, *DAC Principles for Effective Aid: Development Assistance Manual* (Paris: Organisation for Economic Co-operation and Development, 1992)

OECD, *Managing Public Expenditure: A Reference Book for Transition Countries* (Paris: Organisation for Economic Co-operation and Development, 2001)

OECD, *Harmonising Donor Practices for Effective Aid Delivery: Good Practice Papers*, DAC Guidelines and Reference Series (Paris: Organisation for Economic Co-operation and Development, 2003)

OECD, *Paris Declaration on Aid Effectiveness, High Level Forum, February 28–March 2* (Paris: Organisation for Economic Co-operation and Development, 2005)

OECD, *The Challenge of Capacity Development: Working Towards Good Practice*, DAC Guildelines and Reference Series (Paris: Organisation for Economic Co-operation and Development, 2006)

OECD, 'Technical cooperation' in *2005 Development Cooperation Report* (Paris: Organisation for Economic Co-operation and Development, 2006)

OECD, *Aid Effectiveness 2005–2010: Progress in Implementing the Paris Declaration* (Paris: Organisation for Economic Co-operation and Development, 2011) www.oecd.org/document/1/0,3746,en_2649_3236398_48725569_1_1_1_1,00.html, accessed 30 November 2011

Office of the Auditor General, *Annual Audit Report on the Financial Year 2010* (Pristina: Republic of Kosova, 2011)

Office of the Auditor General, *Annual Audit Report 2013* (Pristina: Office of the Auditor General, 2014)

Olden, B., D. Last, S. Ylaoutinen and C. Sateriale, *Fiscal Consolidation in Southeastern European Countries: The Role of Budget Institutions*, IMF Working Paper WP/12/113 (Washington, DC: International Monetary Fund, 2012)

Osborne, D. and T. Gaebler, *Reinventing Government: How the Entrepreneurial Spirit is Transforming the Public Sector* (New York: Plume, 1992)

OSCE, 'Helping Kosovo's institutions improve public service' web page (Pristina: Organization for Security and Co-operation in Europe, 2008) www.osce.org/kosovo/57654, accessed 23 January 2016

OSCE, *The Implementation of Civil Service Legislation in Kosovo* (Pristina: Organization for Security and Co-operation in Europe: Mission in Kosovo, 2013)

Papadimitriou, D., 'The EU's strategy in the post-communist Balkans', *Southeast European and Black Sea Studies* 1: 3 (2001) 69–94

Papadimitriou, D., P. Petrov and L. GreiÇivci, 'To build a state: Europeanization, EU actorness and state-building in Kosovo', *European Foreign Affairs Review* 12 (2007) 219–38

Paris, R., *At War's End: Building Peace after Civil Conflict* (Cambridge: Cambridge University Press, 2004)

Paris, R., 'Saving liberal peacebuilding', *Review of International Studies* 36 (2010) 337–65

Parthasarathi, P., *Why Europe Grew Rich and Asia Did Not: Global Economic Divergence, 1600–1850* (Cambridge: Cambridge University Press, 2011)

Pearson, L. B., *Partners in Development: Report of the Commission on International Development* (New York: Praeger, 1969)

PEFA, *Public Financial Management Performance Measurement Framework* (Washington, DC: World Bank, 2011) www.pefa.org, accessed 10 April 2015
Phillips, L. and S. Ilcan, 'Capacity-building: The neoliberal governance of development', *Canadian Journal of Development Studies* 23: 3 (2004) 393–409
Piselli, E., 'The establishment and development of a public procurement system for Kosovo' in S. Arrowsmith and M. Trybus (eds), *Public Procurement: The Continuing Revolution* (The Hague; London; New York: Kluwer Law International, 2003) 47–59
Pomeranz, K. and S. Topik, *The World That Trade Created* (Armonk, NY; London: M. E. Sharpe, 1999)
Porter, D., B. Allen and G. Thompson, *Development in Practice: Paved with Good Intentions* (London; New York: Routledge, 1991)
Power, S., 'Kosovo dispatch: Breathing room', *The New Republic* (9 August 1999) 18–20
Premchand, A., *Public Expenditure Management* (Washington, DC: International Monetary Fund, 1993)
Pritchett, L. and M. Woolcock, *Solutions when the Solution is the Problem: Arraying the Disarray in Development*, Working Paper No. 10 (Washington, DC: Center for Global Development, 2002)
Pritchett, L., M. Woolcock and M. Andrews, *Capability Traps? The Mechanisms of Persistent Implementation Failure*, Working Paper 234 (Washington, DC: Center for Global Development, 2010)
Public Pulse, *Public Pulse Report No. 6, August 2013* (Pristina: UNDP, 2013) www.undp.org/content/dam/kosovo/docs/Procurement/PPR6_Anglisht.pdf, accessed 3 February 2014
Public Pulse, *Public Pulse Report No. 7 – June 2014* (Pristina: UNDP, 2014)
Public Pulse, *Public Pulse Report No. 8 – November 2014* (Pristina: UNDP, 2014)
Pula, B., 'The UN in Kosova: Administering democratization?' in F. Bieber and Z. Daskalovski (eds), *Understanding the War in Kosovo* (London; Portland, OH: Frank Cass, 2003) 199–216
Rapley, J., *Understanding Development: Theory and Practice in the Third World* (Boulder, CO: Lynne Rienner, 2002)
Republic of Kosovo, *Zgjedhjet për Kuvendin e Kosovës 2014: Rezultatet për Kosovë*, (Pristina: Republic of Kosovo, 2014) www.kqz-ks.org/Uploads/Documents/Rezultatet%20sipas%20Subjeketeve%20-%2020140526%20Party%20Results%20-%20Kosovo%20Level_jywcwsfyts.pdf, accessed 16 June 2015
Rist, G., *The History of Development: From Western Origins to Global Faith* (Atlantic Highlands, NJ: Zed Books, 1997)
Roccia, M., 'Reforming property law in Kosovo: A clash of legal orders', *European Review* 23: 4 (2015) 566–82
Rose, R., 'What is lesson drawing?' *Journal of Public Policy* 11: 1 (1991) 3–30
Rostow, W. W., *The Stages of Economic Growth: A Non-communist Manifesto* (Cambridge: Cambridge University Press, 1960)
Schick, A., *A Contemporary Approach to Public Expenditure Management* (Washington, DC: World Bank Institute, 1998)
Schick, A., 'Why most developing countries should not try New Zealand's reforms', *World Bank Research Observer* 13: 1 (1998) 123–31
Seale, L. C., 'Establishing financial management in the Kosovo interim administration' (unpublished report in possession of author, 2000)
Seers, D., 'Why visiting economists fail', *The Journal of Political Economy* 70: 4 (1962) 325–38
Shepherd, A. J. K., '"A milestone in the history of the EU": Kosovo and the EU's international role', *International Affairs* 85: 3 (2009) 513–30

SIGMA, *Kosovo Public Internal Financial Control (PIFC) Assessment 2007* (Paris: OECD, Support for Improvement in Governance and Management, 2007)

SIGMA, *Assessment: Kosovo 2012* (Paris: OECD, Support for Improvement in Governance and Management, 2012)

SIGMA, *Assessment Kosovo 2013* (Paris: OECD, Support for Improvement in Governance and Management, 2013)

SIGMA, *The Principles of Public Administration* (Paris: OECD, Support for Improvement in Governance and Management, 2014)

SIGMA, *Public Administration Reform Assessment of Kosovo 2014* (Paris: OECD, Support for Improvement in Governance and Management, 2014)

Simonsen, S. G., 'Nationbuilding as peacebuilding: Racing to define the Kosovar', *International Peacekeeping* 11: 2 (2004) 289–311

Skendaj, E., *Creating Kosovo: International Oversight and the Making of Ethical Institutions* (Ithaca, NY: Cornell University Press, 2014)

Sommers, M. and P. Buckland, 'Negotiating Kosovo's education minefield', *Forced Migration Review* 22 (2005) 38–9

Stability Pact for South East Europe, 'About the stability pact' archived web page (2008) www.stability-pact.org/, accessed 23 January 2016

Statistics Office of Kosovo, *Population and Housing Census in Kosovo Preliminary Results – June 2011* (Pristina: Republic of Kosovo, 2011) http://esk.rks-gov.net/rekos2011/?cid=2,40,276, accessed 25 September 2012

Stiglitz, J. E., *Globalization and its Discontents* (New York; London: W W Norton & Company, 2002)

Stone, D., 'Learning lessons and transferring policy across time, space and disciplines', *Politics* 19: 1 (1999) 51–9

Strazzari, F. and B. Kamphuis, 'Hybrid economies and statebuilding: On the resilience of the extralegal', *Global Governance* 18 (2012) 57–72

Symansky, S., *Donor Funding and Public Finance Management Reform in Post Conflict Countries: Recommendations Derived from Personal Observations* (London: Centre for Aid and Public Expenditure, Overseas Development Institute, 2010) http://www.odi.org.uk/sites/odi.org.uk/files/odi-assets/events-documents/4518.pdf, accessed 11 February 2014

TAFKO, *Monthly Summary of Task Force Activities: July–August 1999* (Pristina: European Commission Task Force Kosovo, 1999)

Task Force on Overseas Economic Operations, *Report on Overseas Economic Operations for the Commission on Organisation of the Executive Branch of Government* (Washington, DC: United States Government, 1955)

Tavakoli, H. and S. Saneja, *Public Financial Management Reforms in Fragile States: The Case of Kosovo* (London: Overseas Development Institute, 2012)

Temple, J. and P. A. Johnson, 'Social capability and economic growth', *The Quarterly Journal of Economics* 113: 3 (1998) 965–90

Todorova, M., *Imagining the Balkans* (New York; Oxford: Oxford University Press, 1997)

Torbiorn, K. M., *Destination Europe: The Political and Economic Growth of a Continent* (Manchester; New York: Manchester University Press, 2003)

Toye, J., *Dilemmas of Development: Reflections on the Counter-Revolution in Development Economics* (2nd edn, Oxford: Blackwell, 1993)

Trybus, M., 'The reform of public procurement law in the Western Balkans' in G. Piga and K. V. Thai (eds), *Advancing Public Procurement: Experiences, Innovation and Knowledge Sharing* (Boca Raton: PrAcademics Press, 2006) 392–412

Turner, M. and M. Pugh, 'Towards a new agenda for transforming war economies', *Conflict, Security and Development* 6: 3 (2006) 471–9

UN, *Convention on Privileges and Immunities of the United Nations* (New York: United Nations, 1946) www.unog.ch/80256EDD006B8954/(httpAssets)/C8297DB1DE8566F2C1256F2600348A73, accessed 23 March 2012

UN General Assembly, *Financing of the United Nations Interim Administration Mission in Kosovo: Report of the Secretary General, 22 October 1999* (New York: United Nations, 1999)

UN General Assembly, *Report of the Panel on United Nations Peace Operations (Brahimi Report)* (New York: United Nations, 2000)

UN General Assembly, *Performance Report on the Budget of the United Nations Interim Administration Mission in Kosovo for the Period from 1 July 2003 to 30 June 2004, Report of the Secretary General* (New York: United Nations, 2004)

UN General Assembly, *Performance Report on the Budget of the United Nations Interim Administration Mission in Kosovo for the Period from 1 July 2004 to 30 June 2005, Report of the Secretary-General* (New York: United Nations, 2005)

UN General Assembly, *Budget for the United Nations Interim Administration Mission in Kosovo for the period from 1 July 2006 to 30 June 2007, Report of the Secretary-General* (New York: United Nations, 2006)

UN General Assembly, *Performance Report on the Budget of the United Nations Interim Administration Mission in Kosovo for the Period from 1 July 2005 to 30 June 2006, Report of the Secretary-General* (New York: United Nations, 2006)

UNDESA, *Public Administration in Kosovo: Situational Analysis and Strategy, Draft Discussion Paper* (New York: UN Department of Economic and Social Affairs, 2003)

UNDP, *Capacity Development*, Technical Advisory Paper 2 (New York: United Nations Development Program, 1997)

UNDP, *Assessment of Administrative Capacity in Kosovo* (Prepared for the United Nations Development Program by the Kosovo Capacity Assessment Project (KCAP) Team 2005) http://cv.jmellon.com/kcap.pdf, accessed 21 January 2016

UNMIK, *UNMIK News Archive 1999* (Pristina: United Nations Mission in Kosovo, 1999) http://web.archive.org/web/20020715111303/http://www.unmikonline.org/archive.htm#1999, accessed 24 January 2016

UNMIK, *Kosovo: Reconstruction 2000*, Public Reconstruction and Investment Programme (Pristina: Department of Reconstruction, EU Pillar IV, 2000)

UNMIK, *UNMIK News Archive 2000* (Pristina: United Nations Mission in Kosovo, 2000) http://web.archive.org/web/20020715111303/http://www.unmikonline.org/archive.htm#1999, accessed 24 January 2016

UNMIK, *Partnership in Kosovo: Reconstruction 1999–2000, An Overview by the Department of Reconstruction* (Pristina: United Nations Mission in Kosovo, 2001)

UNMIK, *Kosovo: UNMIK-Government Report for the Donor Coordination Meeting for Kosovo, Brussels, 5 November 2002* (Pristina: United Nations Mission in Kosovo, 2002)

UNMIK, *The New Kosovo Government 2002 Budget* (Pristina: Central Fiscal Authority, United Nations Mission in Kosovo, 2002)

UNMIK, *Kosovo Standards Implementation Plan (KSIP)* (Pristina: United Nations Mission in Kosovo, 2004) http://operationkosovo.kentlaw.edu/symposium/resources/KSIP%20final%20draft%2031%20March%202004b.htm, accessed 24 January 2016

UNMIK, *UNMIK's Impact on the Kosovo Economy: Spending Effects 1999–2006 and Potential Consequences of Downsizing* (Pristina: EU Pillar Economic Policy Office, 2006)

UNMIK/European Union, *Kosovo Consolidated Budget 1 January–31 December 2000* (Pristina: Central Fiscal Authority, Pillar IV, 1999)

UNMIK/European Union, *EU Pillar Annual Report 2005* (Pristina: EU Pillar IV, 2006)

UNMIK/European Union, *The 10 Key Achievements: End of Mission Report 1999–2008* (Pristina: EU Pillar IV, 2008)

UNMIK/PISG, *Kosovo: Public Administration Strategy 2004–2006, Towards a Professional, Responsive and Impartial Public Service (Draft)* (Pristina: United Nations Mission in Kosovo; Provisional Institutions for Self Government, 2004)

UNMIK/PISG, *Letter of Intent between UNMIK and PISG to International Donor Community: Kosovo Memorandum of Economic and Financial Policies, 2 November 2005* (Pristina: United Nations Mission in Kosovo; Provisional Institutions for Self Government, 2005). Formerly available on the UNMIK website. Copy held by author

UNSC, *Report of the Inter-Agency Needs Assessment Mission Dispatched by the Secretary-General of the United Nations to the Federal Republic of Yugoslavia* (New York: United Nations Security Council, 1999)

UNSC, *Report of the Secretary-General Pursuant to Paragraph 10 of Security Council Resolution 1244 (1999) 12 June 1999* (New York: United Nations Security Council, 1999)

UNSC, *Report of the Secretary General on the United Nations Interim Administration Mission in Kosovo, 12 July 1999* (New York: United Nations Security Council, 1999)

UNSC, *Security Council Minutes, 4011th Meeting, Thursday 10 June 1999* (New York: United Nations Security Council, 1999)

UNSC, *Security Council Minutes, 4011th Meeting, Thursday 10 June 1999 (Resumption 1)* (New York: United Nations Security Council, 1999)

UNSC, *Report of the Secretary General on the United Nations Interim Administration Mission in Kosovo, 15 January 2002* (New York: United Nations Security Council, 2002)

UNSC, *Report of the Security Council Mission to Kosovo and Belgrade, 14–17 December 2002* (New York: United Nations Security Council, 2002)

UNSC, *Report of the Secretary General on the United Nations Interim Administration Mission in Kosovo, 29 January 2003* (New York: United Nations Security Council, 2003)

UNSC, *Report of the Secretary General on the United Nations Interim Administration Mission in Kosovo, 14 April 2003* (New York: United Nations Security Council, 2003)

UNSC, *Report of the Secretary-General on the United Nations Interim Administration Mission in Kosovo, 26 January 2004* (New York: United Nations Security Council, 2004)

UNSC, *Report of the Secretary-General on the United Nations Interim Administration Mission in Kosovo, 30 April 2004* (New York: United Nations Security Council, 2004)

UNSC, *A Comprehensive Review of the Situation in Kosovo (Eide Report)* (New York: United Nations Security Council, 2005)

UNSC, *Report of the Special Envoy of the Secretary General on Kosovo's Future Status (Ahtisaari Report)* (New York: United Nations Security Council, 2007)

UNSC, *Report of the Secretary-General on the United Nations Interim Administration Mission in Kosovo, 24 November 2008* (New York: United Nations Security Council, 2008)

US Department of State, *Doing Business in Kosovo: 2012 Country Commercial Guide for U.S. Companies* (Washington, DC: U.S. and Foreign Commercial Service and US Department of State, 2012) http://photos.state.gov/libraries/kosovo/312585/files/2012_Pristina%20CCG_final.pdf, accessed 3 February 2014

US International Development Advisory Board, *Partners in Progress: A Report to the President* (Washington, DC: Govt. Printer, 1951)

USAID, 'Results of Kosova economic sector assessment, July 15 to July 29' (unpublished document, copy held by author, 1999)

USAID, *Strategy for the Federal Republic of Yugoslavia (Serbia, Montenegro, Kosovo) 1999–2000* (Washington, DC: United States Agency for International Development, 1999)

USAID, *Budget Justification, Fiscal Year 2001: Annex III, Europe and Eurasia* (Washington, DC: United States Agency for International Development, 2000)

USAID, *Strategy for Kosovo 2001–2003* (Washington, DC: United States Agency for International Development, 2000)

USAID, *Kosovo: Results Review and Resource Request* (Washington, DC: United States Agency for International Development, 2001)

USAID, *Foreign Aid in the National Interest: Promoting Freedom, Security, and Opportunity* (Washington, DC: United States Agency for International Development, 2002)

USAID, *USAID/Kosovo Annual Report 2002* (Washington, DC: United States Agency for International Development, 2002)

USAID, *Corruption in Kosovo: Observations and Implications for USAID* (Washington, DC: United States Agency for International Development, 2003)

USAID, *Evaluation of the USAID/Kosovo Economic Reconstruction Project* (Washington, DC: United States Agency for International Development, 2003)

USAID, *USAID Mission in Kosovo Strategic Plan 2004–2008* (Pristina: United States Agency for International Development, 2003)

USAID, *USAID/Kosovo Annual Report FY 2004* (Pristina: United States Agency for International Development, 2004)

USAID, *USAID/Kosovo Annual Report FY 2005* (Washington, DC: United States Agency for International Development, 2005)

USAID, *USAID Assistance in Fiscal Reform: The Kosovo Economic Reconstruction Project* (Washington, DC: United States Agency for International Development, 2006)

USAID, *USAID/Kosovo Operational Plan FY 2006* (Washington, DC: United States Agency for International Development, 2006)

USAID, USAID Kosovo Economic Growth Office, presentation slides (unpublished material provided by USAID staff, Pristina, 2010)

USAID, *Human and Institutional Capacity Development (HICD) Assessment: Kosovo* (Washington, DC: United States Agency for International Development, 2012)

USAID, *Human and Institutional Capacity Development Assessment: Kosovo. Final Report, Part II* (Washington, DC: United States Agency for International Development, 2012)

USAID, *Mid-Term Performance Evaluation of the Kosovo Growth and Fiscal Stability Initiative (GFSI) – Final Report* (Washington, DC: United States Agency for International Development, 2012)

USAID, *Kosovo Country Development Cooperation Strategy 2014–2018* (Washington, DC: United States Agency for International Development, 2013)

Venner, M., 'The concept of 'capacity' in development assistance: New paradigm or more of the same?' *Global Change, Peace & Security* 27: 1 (2015) 85–96

Wade, R., *Governing the Market: Economic Theory and the Role of Government in East Asian Industrialization* (Princeton, NJ: Princeton University Press, 1990)

Weber, M., 'Bureaucracy' in H. H. Gerth and C. Mills (eds), *From Max Weber: Essays in Sociology* (London: Routledge & Kegan Paul, 1970) 196–244

Wedgwood, R. and H. K. Jacobson, 'Symposium: State reconstruction after civil conflict: Foreword', *American Journal of International Law* 95: 1 (2001) 1–6

Weinstein, B., 'Developing inequality', *American Historical Review* 113: February (2008) 1–18

Weller, M., *The Crisis in Kosovo 1989–1999: From the Dissolution of Yugoslavia to Rambouillet and the Outbreak of Hostilities. International Documents and Analysis* (Cambridge: University of Cambridge, Centre for International Studies, 1999)

Willis, K., *Theories and Practices of Development* (London; New York: Routledge, 2005)

Wittkowsky, A., 'Squaring the circle: A short history of UNMIK's European Union Pillar, 1999–2008', *Sudosteuropa Mitteilungen* 49: 1 (2009) 16–35

Woodward, S. L., 'Economic priorities for successful peace implementation' in S. J. Stedman, D. Rothchild and E. M. Cousens (eds), *Ending Civil Wars: The Implementation of Peace Agreements* (Boulder, CO; London: Lynne Rienner, 2002)

World Bank, *The International Bank for Reconstruction and Development, 1946–1953* (Baltimore, MD: Johns Hopkins Press, 1954)

World Bank, *The East Asian Miracle: Economic Growth and Public Policy* (New York: Oxford University Press, 1993)

World Bank, The State in a Changing World, World Development Report 1997 (published for the World Bank by Oxford University Press, 1997)

World Bank, *Public Expenditure Management Handbook* (Washington, DC: World Bank, 1998)

World Bank, *Economic Statement by the World Bank*, Second Donors' Conference for Kosovo, Brussels, 17 November (Brussels: Joint Office for South East Europe, 1999) http://ec.europa.eu/enlargement/archives/seerecon/calendar/1999/events/k2dc/sd/wb_econ.htm, accessed 24 January 2016

World Bank, *Kosovo: Building Peace through Sustained Growth. The Economic and Social Policy Agenda* (Brussels: Joint Office for South East Europe, 1999)

World Bank, Rebuilding Kosovo: A Complicated Challenge for the International Community, press conference transcript (Brussels), 12 July (Washington, DC: World Bank, 1999) http://go.worldbank.org/VWCHKJKH40, accessed 23 June 2012

World Bank, *Strategic Directions for the Economic Recovery of Kosovo: First Donors' Conference for Kosovo, Brussels, 26 July* (Washington, DC World Bank, 1999)

World Bank, *World Bank Group Response to Post Conflict Reconstruction in Kosovo: General Framework for an Emergency Assistance Strategy* (Washington, DC: World Bank, 1999)

World Bank, *World Bank Group Transitional Support Strategy for Kosovo* (Washington, DC: World Bank, 1999)

World Bank, *Conflict and Change in Kosovo: Impact on Institutions and Society* (Washington, DC: World Bank, 2000)

World Bank, *Transitional Support Strategy for Kosovo: Progress Report* (Washington, DC: World Bank, 2000)

World Bank, *Implementation Completion Report on Two Grants to the United Nations Interim Administration in Kosovo for the Benefit of Kosovo* (Washington, DC: World Bank, 2001)

World Bank, *Kosovo Poverty Assessment Vol. 1: Main Report* (Washington, DC: World Bank, 2001)

World Bank, *Kosovo, Economic and Social Reforms for Peace and Reconciliation*, vol. I (Washington, DC: World Bank, 2001)

World Bank, *Kosovo: Economic Assistance Grant IV – Project Information Document* (Washington, DC: World Bank, 2002)

World Bank, *Kosovo: Medium Term Public Expenditure Priorities* (Washington, DC: World Bank, 2002)

World Bank, *Program Document: Proposed Fourth Economic Assistance Grant to the United Nations Interim Administration Mission in Kosovo* (Washington, DC: World Bank, 2003)

World Bank, *Economic Policy/Public Expenditure Management, Project Information Document (PID)* (Washington, DC: World Bank, 2004)

World Bank, *Implementation Completion Report: Economic Assistance Grant IV Kosovo* (Washington, DC: World Bank, 2004)

World Bank, *Kosovo Economic Memorandum* (Washington, DC: World Bank, 2004)

World Bank, *Public Expenditure Management Technical Assistance Project (PEMTAG), Project Appraisal Document* (Washington, DC: World Bank, 2005)

World Bank, *Governance Matters: A Decade of Measuring the Quality of Governance* (Washington, DC: World Bank, 2006)

World Bank, *Interim Strategy Note for Kosovo for the Period FY08* (Washington, DC: World Bank, 2007)

World Bank, *IDA/IFC Interim Strategy Note for Republic of Kosovo for the Period FY10-FY11* (Washington, DC: World Bank; International Finance Corporation, 2009)

World Bank, *Public Expenditure Management Technical Assistance Project, Implementation Completion and Results Report* (Washington, DC: World Bank, 2009)

World Bank, *Public Sector Modernization Project, Project Appraisal Document (PAD)* (Washington, DC: World Bank, 2009)

World Bank, *Country Policy and Institutional Assessments: 2010 Assessment Questionnaire* (Washington, DC: World Bank, 2010)

World Bank, *Kosovo Public Expenditure Review* (Washington, DC: World Bank, 2010)

World Bank, *Kosovo Country Fiduciary Assessment* (Washington, DC: World Bank, 2012)

World Bank, *Doing Business 2015: Economy Profile Kosovo* (Washington, DC: World Bank, 2014)

World Bank, *Kosovo Public Finance Review: Fiscal Policies for a Young Nation* (Washington, DC: World Bank, 2014)

World Bank, *Public Sector Modernization Project (P101614) Implementation Status and Results Report* (Washington, DC: World Bank, 2015)

World Bank/European Commission, 'Kosovo: Donors Pledge US$1 Billion in Support of the Reconstruction and Recovery Programme', press release, Second Donors' Conference for Kosovo, Brussels, 17 November (Brussels: Joint Office for South East Europe, 1999) http://go.worldbank.org/2A81BKR370, accessed 23 October 2008

World Bank/European Commission, *Press Release, High Level Steering Group Inaugural Meeting, 13 July* (Brussels: Joint Office for South East Europe, 1999) http://web.archive.org/web/20000930022924/http://www.seerecon.org/PressReleases/press990713.htm, accessed 24 January 2016

World Bank/European Commission, *Press Release: The First Donors' Conference for Kosovo, Brussels 27 July* (Brussels: Joint Office for South East Europe, 1999), http://europa.eu/rapid/press-release_IP-99-571_en.htm, accessed 24 January 2016

World Bank/European Commission, *Rebuilding Kosovo: A Complicated Challenge for the International Community, Press Conference, Brussels, 12 July* (Brussels: Joint Office for South East Europe, 1999) http://web.worldbank.org/WBSITE/EXTERNAL/NEWS/0,,contentMDK:20455872~pagePK:64257043~piPK:437376~theSitePK:4607,00.html, accessed 24 January 2016

World Bank/European Commission, *Towards Stability and Prosperity: A Program for Reconstruction and Recovery in Kosovo* (Brussels: Joint Office for South East Europe, 1999) http://ec.europa.eu/enlargement/archives/seerecon/kosovo/documents/kosovo_toward_stability_and_prosperity_1999.pdf, accessed 24 January 2016

World Bank/European Commission, *Kosovo Donors' Meeting Feb 25–26, 2001 Pristina – Statements* (Brussels: Joint Office for South East Europe, 2001) http://ec.europa.eu/enlargement/archives/seerecon/calendar/2001/events/kdcm/statements/index.html, accessed 24 January 2016

Xinhua News Agency, 'Belgrade protests UN decision to set up budget authority for Kosovo', *People's Daily Online* (17 November 1999) http://english.people.com.cn/english/199911/18/eng19991118W119.html, accessed 17 February 2011

Yannis, A., 'The UN as Government in Kosovo', *Global Governance* 10 (2004) 67–81

Index